11:59...
AND COUNTING!

DR. JACK VAN IMPE

JACK VAN IMPE MINISTRIES
P.O. Box 7004
Troy, Michigan 48007

All Scripture quotations are from the King James Version of the Bible.

Copyright © 1983 by Jack Van Impe Ministries

Printed in the United States of America.

Seventh Printing, 1989

Jack Van Impe Ministries
P.O. Box 7004, Troy, Michigan 48007
In Canada: Box 1717, Postal Station A
Windsor, Ontario N9A 6Y1

ISBN 0-934803-05-6

Table
of Contents

PART VI: The Great Escape

PART VII: The Judgment Seat of Christ

FOREWORD

I n Matthew 24:3, Christ's disciples asked, ". . . what shall be the sign of thy coming, and of the end of the world?" The Saviour then proceeded to describe those world events which would both indicate His return and culminate in the Day of the Lord. He added in Luke 21:28: "And when these things begin to come to pass [or begin to occur simultaneously], then look up, and lift up your heads; for your redemption draweth nigh."

Concerning this great day, the Apostle Paul writes in I Thessalonians 5:1-3: "But of the times and the seasons, brethren, ye have no need that I write unto you. For yourselves know perfectly that the day of the Lord so cometh as a thief in the night. For when they shall say, Peace and safety; then sudden destruction cometh upon them . . . '' II Peter 3:10 pictures this event by stating: '' . . . the day of the Lord will come as a thief in the night; in the which the heavens will pass away with a great noise, and the elements shall melt with fervent heat, the earth also and the works that are therein shall be burned up.''

Never in the annals of world history have we witnessed such a proliferation of the signs Jesus predicted to be in effect immediately prior to His return. No longer are the days of simultaneous war, famine, pestilence, earthquakes and cultic activity limited to the pages of Holy Writ. One need only pick up the evening newspaper or tune to his favorite news broadcast to realize that these signs of Christ's second coming are in evidence worldwide, and increasing both in frequency and intensity. No wonder the scientists who control the famed "doomsday clock" are moving its hands ever closer to midnight!

The pages which follow discuss every major New Testament prophecy relating to Christ's return in the light of current international events. Parts VI and VII, in particular, concern the future of both the Christian and the unbeliever as revealed by God Himself. Remember that prophecy is but history written in advance. It is God's declaration and description of future events. As such, it cannot, has not and will not fail in even the smallest detail until all has been fulfilled.

My personal prayer is that, upon completing

this book, every Christian will renew his vows of love and service to the Saviour, and that every unbeliever will give his heart and life to the only One who is able to save him from the wrath to come (Revelation 3:10).

Dr. Jack Van Impe

PART

1

Signs of the Times and Christ's Return

1
The Blessed Hope

Christ's return is described as the "blessed hope" in Titus 2:13 which states: "Looking for that blessed hope, and the glorious appearing of the great God and our Saviour Jesus Christ."

The happiness of the greatest event in world history has to do with seeing Jesus. John said in Revelation 22:4: "And they shall see his face . . . " If this thought does not affect one's emotions positively, something is drastically wrong. The song often sung by believers should be the position of every child of God. This song declares: "Friends will be there I have loved long ago; joy like a river around me will flow. Yet just a smile from my Saviour, I know, will through the ages be glory for me." Amen. Even so, come quickly, Lord Jesus.

The Rapture

Multitudes today are unaware of the fact that there are two stages or phases within the process of the second coming—the Rapture and the Revelation — and that these events are separated by a seven-year period of time. I personally believe that the Rapture is the next occurrence on God's calendar. This Rapture is the literal, visible and bodily return of Christ in the heavenlies. Acts 1:9-11 state: "And when [Jesus] had spoken these things, while they beheld, he was taken up; and a cloud received him out of their sight. And while they looked steadfastly toward heaven as he went up, behold, two men stood by them in white apparel; Which also said, Ye men of Galilee, why stand ye gazing up into heaven? this same Jesus which is taken up from you into heaven, shall so come in like manner as ye have seen him go into heaven."

Has Christ already returned? Some cultists declare that he came in 1914 or 1918 as an invisible spirit. This is nonsense! The Bible declares that He shall return as He left. One can easily know how He left by studying Luke 24:39 where Christ, in His new, resurrected body, said: "Behold my hands and my feet, that it is I myself: handle me, and see; for a spirit hath not flesh and bones, as ye see me have." He adds in verse 41: "Have ye here any meat?" The disciples gave Christ a piece of broiled fish and honeycomb which He took and ate before them (verses 42, 43). The risen Saviour had a body of flesh and bones—a body that could be seen, touched and fed. This same Christ, in the same body, shall come "in like manner" from heaven. When He returns in the heavenlies, all believers, dead and living, will also be taken bodily to meet Him in the clouds. Yes, one day soon, the people of God are going to disappear from the earth in a blaze of glory.

As a new Christian, I painted a message on the glove compartment of my automobile. It said: "The driver of this car is awaiting the return of Christ. At His coming, Christians will disappear bodily from the earth. Should I suddenly vanish, take over the steering wheel!" I can still remember the look on the faces of hitchhikers as they read my startling message. They cried: "Buddy, the next corner is as far as I go!" Yes, the unsaved world has great difficulty accepting the glorious teaching of the Rapture.

The Christian, on the other hand, accepts by faith the declarations of the Word of God concerning this glorious subject. I Thessalonians 4:16-18 state: "For the Lord himself shall descend from heaven with a shout, with the voice of the archangel, and with the trump of God: and the dead in Christ shall rise first: Then we which are alive and remain shall be caught up together with them in the clouds to meet the Lord in the air: and so shall we ever be with the Lord. Wherefore comfort one another with these words."

Verse 14 declares that when Christ comes at the time of the Rapture, He brings those that sleep (the dead) with Him. At this point, someone cries: "I've found my first contradiction in the Bible! How can Christ bring the dead with Him (verse 14) and come after the dead (verse 16)?" Friend, there are no contradictions in the Word of God. Instead, it is the finite, limited intellect of human beings that cannot grasp the infinite, unlimited mind of the Omniscient God. If one is led by the Holy Spirit and burns the midnight oil in study under the direction of the blessed third member of the Trinity, the so-called contradictions immediately fade into obscurity. Christ *can* bring the dead with Him in verse 14 *and* come after the dead in verse 16. Here is the simplistic solution: When a believer dies, his spirit and soul go into the presence of God, but his body goes into the grave. Proof? " . . . To be absent from the body [is] to be present with the Lord" (II Corinthians 5:8). This soul, absent from the body, is with Christ until the great day when body, soul, and spirit are reunited at the coming of Jesus. So, Christ brings the dead (the soul and spirit) with Him in verse 14 to come after the dead (the body) in verse 16. When "the dead rise first," it is the body — *only* the body — that comes out of the grave to be reunited with the soul and spirit brought to the body from heaven. This does away with the unscriptural teaching of "soul sleep."

The next point is of extreme importance. If the Lord comes to receive the bodies of the *dead* in Christ, will He leave the bodies of the *living* in Christ behind? Were this the case, the wisest thing to do at the sound of the trumpet would be to commit suicide. This, however, is not the case, for the text declares: " . . . The dead in Christ shall rise first. Then, we which are alive and remain shall be caught up together with them [the dead] in the clouds to meet the Lord in the air: and so shall we ever be with the Lord." Thus, we see that the Rapture is a *bodily* resurrection for the dead *and* living who are in Christ, or who are born again.

The entire occurrence is going to take place in half a blink. I Corinthians 15:51-54 state: "Behold, I shew you a mystery; We shall not all sleep, [be dead] but we shall all be changed, In a moment, in the twinkling of an eye, at the last trump: for the trumpet shall sound, and the dead shall be raised incorruptible, and we shall be changed. For this corruptible [the dead] must put on incorruption, and this mortal [the living] must put on immortality." General Electric Company calculates the twinkling of an eye to be approximately eleven one-hundredths of a second. In this moment of time, we take upon ourselves immortality, and are transformed to be like Jesus. The Psalmist said in chapter 17:15: " . . . I shall be satisfied, when I awake, with thy likeness." I John 3:2 reports: " . . . When [we see Jesus] we shall be like him; for we shall see him as he is." Again, Philippians 3:20 verifies the fact that our bodies will be changed as we enter into God's presence in whirlwind style. This verse tells us that our citizenship is in heaven, " . . . from whence also we look for the Saviour, . . . Who shall change our vile body, that it may be fashioned like unto His glorious body." This is the Rapture!

There are those who say, "I don't believe in the Rapture, because the word 'rapture' cannot be found in the Bible." Well, the word "Bible" cannot be found in the Bible either, but this does not disprove the Book's existence. Terms are coined to portray the experiences they picture, and the word "rapture" comes from the Latin word "rapio," which means "a snatching away." Surely the preceding material offers proof enough that the Bible teaches a snatching away. Thus, since God tells us that there shall be a snatching away, and since "rapio" translated from Latin to English means "a snatching away," only the willfully ignorant will reject such a clear-cut term to describe the first phase of the second coming of Christ.

The Revelation

The second phase of the second coming, described as "the Revelation," takes place seven years after the Rapture. Again, the term "revelation" is but a coined word, picturing the truth it depicts. "Revelation" comes from the word "revealing." When Christ returns to earth, He reveals Himself to all the inhabitants of the globe, internationally. Hence, this event is called "the Revelation," or "revealing of Christ." Why quibble about labels when they so beautifully describe the doctrinal truths presented?

Scripturally, Revelation 4:1 describes phase one of the return of Christ, while Revelation 19:11 depicts phase two. Fix these two chapters firmly in your mind, and prophecy will become a stabilized blessing in your life. The "come up hither" of Revelation 4:1 is the Rapture, the meeting in the air, and the appearance of the white horse rider and His armies in Revelation 19:11 is the Revelation of Jesus Christ. Chapter 4 removes the believer from the judgments described in chapters 6-18, while chapter 19 restores him to his earthly sojourn after the judgments are completed. Chapter 4, depicting the Rapture, occurs *before* the seven years of tribulation described in chapters 6-18, and chapter 19 describes the return of the King and His people, *after* the horrendous catastrophies of chapters 6-18 occur. We know this to be true because the Book of Revelation is written chronologically, with the Tribulation Hour taking place in chapters 6-18. Four precedes six, and nineteen follows eighteen. It's just that simple. The Church is removed in chapter 4, and the Tribulation follows in chapters 6-18. Then the Saints return at the conclusion of the Tribulation Hour in chapter 19.

In addition, Revelation 3:10 states: "Because thou hast kept the word of my patience, I also will keep thee *from*"—not *through* (preservation) but *from* (the Greek—"ek"—*OUT* of) "the hour of temptation, which shall come upon all the world, to try them that dwell upon the earth." This will be the world's most terrifying hour. All the wars of the past will look like Sunday School picnics in comparison. Jeremiah 30:7 says: "Alas, for that day is great. [There is none] like it." Daniel 12:1: "There shall be a time of trouble such as never was since there was a nation even to that same time." Joel 2:1,2: "Let all the inhabitants of the land tremble: for the day of the Lord cometh; for it is nigh at hand; a day of darkness and gloominess, a day of clouds and of thick darkness . . . there hath [never been the like]." Jesus said in Matthew 24:21: "For then shall be great tribulation such as [never was] since the beginning of the world to this time, no, nor ever shall be." When it occurs, fiery incineration will engulf the globe: " . . . the Lord will come with fire . . . " (Isaiah 66:15). " . . . the flaming flame shall not be quenched . . . " (Ezekiel 20:47). " . . . A fire [devours] before them . . . " (Joel 2:3). " . . . the whole land shall be devoured by the fire of his jealousy . . . " (Zephaniah 1:18). "Their flesh shall consume away while they stand upon their feet, and their eyes shall consume away in their holes, and their tongue shall consume away in their mouth" (Zechariah 14:12). "The third part of the trees was burnt up, and all green grass was burnt up." (Revelation 8:7). "By these three was the third part of men killed, by the fire, and by the smoke, and by the brimstone . . . " (Revelation 9:18).

The Tribulation Hour lies just ahead for the human race. The saved will have been removed before it begins. They are taken in Revelation 4:1, and experience the Judgment Seat of Christ before the chapter ends. In fact, we find them placing crowns (their rewards) at the feet of the Saviour in verses 10 and 11. This is proof that the saved are safe and secure when the judgments begin in chapter 6. (Remember, 4 comes before 6.) Then, when the blitzkrieg ends in chapter 18, the saved return with Christ as He appears to the inhabitants of the earth and becomes their King. Revelation 19:11-16 give us a glimpse of the momentous event: "And I saw heaven opened, and behold a white horse, and he that sat upon him was called Faithful and True, and in righteousness he doth judge and make war. His eyes were as a flame of fire, and on his head were many crowns, and he had a name written, that no man knew, but he himself. And he was clothed with a vesture dipped in blood: and his name is called The Word of God. And the armies which were in heaven followed him upon white horses, clothed in fine linen, white and clean. And out of his mouth goeth a sharp sword, that with it he should smite the nations: and he shall rule them with a rod of iron: and he treadeth the winepress of the fierceness and wrath of Almighty God. And he hath on his vesture and on his thigh a name written, KING OF KINGS AND LORD OF LORDS."

This, my friend, is the revealing of Christ to the nations. At His revelation, every eye sees His glory. "Behold He cometh with clouds and every eye shall see Him . . . " (Revelation 1:7). The armies following Him from heaven to earth are the saints who were removed from earth in Revelation 4:11. They were evacuated before the great holocaust began. They are the same crowd mentioned in Jude, verse 14: " . . . Behold the Lord cometh with ten thousands of His saints." The Hebrews and Greeks had no terminology to describe millions, billions, trillions, quadrillions, etc. They simply said, "ten thousands." Thus, the innumerable company of saints following the Lord to earth are the redeemed.

We now come to a pivotal point of this message. If the following information is missed, confusion will reign. Please read it carefully.

The Significance of Prophetic Signs

What relationship exists between the Rapture, the Revelation, and prophetical signs? Where do they fit into the schedule of events of God's Word? Many think that the signs point to phase one, the Rapture, because they identify the snatching away as the second coming of Christ in their minds. Doctrinally speaking, this is not so. The actual second coming of Christ is the second phase, the Revelation, or the revealing of Christ to the inhabitants of earth. Since He came to earth at His first advent, He must come to earth at His second advent. The Rapture is not Christ's appearance upon earth, but a meeting in the heavenlies—an intermediary evacuation of believers from earth before the storm. Seven years later, Christ does come to earth, touching

16

down on the Mount of Olives (Zechariah 14:4).

The prophetical signs, then, point to Christ's return to earth with His saints at the close of the Tribulation Hour—not to the Rapture. Can I prove my statements? Yes! Take two Bibles and place them side by side. Open one to the Book of Revelation, chapter 6, where the signs begin to be fulfilled. Then open the other to Matthew 24, Mark 13, or Luke 17 or 21, where Christ's prophetical predictions are recorded. The inescapable conclusion is that the signs are identical! Now get this. The Church is taken in Revelation chapter 4, and the signs take place two chapters later. The signs of Revelation 6 are identical to the predictions of Christ in the four Gospels, proving that the signs Jesus gave point to His *Revelation*, the second phase of the second coming. Even if there were not a sign yet in existence, we believers could be called home imminently or momentarily. Why? Because each of the signs could occur during the seven-year period following the believers' departure. Remember, the signs point to Christ's second coming to earth (Revelation 19).

Now, the reason I believe we may go home at any moment (and this thrilling truth should produce goose pimples on one's duck bumps) is that Jesus said: " . . . When you shall see all these [signs]" not one, not two, but *all* the signs occurring simultaneously, then, "know that it is near, even at the doors" (Matthew 24:33). What is near when one sees all the signs occurring? Christ's return to earth, the Revelation, phase two. Wait! When this event takes place, we Christians will return with Him, and all the signs pointing to the return of Christ with His saints — the return of the King with His armies — are *already* in their initiatory or *beginning* stages. Yes, the signs say that you and I are coming back with the Lord soon. How can this be, as long as we are still present on earth? There is but one logical conclusion. We must be removed *very soon* via phase one, the Rapture, in order to return with Christ, via phase two, the Revelation. Be ready! It may happen at any moment!

2
Signs of Christ's Return

We are now ready to begin our study of the signs themselves. My desire is to deal with every major sign of the New Testament in order to conclusively prove that the statement of Jesus, " . . . When you shall see *all* these things, know that it is near, even at the doors," is in the process of fulfillment in our day and age. Matthew 24:3-14 states: "And as he [Jesus] sat upon the mount of Olives, the disciples came unto him privately, saying, Tell us, when shall these things be? and what shall be the sign of thy coming, and of the end of the world? And Jesus answered and said unto them, Take heed that no man deceive you. For many shall come in my name, saying, I am Christ; and shall deceive many. And ye shall hear of wars and rumours of wars: see that ye be not troubled: for all these things must come to pass, but the end is not yet. For nation shall rise against nation, and kingdom against kingdom: and there shall be famines, and pestilences, and earthquakes, in divers places. All of these are the beginning of sorrows. Then shall they deliver you up to be afflicted, and shall kill you: and ye shall be hated of all nations for my name's sake. And then shall many be offended, and shall betray one another, and shall hate one another. And many false prophets shall rise, and shall deceive many. And because iniquity shall abound, the love of many shall wax cold. But he that shall endure unto the end, the same shall be saved. And this gospel of the kingdom shall be preached in all the world for a witness unto all nations; and then shall the end come."

This text undoubtedly has been the most misunderstood of all prophetic pronouncements. The problem has arisen because multitudes fail to see that God has two elect groups upon earth — Israel (Romans 11:28) and the Church (I Peter 1:2). Romans 9-11 tell the entire story of God's chosen people, Israel. Chapter 9 concerns Israel's past, chapter 10 her present, and chapter 11 her future. Regarding her glorious past, Romans 9:4 declares that Israel was given the promises, including prophetic pledges. In chapter 10, verse 16, we find: "But they have not all obeyed the gospel. For Esaias saith, Lord, who [among them] hath believed our report?" Presently they are blinded to their calling and promises, but in the future, chapter 11, verse 26: " . . . all Israel shall be saved: as it is written, There shall come out of Sion the Deliverer, and shall turn away ungodliness from Jacob." Why will God perform this? Verse 29 contains the answer: "For the gifts and calling of God are without repentance." God chose Israel (see Deuteronomy 7:7) and He has never abrogated His selection. Therefore, Israel remains God's chosen people and heir to His promises as stated in verse 28.

The signs of Matthew 24 are presented to the elect — yes, elect Israel. We know this to be true in this chapter because of the regard for the Sabbath day (verse 20), because of the connection with synagogues (Luke 21:12), and because the setting of Matthew 24 is Jerusalem (verse 20).

Only Bible manipulators, anti-dispensationalists, anti-literalists, British Israelites, and Garner Ted Armstrongites could make Gentiles out of these Jews.

Included in this group are the twelve tribes of the children of Israel. Twelve thousand shall be chosen from each of the twelve tribes. Twelve thousand times twelve equals one hundred fourty-four thousand. The tribes are Juda, Reuben, Gad, Aser, Nepthalim, Manasses, Simeon, Levi, Issachar, Zabulon, Joseph, and Benjamin (Revelation 7). The names even sound Jewish. Smith, Olson, Dillon, and Deboer do not fit the bill. Quit listening to men. The proof is before you. Believe it! Don't miss it! These signs are for Israel who is looking for the return of her King in Revelation 19. They are not signposts for the Rapture. They fit into the Book of Revelation in chapters 6-18. The church is gone in chapter 4, and 6 follows 4.

This is also why the crowd looking for the fulfillment of the signs in Matthew 24 is preaching a different Gospel in verse 14. Gospel means "good news," and their good news is the Gospel of the Kingdom, or the good news that their King is about to return (Revelation 19:16). They will be traveling around the globe, 144,000 strong, singing "The King is Coming! The King is Coming!"

Although the signs are all fulfilled *after* the Christians are gone, we already see the *beginnings* of every one of these signs. Again, this means that if these signs pointing to our return

21

with the King are already in their initial stages, we must be gone very soon in order to prepare for our return to earth *with* Christ the King.

False Christs

In Matthew 24:3, Jesus was asked: " . . . when shall these things be? and what shall be the sign of thy coming [to earth], and of the end of the world [or Age of Grace]?" He replied in verse 5: " . . . many shall come in my name, saying, I am Christ; and shall deceive many." Has it happened? Since the year 1900, over 1,100 false Christs have appeared on the scene: Father Divine, New York City; Prophet Jones, Detroit, Michigan; Sweet Daddy Grace, southern states; Father Riker, Holy City, California; Daniel Swalt, Seattle, Washington; Moses Guibbory, Israel; Maharaj Ji, India, and Dr. Sun Myung Moon, Korea, not to mention scores of lesser-known, self-proclaimed messiahs.

Eventually, a false Christ — one who is probably alive even at this moment — will proclaim himself as the true Christ and become accepted on an international scale. The Bible predicts such an hour in II Thessalonians 2:4, when the Antichrist "Who opposeth and exalteth himself above all that is called God, or that is worshipped . . . sitteth in the temple of God, shewing himself that he is God." This internationally deified dictator will inaugurate a world peace program which holds the world spellbound for 42 months, or 3½ years. Then, in the middle of

the seven-year period of Tribulation, he breaks all
of his pledges and destroys his contractual obliga-
tions with Israel (Daniel 9:27). At this time, Russia
begins a world war as she invades Israel (Ezekiel
38). This war involves all nations (Zechariah 14).
This is God's outline from the Bible. First, the
international dictator establishes global peace,
and, when the world believes that Utopia has
arrived, the bottom falls out of their hopes and
aspirations: "For when they shall say, Peace and
safety; then sudden destruction cometh upon them
. . . " (I Thessalonians 5:3). This thought leads into
the next sign Christ mentioned.

Wars and Rumours of Wars

" . . . ye shall hear of wars and rumours of wars:
see that ye be not troubled: for all these things must
come to pass, but the end is not yet. For nation
shall rise against nation, and kingdom against
kingdom . . . " (Matthew 24:6).

From this proclamation one sees that the world
can expect nothing but rivalry and battles until the
Antichrist produces the false peace of the Tribulation Era. Thirty to forty limited wars have been
fought since the end of the second World War, and
presently one out of every four nations on earth is
engaged in conflict. Soon, we will experience the
greatest global confrontation in the annals of history, for we are marching toward Armageddon at
this very moment.

Admiral Sharpe recently said: "The American

people are being misled. The Soviets are building up their armed forces at a furious pace. They can, from 400 miles out at sea, hit all of our coastal cities and more than 60% of our population with their nuclear warheads. The American people must be jarred out of their euphoria and made to realize that our way of life is threatened. We must wake up and get on with the job if we are to survive as a nation."

Lord Shear, reporting on the recent meeting of the Stockholm International Peace Research Institute said: "Thirty-five nations will have developed nuclear bombs by 1985, and war will become inevitable." The 200 experts from 25 nations believe that, by 1985, deterrents as we have known them will have become impossible and war will become a reality.

Dr. David Lillianthal, first Chairman of the Atomic Energy Commission, stated in the *New York Times:* "I am glad I am not a young man, and I am sorry for my grandchildren." His statement was made in the connection with the rapid and terrifying spread of nuclear explosives around the globe.

As if these statements were not fearsome enough, a recent UPI release out of Moscow declares: "Top ranking party officials believe today that the Soviet Union is mightier that it ever has been, and is no longer threatened by force, making the triumph of Communism inevitable." Janos Kadar, Hungary's Communist leader, told 5,000 delegates to the Soviet Party Congress, "There is no force on earth that can stop the

Soviet Union's advance and the triumph of Communism.''

The latest CIA and British Intelligence reports concerning the Soviet Union are also very grim. They state that the development of new weapons systems, located throughout the Soviet Union, along with expenditures of enormous sums for underground civil defense shelters can only mean that Russia is preparing for war. Ezekiel, chapters 38 & 39, picture the Russian hordes from the north swarming to the Middle East. The Red Horse of the Apocalypse is about to appear. Revelation 6:4 states: ''There went out another horse that was red, and power was given to him that sat thereon, to take peace from the earth, that they should kill one another. And there was given unto him a great sword.'' The signs abound — come quickly, Lord Jesus.

Famines and Pestilences

Christ added in Matthew 24:7: '' . . . and there shall be famines, and pestilences . . . ''

Presently, two billion of the world's inhabitants are going to bed hungry each night. Thousands are dying painful deaths, while scores of others are too numb with hunger to realize what is happening. *U.S. News and World Report* featured an article describing starvation which stated: ''First the belly swells, then the hair turns gray and the skin cracks; after a while the victim dies in mute misery.'' Such an experience will soon be the fate of millions upon millions. Dr.

25

Paul Erlich, a biochemist at Stanford University, says: "It is already too late to prevent famines that will kill millions. Already one-half billion are starving and another billion are malnourished. There is no possible solution in the near future because it is too late to produce enough food, so mass starvation is under way."

America will undoubtedly be a part and parcel of this suffering in the days ahead. In fact, the number of the beast, 666, may come into existence through an international rationing plan. Soon the voice of Revelation 6:6 will sound: " . . . A measure of wheat for a penny . . . " A measure in Bible times was a quart, and a penny was a day's wages. Imagine, a loaf of bread for a day's labor. It's coming — and SOON!

Pestilence, the twin sister of hunger, is also on the rampage. The swine flu scare, legionnaire's disease and other maladies were but the beginning. *Reader's Digest* reprinted an article from *Time* entitled, "The Bugs are Coming," indicating yet another pestilential plague in its preparatory stages. This report stated that the South American fire ant has advanced from its initial beachhead in Mobile, Alabama, and now infests one hundred billion acres in nine southern states, sometimes driving farm workers from the fields because of its fiery sting. In forest areas, the gypsy moth, the Spruce budworm and the Southern Pine beetle are wreaking devastation on huge areas of woodland, defoliating and killing millions of valuable trees — enough, in fact, to build 910,000 houses per year! Corn boars and rootworms are attacking crops in the corn belt at an incredible rate, and the boll weevil costs United States farmers $260,000,000 annually in crop losses. The mosquito is infecting one million humans per year in sub-Sahara Africa, and killing 100,000 annually with malaria while the black fly in the Volta River Basin blinds 700,000 each year.

Yes, the insect world is multiplying unbelievably. Entomologists estimate that the number has now climbed to one quintillion among five million different species. In fact, if one could weigh all insects together, their combined weight would be *twelve times that of the entire human race.* Undoubtedly, the pestilence that Jesus predicted will soon rear its head in monstrous proportions, and world hunger will be felt by every country on earth. This, along with what comes out of the bottomless pit in Revelation 9:2 (causing the plague of verse 3) is just around the corner. Listen to the prediction: " . . . there came out of the smoke locusts upon the earth: and unto them was given power, as the scorpions of the earth have power." The purpose is to destroy and kill. Oh, it's wonderful to be saved, awaiting the hour of deliverance via the Rapture.

Earthquakes

Jesus also said: "[There shall be] earthquakes, in divers places" (Matthew 24:7).

Men foolishly say: "We've always had earthquakes. How can this be a sign?'' Get ready Mr. skeptic! The Lord made this prediction around 30 A.D. From the year He made the statement until 1959, a total of 24 major earthquakes were recorded. Since 1960, however, more than 30 major quakes have jolted and jostled the earth. Think of it! Twenty-four major quakes in 1,929 years, and over 30 in less than 25 years. Furthermore, seismologists inform us that when the North Pole wobbles off center ten degrees, devastating earthquakes are imminent. Presently, the Pole wobbles almost *15* degrees off center! How quickly could the hour of Tribulation soon engulf the world!

Iniquity

Christ went on to say in His pronouncement of signs: "And because iniquity shall abound, the love of many shall wax cold" (Matthew 24:12).

What a portrait of modern-day America and the world! The U.S. Justice Department reports that in 1980, 30 percent of the nation's households were victimized by serious crime. The U.S. attorney general says that one of every 16 American families is brutalized by violent crimes such as murder, rape, and aggravated assault.

The FBI index for 1979 also paints a grim portrait: " . . . a murder every 24 minutes; a forcible rape each seven minutes; a robbery every 68 seconds; and an aggravated assault each 51 seconds. The total figures show that a violent crime was committed every 27 seconds, a property crime every three seconds."

The book, *American Averages: Amazing Facts of Everyday Life,* written by Mike Feinsilber and William B. Mead and published by Doubleday, presents additional facts concerning the current scene in our nation. The authors inform us that on an average day in America: (1) 1,282 illegitimate babies are born; (2) 2,740 children run away from home; (3) 1,986 couples divorce; (4) 68,493 teenagers come down with venereal disease; (5) 2,740 teenagers become pregnant; (6) 3,231 women have abortions; (7) people drink 90 million cans of beer; (8) people smoke 1.6 billion cigarettes.

As a result of this present situation, coldness saturates the church of the Lord Jesus Christ. Some churches are so cold that the sign above the entrance should read: "First Church of the Deep Freeze, pastored by Dr. Jack Frost." The situation has become so drastic that the verse, "Many [are] called, but few [are] chosen," might well state: "Many are cold, and a few are frozen." We need an old-fashioned Holy Ghost revival to put the fire of God back into His people. Sin abounds and silence prevails because men of the cloth do not have enough backbone to take a chiropractic adjustment. Oh, Jesus is coming soon!

Signs in Space

Verses 27-31 of the 24th chapter of Matthew tell us: "For as the lightning cometh out of the east, and shineth even unto the west; so shall also the coming of the Son of man be. For wheresoever the carcase is, there will the eagles be gathered together. Immediately after the tribulation of those days shall the sun be darkened, and the moon shall not give her light, and the stars shall fall from heaven, and the powers of the heavens shall be shaken: And then shall appear the sign of the Son of man in heaven: and then shall all the tribes of the earth mourn, and they shall see the Son of man coming in the clouds of heaven with power and great glory. And he shall send his angels with a great sound of a trumpet, and they shall gather together his elect from the four winds, from one end of heaven to the other."

This awe-inspiring picture is not the Rapture but the Revelation, or revealing of Christ to all the world as He returns to earth as King of Kings. The elect mentioned in this text are the elect Israelites of Romans 11:28 discussed earlier. They are converted nationally (Romans 11:26), and He gathers them together "from the four winds." Gentile believers are not listed with the twelve tribes who mourn as Christ returns.

Again, these are Jewish signs pointing to Christ's coming as King of Kings and Lord of Lords, and the people of the Tribulation Hour will know when the momentous event is near because verse 29 pinpoints the time: "Immediately after the tribulation of those days shall the sun be darkened, and the moon shall not give her light, and the stars shall fall from heaven,

and the powers of the heavens shall be shaken."
No doubt about it. The space signs are for the
close of the Tribulation Hour. There is no way
that they could point to the pre-Tribulation Rapture, for we Christians are gone when the dreadful bombardment of earth from space occurs.

Luke adds to this account in chapter 21:25-26:
"And there shall be signs in the sun, and in the
moon, and in the stars; and upon the earth
distress of nations, with perplexity; the sea and
the waves roaring; Men's hearts failing them for
fear, and for looking after those things which are
coming on the earth: for the powers of heaven
shall be shaken." Now watch it. These signs
point to the close of the Tribulation Hour
because they signal the return of the King to
earth. Verse 27 says: " . . . then shall they see
the Son of man coming in a cloud with power
and great glory." This is the coming of Christ to
set up His glorious millennial reign for 1,000
years (Revelation 20:6).

The Signs and Space Activities

As stated previously, these space signs, which
are to take place at the conclusion of the Tribulation Hour or almost seven years after the
believer's departure via the Rapture, are *already*
showing partial fulfillment. Humans walking,
driving and planting a flag on the moon certainly
make one realize that the signs are only for twentieth century citizens. Had one made such a
prediction at the turn of the century, he would

have become a candidate for a mental institute. Today, space activity has become so commonplace that no one even talks about the first step Neil Armstrong took on the moon in 1969.

To the argumentative skeptic who ridiculously states: "Oh we have always had signs — nothing has changed. It's the same as it was in grandma's day," I say, "get your head out of the sand, Mr. Ostrich, and fix your eyes on the heavenlies. The space age is with us, and Christ's prophecies are occurring with such alarming rapidity that only a hardened heart could doubt it." *U.S. News & World Report,* October 3, 1977, carried an article entitled, **"From Sputnik to Shuttle."** This informational report proved that all thrilling feats in space have occurred within the last 20 years — our generation. I list the facts:

1. **August 12, 1960**: The first communications satellite to transmit television, Echo 1, was orbited.

2. **November 29, 1961**: The first chimpanzee, Enos, was launched into space.

3. **June 28, 1965**: The first commercial communications satellite was propelled into the heavenlies.

4. **April, 1967**: The first pictures from the surface of the moon were taken by Surveyor 3.

5. **December, 1968**: Apollo 8 became the first manned space flight to orbit the moon.

6. **July, 1969**: The first low pass over Mars was made by Mariner 6.

7. **July 20, 1969**: The first man arrived on the moon via Apollo 11.

8. **August, 1971**: The first use of a motor-driven vehicle carrying astronauts on the surface of the moon took place.

9. **December 31, 1973**: The first spacecraft investigation of Jupiter, by Pioneer 10, was made.

10. **July 20, 1976**: The first successful, long duration mission to the surface of Mars was completed by Vikings 1 and 2.

11. **September, 1977**: The first mission to attempt the examination of Uranus was launched, and is set to encounter the planet in 1986.

Since this article appeared, of course, America has successfully begun her space shuttle program. Scientists and engineers anticipate that during the present decade these shuttles will make weekly flights out of earth's atmosphere. Technicians on board will attempt the manufacturing of metals, crystals and drugs in a weightless environment — a pioneering project which will lead to the establishment of work camps and space laboratories which will serve as man's first outposts on a new frontier. Eventually, scientists and engineers will shoot solar cells across miles of space to beam electricity to earth via microwaves. Each new venture will incorporate additional methods of placing the potentials of space on earth. **Wow! What a day to be alive!**

If one thinks that he has observed frightening signs in the twentieth century, let him study the predictions for the future. Through these he will certainly come to the conclusion that Christ's astounding prophetic statements about space are beginning to fill the skies in an alarming way. Aerospace writer Edwin G. Pipp recently stated that the next war could be fought *entirely* in space. He reports: "Military experts laughed at mention of space warfare only two years ago, but today it is neither a laughing matter nor the figment of comic book, movie serial or science fiction imaginings. In fact, inquiries by the *Detroit News* have led to the conclusion that the United States and Russia are now spending millions of dollars on equipment that could be used in future battles between spacecraft hundreds of miles above the earth." Articles such as these help one realize that Satan and his demonic hosts could use the world's inventions for the war of wars described in Revelation 12:7-9: "And there was war in heaven: Michael and his angels fought against the dragon; and the dragon fought and his angels, And prevailed not; neither was their place found any more in heaven. And the great dragon was cast out, that old serpent, called the Devil, and Satan, which deceiveth the whole world: he was cast out into the earth, and his angels were cast out with him."

The Signs and Space Phenomena

I also have no doubt that the rash of reports about UFOs are connected with the spirit world. One need not ask, "Is there life on other planets?" This is unimportant. There is life in the heavenlies, for the stratosphere is full of demonic spirits, and they are alive. This could

34

easily explain the thousands of saucer sightings. For instance, Santa Cruz, California (UPI): "It is now known that two Apollo crews were followed by unidentified flying objects during their lunar missions. Professor James Harder, an engineering professor at the University of California at Berkeley, told a symposium that Apollo 11 was followed halfway to the moon and that a UFO trailed Apollo 12 on three orbits around the moon. He stressed that the Space Administration suppressed the UFO incidents to avert panic. He said that he had discovered the Apollo 11 incident while reviewing tape recorded conversations between the spacecraft and Houston space control. He also said that Apollo 12's report was disclosed by a member of the space team. Official explanations that the objects were part of the spacecraft trailing behind were not supported by the speed observed on NASA instruments."

Whatever these UFOs are, I definitely believe they are connected with the spirit world. Ezekiel 1 and II Kings 2:11 talk about "angels in chariots of fire." Whoever mans them is not the important point. The fact that weird signs in space are prophesied for the latter days is. It makes one realize that the coming of the Lord is near. Because of it one should live as though he could meet the Saviour at any moment.

3
Signs Within Man

The signs indicating Christ's return are not limited to happenings on the earth and in space. The Bible also tells us that man himself will play a most significant role in declaring the end of the age.

Describing the attitude of mankind and the conditions which will prevail upon the earth at the time of His return, the Lord Jesus said: "But as the days of Noah were, so shall also the coming of the Son of man be. For as in the days that were before the flood they were eating and drinking, marrying and giving in marriage, until the day that Noah entered into the ark, And knew not until the flood came, and took them all away; so shall also the coming of the Son of man be. Then shall two be in the field; the one shall be taken, and the other left. Two women shall be grinding at the mill; the one shall be taken, and the other left. Watch therefore: for ye know not what hour your Lord doth come" (Matthew 24:37-42).

We discover in this portion of Scripture that, upon Christ's return, conditions on earth will be exactly as they were during Noah's era of time: "And it came to pass, when men began to multiply on the face of the earth, and daughters were born unto them, That the sons of God saw the daughters of men that they were fair; and they took them wives of all which they chose . . . And God saw that the wickedness of man was great in the earth, and that every imagination of the thoughts of his heart was only evil continually . . . The earth also was corrupt before God, and the earth was filled with violence" (Genesis 6:1, 2, 5, 11).

Illicit Sex

The first sign in this listing has to do with sex. "They took them wives . . . " (Genesis 6:2). In so doing, they went against the lesson God had given them at creation. God said, " . . . It is not good that the man should be alone; I will make him an help meet for him" (Genesis 2:18). Now what did God create? He did not create a man for a man. Instead, He created ONE WOMAN for ONE MAN. This is God's instituted order for the universe. Lust and sin have, however, changed the Almighty's program.

Presently, men and women are running away from one another, leaving children destitute and homes broken — all because they must satisfy the flesh. Someone compliments them, they become enamored, and suddenly find themselves infatuated with the *idea* of love rather than genuine love. Soon it is adultery, divorce and remarriage, only to discover that the second and third choices were no better than the first. The trouble is not the first mate, but sin! Today, one-third of all American marriages end up on the casualty listings. The signs of Noah's era are repeating with great prolificacy.

Jesus also added that they were "giving in marriage." Dr. M.R. DeHaan and other scholars render this as "exchanging mates" or "wife swapping." Swingers are the rage of the day. They get together for a supper bash and end up exchanging their mates for a night of glorified orgies. How low can humans go? The situation dominates modern society and has the curse of God upon it. Hebrews 13:4 states: "Marriage is honourable in all, and the bed undefiled: but whoremongers and adulterers God will judge."

Despite God's warning, millions disobey His commandments. They live life loosely and laugh it off. Sin, however, will bring it's reward. The mills of God grind slowly, but exceedingly fine. The day of sifting and judgment is coming. Soon a sin-crazy, hell-bent generation will meet the God of holiness and the joke will end. May I ask you a personal question? Is an hour of sin worth an eternity of fire? Think it over.

Gluttony and Drunkenness

Christ also mentioned gluttony and drunkenness as signs foreshadowing His return. He said, " . . . they were eating and drinking . . . " and "For as [it was] in the days that were before the flood . . . so shall also the coming of the Son of man be" (Matthew 24:37-39).

The fool's motto is, "eat, drink and be merry, for tomorrow we die." Bars and nightclubs throughout the nation advertise the "happy hour," meaning drinks for half price during a specified time. All it means is that one can go into an eternal hell at a savings. The signs are here and overindulgence is seen everywhere. Millions of Americans are also following scores of diet plans. If one really desires to succeed, he should try fasting and praying two days each week. God's program works miracles!

Again, never have we had so many alcoholics or drug addicts during any similar period of world history. America's combined total exceeds 20 million. Belgium, Holland, France — yea, all Europe, Asia and the continents of the world are in the same dilemma. An epidemic of intoxication prevails. Satan's brew is eye-enticing and nose-appealing and millions have fallen victim to his seduction. However, it will not last forever! The third and fourth seals of the apocalypse picture shortages, poverty, hunger and death.

Revelation 6:7, 8 state: "And when he had opened the fourth seal, I heard the voice of the fourth beast say, Come and see. And I looked, and behold a pale horse: and his name that sat on him was Death, and Hell followed with him. And power was given unto them over the fourth part of the earth, to kill with sword, and with hunger, and with death, and with the beasts of the earth." Tragic isn't it? Wait, there's more. When life ends, as it must for all mortals, because " . . . it is appointed unto men once to die" (Hebrews 9:27), the sinner must enter a place where even water is unattainable. Christ told of a lost sinner crying out from hell, saying, " . . . send Lazarus, that he may dip the tip of his finger in water, and cool my tongue; for I am tormented in this flame" (Luke 16:24). Is liquor worth eternal thirst? Think and rethink the issue.

The sign is with us. Christ is coming soon!

Corruption

Noah's era was also one of corruption. Genesis 6:5 reports: " . . . every imagination of the thoughts of [man's] heart was only evil continually." The result: "The earth also was corrupt before God . . . " (Genesis 6:11).

It takes no stretch of one's imagination to see a world of men filled with vile imaginations. This is history's worst hour. Undoubtedly, filthy, pornographic magazines and R and X-rated movies have brainwashed the depraved into submission. Vile, lewd and licentious pornography floods the world and is having its effect. Savages are roaming the streets raping and sodomizing victims. It is portrayed on the silver screen. If actors can get away with it, why not the average citizens?

Since morality is the essence of God's Ten Commandments, as well as the entire teaching of the Holy Bible, Christians should be crusaders in the battle against the world, the flesh and the devil. How sad to see many pornographic bookstores within a few doors of gospel-preaching churches. Does Rev. Milquetoast do anything about it? No. He wants peace with the world — an armistice with iniquity. This is contrary to the Almighty God who, in Isaiah 58:1, demands that His servants: *"Cry aloud, spare not, lift up thy voice like a trumpet, and shew my people their transgression, and the house of Jacob their sins. "* Pastor Gareth B. Miller, president of FARMS, International, states: "If you don't want child porn and its sister, prostitution, then you've got to get rid of obscenity at every level, for eventually it *will* reach out to children. Even the Supreme Court has stated emphatically that the First Amendment does not protect obscenity. But the laws must be enforced at all levels; local, State, and Federal."

Pastor Miller goes on to say that Christians are not speaking out against obscenity. "It is a devilish deception when Christians think *their* children are safe because they are in a Christian school and church," he says. "The home is being invaded through television and popular magazines." His views are supported by Mortan A. Hill, president of Morality in Media and a member of the Presidential Commission on Obscenity and Pornography. He states that the influence of secular humanism in America has duped the public into believing that it has to accept everything with no right of dissent. Millions of Americans have accepted the philosophy that there is no right or wrong. Thus, the purveyors of smut capitalize on the opportunities that an uncaring public hands them on a silver platter. "We already have Federal, State and local laws making it a crime to traffic in obscenity," states Mr. Hill, "but the public does not care enough to demand law enforcement."

The present scene has become so nauseating that celebrities, professional counselors and media executives themselves are speaking out. Actor and Comedian Steve Allen states: "TV has

41

gotten too dirty. Much of television is what I call junk food for the mind. The people who run the networks are perfectly intelligent people — responsible citizens. However, they run junk to keep the ratings high." In turn, a Yale University psychiatrist, Dr. Robert Abramovitz says: "Kids learn aggression from TV. Anyone who has been brainwashed 15,000 hours via television by the age of 18 has learned aggression, profanity and filthiness." Likewise, Gene Rogers, a Chicago broadcasting executive, has stated: "The day of filth has arrived. Every other record I receive has cursing in it. The majority of TV shows have cursing in them . . . Have we sunk so low that we have sold our children to the dogs in order to make a dollar?"

A radio station disc jockey in Michigan just sent a shocking report to me. Several months ago he began a project geared to investigating "hidden messages" in the music of many popular rock groups and artists. He had been informed that by playing the recordings backward on the station's sophisticated electronic equipment, concealed messages could be discovered. It is contended that these messages are subliminally implanted into the mind of a person listening to the recording in normal fashion via a record or tape player. The first album so investigated was, *Stairway to Heaven*, recorded by Led Zeppelin. The result? Eight distinct words and phrases through the course of the album. When placed together, these items produced the following message: "Listen, we've been there. Because I live, serve me. There's no escaping it, Satan. If we got to live for Satan, Master Satan." A second album investigated contained the message: "The music is reversible, but time is not. Turn back, turn back, turn back!" These words were camouflaged within the music itself as the recording was played in normal fashion, appearing as a background distortion to the keen musical ear. However, when the recording was played in reverse, the message was spoken in clear, crisp reverberating words.

This report is corroborated by a *Detroit News* article of December, 1981, entitled: **"Satan's Messages."** In it, UPI writer Betty A. Luman states: "A technique of hiding backwards lyrics in rock music is placing evil messages in the subconscious minds of listeners, said a minister who is angry at what he said these messages can do to young people. James Gilbert, the minister of youth at the Church of Christ in Kaufman, a town of 5,000 southeast of Dallas, said he is intrigued 'and scared' by the subliminal message hidden in some rock music. He is especially appalled at the technique of 'backward masking.' 'They're messing with your mind and you don't even know it. Subliminal persuasion is as close to mind control as you can get,' he states.

"The technique of backward masking is confirmed by recording industry spokesmen in Dallas. 'Quite often on certain pieces of music they will put something in backwards,' said Tom Gondolf, chief engineer for Goodnight Audio. 'The Beatles used to put voices on backwards all the time, especially during the "Paul is dead" thing.'

"Songs by the Beatles, Led Zeppelin, Black Oak Arkansas and Queen include hidden messages . . . [others] are listed in a book by Bob Larson, *Rock — Practical Help for Those Who Listen to the Words and Don't Like What They Hear.* In Queen's song, *Another One Bites the Dust,* the words of the title are repeated several times at the end. But played backwards, one hears 'decide to smoke marijuana' over and over, Gilbert said. The Beatles song, *Revolution No. 9,* repeats the words 'number nine' over and over. When played backwards, it plainly repeats 'turn me on dead man.' When the Black Oak Arkansas song, *The Day Electricity Came To Arkansas,* is played backwards it says, 'Satan, Satan, Satan. He is God, He is God. He is God.' "

Columnists Jack Anderson and Joe Spear inform us that even the government has fallen prey to psychic phenomenon, stating: "We have been reporting for months that the Pentagon is experimenting with psychic warfare. The projects had been cloaked in the deepest secrecy; the ostensible reason was national security. But the projects are so bizarre that another possibility for secrecy suggests itself: sheer embarrassment.

"The Navy, for example, paid 34 psychics $400 a month each to try to read the minds of Soviet submarine commanders under the seven seas. The Air Force tried to determine whether a psychic could move the quarter-ounce trigger of a nuclear bomb by sheer willpower. The Pentagon even discussed the possibility of a time warp which would intercept incoming Soviet missiles over the North Pole and cause them to detonate thousands of years ago.

"Now we've learned that the Army is providing financial support for the 'First Earth Battalion' which may be schooled at a monastery in Santa Fe, New Mexico. Members of this elite unit will be trained to meditate while marching, communicate with each other by ESP and to combat the enemy with the 'force of love.' The First Earth Battalion will also be armed with tanks and armored personnel carriers equipped with stereo speakers that will blast loud rock music."

These reports amplify the admonition of the Apostle Paul who said in Ephesians 6:11, 12: *"Put on the whole armour of God, that ye may be able to stand against the wiles of the devil. For we wrestle not against flesh and blood, but against principalities, against powers, against the rulers of the darkness of this world, against spiritual wickedness in high places."* I could present scores of additional reports as studies have shown that most major rock groups and songs reflect association with the occult, drugs and/or religious cults. The point I am making is that millions of children have parents who allow them to watch anything on television or listen to any kind of music they desire. Hundreds of thousands of children have their own TV sets and stereo equipment.

This bombardment of continual wickedness,

implanting filth and false values in the individual minds of America, is presently reaping the harvest morally, spiritually and socially. Just as the degenerated values of society in Noah's day filled the world with violence, so sin, crime and fear increasingly stalk the citizens of this twentieth century.

I believe this present situation will become increasingly worse because the sign breaks forth in all of its debauchery during the Tribulation Hour. We are but observing the preview of coming events. Life will not be worth living during the Tribulation, because Satan will have been cast out of the heavens and will be enthroned upon the earth. Because he knows that he has but a short time to perform his heinous acts, and because of his impending incarceration for 1,000 years (Revelation 20:3), he will unleash all of his brutality and uncleanness upon earth's teeming millions. That is why Revelation 12:12 states: " . . . Woe to the inhabitants of the earth and of the sea! for the devil is come down unto you, having great wrath, because he knoweth that he hath but a short time."

I do not want to be around for earth's goriest, blood-soaked hour, do you? One does not have to experience earth's judgment pangs because the Rapture precedes this holocaust. Those who have trusted in Christ will be removed before the dreadful proceedings begin. Get saved now!

Signs of the Times and Christ's Return

Violence

If you procrastinate, violence will be the criteria of the hour. Christ said, " . . . as the days of Noah were, so shall also the coming of the Son of man be" (Matthew 24:37). Remember that Noah's day was one of violence (Genesis 6:11). Is it coming? Listen to the following leaders and think seriously:

Ron Newhouser, supervisor of anti-terrorist projects for the International Association of Chiefs of Police said: "We are ripe for terrorism and what we are seeing is only the beginning." J.F. TerHorst: "The U.S. is a likely target of terrorist groups. There is evidence that cooperation exists among American and foreign groups which could lead to a world revolutionary coup." Victor Riesel: "Revolutionary specters are stalking Capitol Hill. They range our nation and most of Europe." Paul Harvey: "When the Bolsheviks took over Russia they were a fraction of the population. This handful worked millions into a frenzy over working conditions. It may happen in America." *Skeptic Magazine* No. 11: "Militants may soon shoot down civilian jets. They may soon have the Sam 7 missile which weighs 25 pounds and can be fired from the shoulder in a field or from a house." Sir Brian Flowers, the British nuclear physicist says: "Terrorists will eventually get nuclear weapons. It is not a question of if, but when."

Colonel R.D. Heinl, Jr., *Detroit News* Military Analyst, reports: "Newly discovered information coming to the intelligence community is providing further evidence and much detail on the operations of a worldwide international terrorist network which has been functioning since 1969. They are an organized alliance with roots in Asia, the Middle East, Western Europe, Latin America and the U.S.A. The network's ideological cement is mixed from Marx and Mao, with proclaimed goals of 'world revolution,' to be attained through a worldwide war of terror against the advanced states in attempts to undermine their normal way of life and institutions. Libya is considered as the armorer of world terrorists, using stocks obtained from Moscow. While the scope of the terrorist alliance now is attaining global proportions, the Middle East remains its main base and sanctuary area — backed by Russian arms and manipulation."

Presently, a total of 370 terrorist groups are operating in 63 countries — and the casualties have reached an all-time high! Aside from the continuing problems in Afghanistan, Northern Ireland and Poland, the following sketches but skim the surface of the international scene:

• **Africa** —.From north to south, conflict has become a way of life as ambitious leaders vie for power.

• **China** — Chinese troops have killed scores of protesting workers on state farms in the western province of Xinjiang. A government memo stated: "Such incidences are warnings of the severity of measures we must take."

• **England** — Paralleled with the rise of

unemployment is a widespread wave of violence.

• **Italy** — The murder of prison guard Cinotti and the attempted assassination of Pope John Paul II are grim reminders that Italy's war on terrorism is far from over.

• **Latin America** — From Argentina to El Salvador, governments are in a state of turmoil and terrorism reigns.

• **The Middle East** — The clearest evidence of substantial Russian investment in terrorism can be found in the training camps of South Yemen, Libya, Iraq, Algeria, Syria and Lebanon.

A recent CIA study predicts an increasing number of casualties as terrorists become more sophisticated in their approach. The *New York Times News Service* reports that terrorists "may believe that a larger number of casualties are now necessary to generate the amount of publicity formerly evoked by less bloody operations."

There is no doubt that the world is in the most precarious position ever experienced in the annals of history. Violence is about to rear its ugly head in monstrous proportions. Millions will die. When it does occur, could it not be the Tribulation Hour? Could there really be anything worse than what is on the way?

Whenever the Tribulation Period arrives, two things will happen. First, the church will be kept " . . . from the hour of temptation, which shall come upon all the world . . . " (Revelation 3:10), and Israel will be preserved through the deluge of fire. Jesus said, " . . . as the days of Noah were, so shall also the coming of the Son of man be" (Matthew 24:37). Noah floated above the judgment. He and his loved ones were protected from watery graves. This will also be true of God's chosen people, the Jews. God will miraculously intervene. My question to you is, "are you ready?" Have you trusted in the blood of Christ Jesus shed upon Calvary for the remission of your sins? If not, why not? Prepare now and be ready when He returns — first for His own and then as King.

The signs of Mark 13:3-10 are identical to those already discussed in Matthew 24. Therefore, we move on to Luke 17:26-30: "And as it was in the days of Noah, so shall it be also in the days of the Son of man. They did eat, they drank, they married wives, they were given in marriage, until the day that Noah entered into the ark, and the flood came, and destroyed them all. Likewise also as it was in the days of Lot; they did eat, they drank, they bought, they sold, they planted, they builded; But the same day that Lot went out of Sodom it rained fire and brimstone from heaven, and destroyed them all. Even thus shall it be in the day when the Son of man is revealed."

Here we again discover that in the days of both Noah and Lot, overindulgence was the criteria of the hour. The people of both ages lived only to satisfy the cravings of the flesh.

Drunkenness

The Bible also tells us that both Noah and Lot

became intoxicated (Genesis 9:20, 21 and 19:32-35). Jesus said, "As it was, so shall it be," and never in the annals of history have we seen such an international deluge of drunkenness and drug addiction. America alone has 9 million alcoholics and 10 million drug addicts.

Perhaps someone reading this book is enslaved by the bottle, pill or needle. Is it really satisfying? Is it already ruining your home, destroying your marriage and spoiling your happiness? Are your children hungry, your pockets empty and life miserable? Christ can make a difference! St. Augustine said, "There is no peace until one finds the Prince of Peace, the Lord Jesus Christ." The bottle and needle can only destroy your quest for earthly and eternal life.

Proverbs 20:1 states: "Wine is a mocker, strong drink is raging: and whosoever is deceived thereby is not wise." Proverbs 23:29, 30 continue: "Who hath woe? who hath sorrow? who hath contentions? who hath babbling? who hath wounds without cause? who hath redness of eyes? They that tarry long at the wine . . . " Then, when earthly existence ceases, liquor's reward is hell. The Holy Spirit declares in I Corinthians 6:9, 10: "Know ye not that the unrighteous shall not inherit the kingdom of God? Be not deceived: neither fornicators, nor idolators, nor adulterers, nor effeminate, nor abusers of themselves with mankind, nor thieves, nor covetous, nor drunkards, nor revilers, nor extortioners, shall inherit the kingdom of God."

Galatians 5:19-21 mention 17 sins, and the sixteenth is listed as "drunkenness" and brings eternal loss, for the conclusion of the text states: " . . . they which do such things shall not inherit the kingdom of God." Do not let sin rob you of eternal life. This very sign of which you may be a statistic indicates that Christ's return is very near. When He returns, will you be ready?

Three Thrilling Signs

We find another triad of signs mentioned in Luke 21:24-28. Jesus said, "And they shall fall by the edge of the sword, and shall be led away captive into all nations: and Jerusalem shall be trodden down of the Gentiles, until the times of the Gentiles be fulfilled. And there shall be signs in the sun, and in the moon, and in the stars; and upon the earth distress of nations, with perplexity; the sea and the waves roaring; Men's hearts failing them for fear, and for looking after those things which are coming on the earth: for the powers of heaven shall be shaken. And then shall they see the Son of man coming in a cloud with power and great glory. And when these things begin to come to pass, then look up, and lift up your heads; for your redemption draweth nigh."

This portion of Scripture is utterly fantastic. It pinpoints the time of Christ's statement in all of its simplicity. In modern grammar, the Saviour declares: "There is an hour coming when Jerusalem shall be controlled by my people, the Jews. At this moment of time, there shall also be signs in space coupled with a trouble-filled world. When all of these events occur simultaneously, look up because my return to earth is very near.''

Search the annals of history. The conclusion? Jerusalem has always been under the heel of the Gentiles. In fact, the Gentiles controlled the Holy City for 25 centuries, but in our lifetime a miracle happened. Jerusalem was captured by the Jews in a six-day war fought June 5-10, 1967. Space spectaculars have also occurred. Men have walked and driven on the moon and Viking explorers have landed on Mars. In addition, multiplied nations are experiencing distress and turmoil in unbelievable proportions. The meaning? When these things begin to happen — not when they are fulfilled, but when they begin — then look up and lift up your heads, for your redemption draweth nigh. Are you ready?

Verse 34 continues: ''And take heed to yourselves, lest at any time your hearts be overcharged with surfeiting, and drunkenness, and cares of this life, and so that day come upon you unawares.'' Christ is saying, ''Don't be caught unprepared.'' Instead, ''Watch ye therefore, and pray always, the ye may be accounted worthy to escape all these things that shall come to pass, and to stand before the Son of man'' (verse 36). May I ask you some personal questions? Are you saved? If so, are you living completely for Christ? Do you spend time daily with the Lord in prayer and in His Word? Are you winning souls? Do you attend God's house morning and evening on the Lord's day? Are you tithing? Do you run with the world? Are there unclean habits in your life? Would you really like to meet Christ in your present condition? If many of the answers are negative, surrender your life anew to Christ today. Soon you will meet Him face to face.

Judgment

As we have already learned, the period of time which follows the Rapture and precedes Christ's return to earth is called the Tribulation (Revelation 7:14). The Rapture occurs in Revelation 4:1 and the Revelation — His return to the earth — occurs in Revelation 19:11. The chapters between the two events constitute the Tribulation Hour — a seven-year period of judgment. Christ referred to it in the statement: " . . . as it was in the days of Lot . . . Even thus shall it be in the day when the Son of man is revealed" (Luke 17:28, 30). The fire that consumed Sodom and Gomorrah pictures the devastating fire of the Tribulation Hour. Jeremiah 30:7 declares: "Alas! for that day is great, so that none is like it . . . " Daniel 12:1 states: " . . . there shall be a time of trouble, such as never was since there was a nation . . . " Jesus also declared in Matthew 24:21: "For then shall be great tribulation, such as was not since the beginning of the world to this time, no, nor ever shall be."

Included in this horrendous portrayal is a world on fire — similar to the judgment of Lot's day. The Bible says, " . . . the flaming flame shall not be quenched . . . " (Ezekiel 20:47).

Again, " . . . the whole land shall be devoured by the fire of his jealousy . . . " (Zephaniah 1:18). "For, behold, the day cometh, that shall burn as an oven . . . " (Malachi 4:1), " . . . and the third part of the trees was burnt up, and all green grass was burnt up" (Revelation 8:7). "By these three was the third part of men killed, by the fire, and by the smoke, and by the brimstone . . . " (Revelation 9:18).

Currently, a stockpile of nuclear explosives jams the weapons arsenals of the world. Reports indicate that the amount is equivalent to one ton of TNT for every person alive. Think of the mass destruction that shall be unleashed on this world during the Tribulation Hour! Isn't it wonderful to know that God's people will escape this catastrophic judgment? Revelation 3:10 declares: " . . . I also will keep thee from the hour of temptation, which shall come upon all the world to try them that dwell upon the earth." Again, this is what Christ meant when He stated: " . . . as it was in the days of Lot, so shall it be in the day of the Son of man." Lot and his loved ones were evacuated out of the city before the fiery incineration began. This has always been true. In Noah's day, God said to His own, "Come in." To Lot and his loved ones He said, "Come out." To His church or bride, Christ will soon say, "Come up" (Revelation 4:1).

Signs in the Epistles

In addition to those contained in the Gospel

accounts, the New Testament presents many other signs pointing to Christ's return. Let's consider II Timothy 3:1-5: "This know also, that in the last days perilous times shall come. For men shall be lovers of their own selves, covetous, boasters, proud, blasphemers, disobedient to parents, unthankful, unholy, without natural affection, trucebreakers, false accusers, incontinent, fierce, despisers of those that are good, traitors, heady, highminded, lovers of pleasure more than lovers of God; having a form of godliness, but denying the power thereof: from such turn away."

Some say, "Haven't these signs always existed? How can these be signs pointing to His return when we have always experienced some of them?" The answer is found by comparing Romans 1:28-32 with II Timothy 3:1-5. Paul, in Romans 1, is speaking about the pagan world of the ungodly. However, in II Timothy 3 he is speaking about the conditions that shall prevail at the end of the age of Christendom among those who profess the Christian religion. Did you get that? In Romans 1, he is talking about things that are happening among the pagans. In II Timothy 3, he speaks about the deterioration of the professing Church. Never before have we seen signs so drastically predominant in the Christian church than at this present hour. The only comfort we find in these conditions is that they do tell us that the coming of the Lord is at hand. We must be ready every moment. Let's consider these signs one by one.

Signs of the Times and Christ's Return

Selfishness

"Men shall be lovers of their own selves." What a picture of this present hour, when church members are so busy satisfying their flesh with the world's goodies and pleasures, that they have no time to pray or witness to lost souls. God help us!

A certain scribe came to Jesus in Matthew 22:36-40 and said, "Master, which is the great commandment . . . ? Jesus said unto him, Thou shalt love the Lord thy God with all they heart, and with all thy soul, and with all thy mind. This is the first and great commandment. And the second is like unto it, Thou shalt love thy neighbor as thyself. On these two commandments hang all the law and the prophets." Yet, we are so busy satisfying our bodily appetites in the professing church of Jesus Christ at the present hour, that we do not have time to pray or win souls to Him. We are lovers of our own selves. One could expect this in the ungodly world of pagans, but how sad when one sees it among those who are supposedly of the family of God.

The Love of Money

"Covetousness." In the first century, Peter could say: " . . . silver and gold have I none; but such as I have give I thee: In the name of Jesus Christ of Nazareth rise up and walk." The church has wealth untold, but it does not have the power to perform miracles. We are living in

the Laodicean age. Revelation 3:15, 16: "I know thy works, that thou art neither cold nor hot: I would thou wert cold or hot. So then because thou art lukewarm, and neither cold nor hot, I will spue thee out of my mouth." God says, "You make me sick!" Why? "Because thou sayest, I am rich, and increased with goods, and have need of nothing: and knowest not that thou art wretched, and miserable, and poor, and blind, and naked" (verse 17).

So many in our churches today are in the "upper crust." They have money, so they think they are really something. They are so important that they have no time to help people, no time to do things for Christ, no time for the church, no time for devotions, no time for anything except getting a few more dollars. In I Timothy 6:10 God says: "For the love of money is the root of all evil: which while some coveted after, they have erred from the faith, and pierced themselves through with many sorrows."

How sad it is in our day and age to pick up Christian periodicals and read, "Do you want to make $20,000 or $25,000 a year?" as though this was a believer's goal. Thank God when He blesses believers and they use it for His glory. I hope you are not one of the signs of the end. Do not try to get everything you can to build an empire here and neglect the work of Jesus Christ.

"Boasters, proud." God says: "Humble yourselves in the sight of the Lord, and he shall lift you up" (James 4:10). Satan fell because of pride. He said: " . . . I will ascend into heaven, I will exalt my throne above the stars of God: I will sit also upon the mount of the congregation, in the sides of the north: I will ascend above the heights of the clouds; I will be like the most High." (Isaiah 14:13, 14). Too many professing believers are also proud! A man recently came to me with tears in his eyes and said, "I was trying to win this young lady to Christ. Her parents are alcoholics and she had nothing to wear but an old tattered dress. I took her to our church — a fundamental, Bible-believing church. When she walked down the aisle, I heard a few snooty people behind me say, 'Why do they bring that kind of trash to our church!' "

If you are so high and mighty, I pray that God will speak to your heart and show you that you are one of the signs that Jesus Christ is coming soon. Our Saviour said in Matthew 11:28, 29, "Come unto me, all ye that labour and are heavy laden, and I will give you rest. Take my yoke upon you, and learn of me; for I am meek and lowly in heart: and ye shall find rest unto your souls."

Blasphemy

"Blasphemers." Blasphemy is a sin against the

Lord Jesus Christ. Paul said in I Timothy 1:12, 13, "And I thank Christ Jesus our Lord, who hath enabled me, for that he counted me faithful, putting me into the ministry; who was before a blasphemer . . . " What did he do? He murdered Christians and hated the name of Jesus Christ.

There are many doing similar things today. Our seminaries are filled with apostates who mock the doctrine of the Lord Jesus Christ — His virgin birth, His deity, His blood atonement and His bodily resurrection. They talk about higher criticism and blaspheme Christ in the scriptures. Seventy percent of the ministers are either affected or infected by this malady. God Help us! Jesus Christ is coming soon!

Disobedience

"Disobedient to Parents." Some young people say that they love Jesus Christ, yet when their parents ask them to do something, they always answer back with a smart remark. Do they really believe the Bible? Listen, young man and young lady, to Ephesians 6:1-3: "Children, obey your parents in the Lord: for this is right. Honour thy father and mother; which is the first commandment with promise . . . and thou mayest live long on the earth."

I was mightily moved not long ago as I studied John 19: 26, 27. These verses portray Jesus Christ hanging on the cross, dying for our sins. As He was about to expire, He looked down and saw His wonderful mother Mary standing beneath the cross. Do you know what He said? " . . . woman, behold thy son! Then saith he to the disciple, Behold thy mother!" Yes, even in the last moments of life as He was dying for the entire world, the Lord Jesus Christ still loved His mother. He came to fulfill the law, and He said in Matthew 19:19: "Honour thy father and thy mother . . . " Young people who are disobedient and disrespectful are a sign that Jesus is coming soon.

Unthankfulness

"Unthankful." Many church members find it difficult to give credit where credit is due. Because they seek their own glory, they refuse to recognize the accomplishments and contributions of others whom God has sent to share their labor and service.

Others never take the time to say "Thank you, Lord" for answered prayer, and still others are ashamed to pray in a restaurant. When they do bow their heads, they sit there and scratch their eyebrows for a few seconds so that no one will think they are talking to Almighty God.

Unholiness

"Unholy." What a picture of the twentieth century. Godly separation from the world, according to the Bible, is sneered at as bigotry and puritanism. When one preaches against the dirty,

lewd movies, the filthiness of much of this modern music called rock, the uncleanness of tobacco, the soul-damning habits of drug abuse and alcoholism, some church members say, "Let's not talk about secondary issues." My friend, the holiness of God and holy living are not secondary issues. I Thessalonians 4:7: "For God hath not called us unto uncleanness, but unto holiness. I Peter 1:16: " . . . be ye holy; for I am holy." Again, this sign indicates that Jesus is coming soon. I repeat — all of the signs given in II Timothy 3 have to do with Christendom and the professing church in the last days.

Lack of Love

The phrase, *"Without natural affection,"* refers to the dissolution of families because of the lack of love. Look at the divorce rate, the murder of babies through abortion, the stories appearing in the papers concerning parents beating their little ones to death or strangling them, and you will know that this sign is being fulfilled.

Broken Promises

"Trucebreakers." Has someone told you a secret in order that you might pray for them? Did you keep it, or did you spread gossip about that person? Promise breaking is another sign now being fulfilled.

Lying

"False accusers." Churches from one end of America to the other are splitting because of the exaggerated stories (outright lies) church members tell about other people. When one falsely accuses a brother, he breaks God's ninth commandment. Exodus 20:16 says, "Thou shalt not bear false witness . . . " Do you know what is going to happen to false accusers? Revelation 21:8 says: "But the fearful, and unbelieving, and the abominable, and murderers, and whoremongers, and sorcerers, and idolators, and all *liars* shall have their part in the lake which burneth with fire and brimstone . . . "

No Self-Control

"Incontinent." This term speaks of the lack of control over one's sexual appetites. The world says: "Live it up. Premarital and extra-marital sex is good and healthy. I say: " . . . let God be true, but every man a liar . . . " (Romans 3:4). Sex is pure and holy in marriage, for Hebrews 13:4 states: "Marriage is honourable in all, and the bed undefiled . . . " However, the verse continues: " . . . but whoremongers and adulterers God will judge."

I see so much of this debauchery taking place among church members as I travel across this land. Sins of all kinds are being condoned in this hour. Why? Because Jesus Christ is coming soon!

Temper

"Fierce." Some men would be minus their teeth if they talked to the waiter in the restaurant like they talk to their wives at home. Oh, they say they love Jesus Christ. They are great Christians at church, but what a fierce, vicious temper they exhibit at home and at work. "Let all bitterness, and wrath, and anger, and clamour, and evil speaking, be put away from you, with all malice" (Ephesians 4:31).

The signs "despisers of those that are good, traitors, heady, highminded: are all self-explanatory.

Pleasure

"Lovers of pleasure more than lovers of God." In the last days, men — professing Christians included — will be lovers of pleasure more than lovers of God.

This sign is becoming increasingly evident as churches go into the entertainment business in order to draw crowds. People want to be amused, and the church must meet the cravings of pleasure-mad members. How else are godless hypocrites going to be held together? How else can half-hearted members be attracted to the services? As a result, the latest Christian movie and the Christian minstrel show take the place of the Word of God. Beloved, God has not called us to run a showboat, but a lifeboat. We need to get souls into the kingdom of God.

Today, many religious telecasts and crusades feature pagan movie stars whose lives are a mockery to God. Still, their appearance is deemed appropriate because entertainers draw crowds. Some evangelistic meetings even feature people who are still working full time in nightclubs where drinking, gambling, filthy jokes, and solicitation for sex are prevalent. The organizers say, "It does not matter, because the end justifies the means. If these religious fakes draw crowds, then it is the right thing to do." God forgive us! Through it all, Christless souls are lulled to sleep and made to feel religious while every carnal desire of the flesh is gratified under the sanction of the church.

What is God's way to reach souls in the last days? "They that sow in tears shall reap in joy. He that goeth forth and weepeth, bearing precious seed, shall doubtless come again with rejoicing, bringing his sheaves with him" (Psalm 126:5, 6).

Lack of Power

"Having a form of godliness, but denying the power thereof" There is so little power in the church of God today. Again, Romans 1 is a picture of the pagan world while II Timothy 3 pictures the professing church just before Jesus comes.

Study all the signs and you will come to one conclusion: soon the trumpet of God shall sound and we shall hear three words, " . . . come up hither . . ." (Revelation 4:1). Then, in the twinkling of an eye, we will sweep through the heavenlies to meet Jesus. Are you saved? Are you ready? Jesus is coming soon! Sinner, let Him into your heart right now. Christian, let Jesus Christ have first place in your life. Soon we will see Him face to face.

Other New Testament Signs

Numerous New Testament passages speak about Christ's return. For instance, Titus 2:13 states: "Looking for that blessed hope, [the Rapture] and the glorious appearing [the Revelation] of the great God and our Saviour Jesus Christ." Hebrews 10:25 speaks about that great "approaching" day. James mentions the hoarding of gold and silver in the last days, stating: "Ye have heaped treasure, [gold and silver] together for the last days" (5:3). Likewise, Jude declares that, as the Lord returns with His saints, filthy dreamers or false prophets who have denied the Bible will be destroyed (verse 15).

Scoffers

Since the majority of texts we bypassed deal with the Rapture, Revelation or signs already discussed, we continue our study by investigating II Peter 3:1-4: "This second epistle, beloved, I now write unto you; in both which I stir up your pure minds by way of remembrance: That ye may be mindful of the words which were spoken before by the holy prophets, and of the commandment of us the apostles of the Lord and Saviour: Knowing this first, that there shall come in the last days scoffers, walking after their own lusts, And saying, Where is the promise of his coming? for since the fathers fell asleep, all things continue as they were from the beginning of the creation."

This sign has been misused, abused and confused beyond reality. I have personally encountered scores of duped sinners who said, "There is nothing new under the sun. My grandparents often told me that Christ was coming soon. They discussed the signs you are mentioning. Now they are dead and gone and everything is still status quo — nothing has changed. Therefore, it cannot happen — Christ will not return." Most of these hardened sinners talk this way — in nonsensical riddles — because of their lustful, worldly pursuits. If anyone reading this book is guilty of making such statements, may I try to help you mentally and spiritually.

Do you really think nothing has changed since your forefathers passed from the scene? In the light of current events, could you really be that blind? If so, read the following carefully. Christ did not say, "When wars, famines, pestilences and earthquakes occur, look . . . my return is near." Instead, He said, "When you shall see all [ALL — not one, or two, or even three signs transpiring, but when ALL are happening simultaneously], then know that it is near, even at the doors" (Matthew 24:33). Our generation is the only one in the annals of history to witness the initial stages of every prediction.

Jerusalem and the Gentiles

Greater still is the fact that signs no one has ever before observed are presently being witnessed. For instance, Luke 21:24: " . . . Jerusalem shall be trodden down of the Gentiles, until the times of the Gentiles be fulfilled." In modern English, Christ stated: "Jerusalem will be controlled by Gentile nations and powers until the time of my return." Timothy's grandmother, Lois, in II Timothy 1:5 may have mentioned this fantastic prophetical utterance to her grandson, but it did not happen in his lifetime. Generations of grandmothers continued to mention this sign to their loved ones and it never occurred. The mockers continued their abusive assaults crying, "Where is the promise of this coming? Since our grandparents departure, all things continue as they were." But God cannot lie (Titus 1:2). Finally, after 1,900 years of waiting, yea, after 75 to 100 generations of grandparents had lived and died, it happened. A six-day war was fought June 5-10, 1967. During the battle, the Jews took Jerusalem. Quit laughing and get saved — tomorrow may be too late!

A Day as a Thousand Years

As we continue our study in II Peter, we find a tremendous mathematical formula mentioned in verses 8 and 9: "But, beloved, be not ignorant of this one thing, that one day is with the Lord as a thousand years, and a thousand years as one day. The Lord is not slack concerning his promise, as some men count slackness; but is longsuffering to us-ward, not willing that any should perish, but that all should come to repentance." Let's analyze this mathematical masterpiece.

The promise God will keep is located in verse 4. It is the promise of His coming. Because God cannot lie (Titus 1:2), He *will* come again! His heart of love toward sinners is filled with patience, but soon the day of grace will end. The patience shown presently cannot go on eternally. His prearranged or predestined timetable must be fulfilled. What is it? Can mortals know such secrets? Yes! Jesus said, " . . . when ye shall see all these things, know that it is near, even at the doors" (Matthew 24:33). Though we will never know the day or hour (Matthew 24:36), we can know God's approximate schedule. How? "A thousand years is as a day and a day is as a thousand years." This is not as mysterious as it sounds. In fact, a small amount of mental calisthenics solves the equation. Are you ready?

God created the world in six days (Genesis 1:31) and rested on the seventh day (Genesis 2:2). So far so good. Since a day is as a thousand years and a thousand years is as a day, we have six days of labour, signifying six thousand years of burdensome toil for humanity, and a final seventh day of rest, or the millennial reign of Christ. Revelation 20:4 declares: " . . . they

lived and reigned with Christ a thousand years.''
Friend, the calendar on your wall indicates that
this prophecy is practically fulfilled.

Chronologists such as Ussher have worked
strenuously on historical timetables to produce
the following information: From Adam's creation to Christ's birth 4,004 years have passed.
From Christ's birth to our day, 1,983 years have
transpired. This gives us a total of 5,987 years.
The 13 years needed to complete the remaining
six days need explanation. Why? The Jewish
calendar contained 360 days per year. Revelation
11:2 mentions 42 months as a total of 1,260 days.
Each month, then, contained 30 days. Prove it to
yourselves: 42 x 30 equals 1,260. This is a five
day shortage annually on modern calendars.
When did the change occur? Approximately 400
years ago. This gives us 400 years of extra days or
a total of 2,000 24-hour days. In years, this totals
six. We now have 5,987 years from Adam to the
present, plus six extra years created by a calendar
change, plus seven years of tribulation, for a
grand total of 6,000 years.

We are on the threshold of the final day of rest!

The chronological tables could be off by five
years. However, we know that it is near, even at
the doors, though we know not the day and
hour. Beloved, just minutes remain before midnight. The closing day is upon us. Work is about
to cease and we believers are about to rule and
reign with the Lord Jesus Christ. Will you be

with Him then, and throughout eternity? Or will you share the reign of Antichrist 'and then a devil's eternal hell? These are serious questions! Prepare·to meet thy God (Amos 4:12).

Atoms and the End

In concluding this study, let's look at II Peter 3:10: "But the day of the Lord will come as a thief in the night; in which the heavens shall pass away with a great noise, and the elements shall melt with fervent heat, the earth also and the works that are therein shall be burned up."

Now, consider two interesting observations. First, God does not need man's modern inventions to produce the mass devastation in this text. The atoms have been here since " . . . God created the heaven and the earth" (Genesis 1:1). Only in our day have scientific geniuses learned to harness what has always existed. God could have brought the components together at any given point in history and produced the effects predicted in this prophecy. Secondly, this text pictures the total annihilation of the world. Since God's Word promises a final day of rest, there can be no complete obliteration of the earth until Christ has ruled and reigned for 1,000 years. Therefore, I believe this text is fulfilled after the Millennium.

The startling truth portrayed in this portion of scripture is that, presently, mankind has the potential to carry out that which prophecy predicts for humanity. Because he has harnessed this power, and because God's predictions for the Tribulation Hour concern themselves with fiery devastation, the hour most certainly is at hand.

Let me again point out that God is able to do everything mentioned in II Peter 3:10. He, the omnipotent One, needs no one else especially insignificant, puny men! Nevertheless, our text indicates that humans will use atoms during the Tribulation period, and at the end of the Millennium. My assumption is based on the fact that the very effects discovered in this can presently be fulfilled through created inventions.

Scientists tell us that there are three major effects of an A or H Bomb blast. First, there is the tremendous mushrooming effect as it ascends into the heavens upon detonation. Secondly, as it begins to descend, it disintegrates, dissolves and melts even steel. In fact, a 500-foot steel tower melted into nothingness in the desert of New Mexico during past experiments. Finally, the heat made the same desert a blazing inferno.

Now, observe carefully the statement that the Apostle Peter made under the direction of the Holy Spirit. First, " . . . the heavens shall pass away with a great noise." Second, " . . . the elements shall melt with fervent heat." This is utterly fantastic because the twentieth century scientists are using the very word God used 1,900 years ago. Imagine, God said, " . . . the ELEMENTS shall melt." Go to any library and make a study of atomic weaponry. Surprise! The materials will be classified under the letter "E"

— yes, under the word "Elements." Would you please tell me how man chose the very word God used 19 centuries ago? The answer is simple. God wrote the Bible. Finally, Peter states: " . . . the earth also and the works that are therein shall be burned up" (II Peter 3:10). Yes, the three effects of nuclear detonations are identical to Peter's prophecies and the catastrophic bombardments of earth predicted for the coming Tribulation Hour. Oh, hear the word of the Lord!

Undoubtedly, World War III will be one of incineration. Revelation 9:18 states: "By these three was the third part of men killed, by the fire, and by the smoke, and by the brimstone . . . "

I have stood in Japan, near Hiroshima, and remembered with sadness the reports of woe that emanated from the two Japanese cities struck by the atomic bomb during World War II. My mind was troubled. Then I thought about the Tribulation Hour. Zechariah 14:12 pictures the atomic devastation beyond comprehension. The prophet said, " . . . Their flesh shall consume away while they stand upon their feet, and their eyes shall consume away in their holes, and their tongues shall consume away in their mouth." This is the exact effect of mankind's newest weapon — the Neutron Bomb which destroys people, but not property! All of this is for the near future. Then, after the millennial reign of Christ, the final atomic detonation of II Peter 3:10 occurs.

The prophecies in this startling chapter again make us realize that the coming of our Lord

11:59 and Counting

Jesus Christ is very near. At a time when the world mocks His return and is in possession of atomic weaponry, and at an hour when the sixth day is about to expire, He will return. At best, the clock is ticking off its last seconds. Sinner, there is little time left. Soon you will be left behind with the scoffers. Then laughing will cease when the fire begins to fall. Then it will be eternally too late. Do something about your salvation while you can. " . . . behold, now is the accepted time; behold, now is the day of salvation" (II Corinthians 6:2). Christ died for your sins as He shed His precious blood 1,900 years ago. Everlasting life can be yours today if you will but trust Him.

4
Signs and the Revelation

In this final chapter of our study, let's examine portions of the Book of Revelation — the spoken testimony of the risen Christ concerning the course of history until His return to earth, the Millennium and the eternal state. (For a verse-by-verse explanation of this thrilling book, request my study, *Revelation Revealed,* on cassette or in paperback form).

Chronological Order

The Book of Revelation, penned through the instrumentality of John by the Holy Spirit, is presented in chronological order. In Revelation 1:19, God states: "Write the things which thou hast seen, and the things which are, and the things which shall be hereafter." One immediately notices three tenses — past, present and future. Past — "Write the things which thou hast seen . . . " (chapter 1); present — " . . . and the things which are . . . " (chapters 2 and 3); and future — " . . . and the things which shall be hereafter" (chapters 4-22).

In chapters 2 and 3, the panoramic historical view of the seven churches is presented. Presently, we are living in the Laodicean church period described in Revelation 3:15-17. God's statement concerning this age-ending church is, " . . . I would thou wert cold or hot. So, then because thou art lukewarm, and neither cold nor hot, I will spue thee out of my mouth. Because thou sayest, I am rich, and increased with goods, and have need of nothing; and knowest not that thou art wretched, and miserable, and poor, and blind, and naked."

What a graphic description of twentieth century Christendom. Our ranks are filled with lukewarm indifferent, lackadaisical members. Our services are deluged with formalism, ceremonialism and ritualism — all life-destroying procedures. Most sermons, extravagantly spiced with pleasing platitudes to enamor sinners, are void of effectiveness. No wonder God wants to regurgitate, spewing the distasteful mass of humans out of His mouth.

All of this precedes Christ's return. In fact, this attitude of the church may be the one pre-Rapture sign, if there are any. Why? In Revelation 4:1, we find the words, "After this [after what? After the pitiful situation of the end-time church is observed. Then John continues] I looked, and behold, a door was opened in heaven: and the first voice which I heard was as it were of a trumpet talking with me; which said, Come up hither . . . " This is the Rapture, the snatching away, the call of the Bridegroom for His bride. This must be so because the rewarded believers are already casting their crowns at Christ's feet in verses 10 and 11. What is next?

A World on Fire

As we progress to the eighth and ninth chapters of the Book of Revelation, we have two unusual predictions concerning the woes of the

Tribulation Hour. First, Revelation 8:7 mentions the burning of one-third of the earth. Second, Revelation 9:18 depicts the extinction of one third of the world's inhabitants. Could these prophetic and astronomical figures find fulfillment in our day? The answer is an unequivocal "yes!"

Recently, I studied an amazing statistical survey in *The Life Pictorial Atlas.* The continents, land areas and population figures were presented for every country in the world. In fact, I discovered that Africa, Antarctica, Asia, Australia, Europe, North America and South America covered a total of 56,889,581 square miles. I then decided to divide this figure by three, and the resulting sum was 18,963,194 square miles. This is the amount of land that will burn during the Tribulation period, according to our text. None of this was shocking until I futher studied the predicted alignment of nations mentioned in Daniel, chapters 2, 7 and 11, and in Ezekiel, chapters 38 and 39, for the Middle East confrontation. Their combined land area totaled — believe it or not — one third of the globe to the exact mile.

Rather than quote mind-boggling statistics for the next five pages in order to prove my findings, let me turn your attention to the following charts:

Life Pictorial Atlas of the World

Continent	Land Area (square miles):
Africa	11,635,000

Continent	Land Area (square miles):
Antarctica	5,100,000
Asia	17,035,000
Australia	2,974,581
Europe	3,850,000
North America	9,435,000
South America	6,860,000

One third is: 18,963,194

Nation:	Land Area (square miles):
Israel	7,990
Persian Empire (including West Pakistan)	1,996,145
Arab areas (Ethiopia, Libya)	3,487,943
U.S.S.R.	8,650,140
Gomer and his bands (Warsaw Pact nations)	381,934
The ten nation pact	763,412
U.S.A.	3,675,630
TOTAL:	**18,963,194**

If you find this information startling, let me go one step farther. The same atlas lists the population figures for the nations of the earth. The same alignment of pro and anti-Russian nations for the war of wars total one third of earth's inhabitants. Thus, Revelation 8:7 and 9:18 could become factual events in the near future.

Think of it! This is the war that leads to — not is — but leads to Armageddon. It also occurs, according to major Bible scholars, during the

Tribulation Hour. The signs of the times are present. How much more proof is needed to convince the lost that Christ's return is very near?

Murder, Drug Addiction, Sex and Burglary

Since horrible judgment has just been described, what is its cause? What sins are flooding the world in horrendous proportions during the Tribulation Hour? Why is a God of holiness angry?

Revelation 9:18-21 predicts the destruction of one-third of earth's billions, and states the reason: "Neither repented they of their murders, nor of their sorceries, nor of their fornication, nor of their thefts." This is certainly a portrait of today's society. These sins are already inundating the world. Thus, if this depiction of sordid sins finds its culmination during the Tribulation era, and presently the identical iniquities are flooding the earth, the logical conclusion is that we are swiftly moving toward the time of Tribulation.

The abominations mentioned in verse 21 are practically self-explanatory, especially the first, third and fourth sins. They are murder, fornication (or prolonged immorality) and stealing. The second, however, needs further elucidation.

In 27 texts of the Bible, "sorcery" usually means "magic" or "witchcraft." However, there are five instances in scripture when it definitely means drugs: Galatians 5:19; Revelation 9:21; Revelation 18:23; Revelation 21:8; and Revelation 22:15. In these texts the Greek root word is "pharmakeia." When it is translated into English, we have "pharmacy," or simply, "drugstore." The literal meaning is "to become enchanted with drugs." In other words, the world is enchanted with, high on, and getting its kicks out of drugs during this terrible era of time. Notice the outline of Revelation 9:21. In order to get their kicks out of drugs, the people turn to fornication — the selling of their bodies — to pay for their drugs. Thousands of others turn to thievery to support the deadly habit.

One further point of interest in this chapter is the tie-in of drugs, fornication and thievery with demon worship. Revelation 9:20: " . . . yet repented not of the works of their hands, that they should not worship devils . . . " I Timothy 4:1 predicts: "Now the [Holy] Spirit speaketh expressly, that in the latter times some shall depart from the faith, giving heed to seducing spirits, and doctrines of devils." This is also happening. The world is experiencing the initial preparations of a demonic invasion as Satan and his cohorts come from space to earth to wreak havoc (Revelation 12:9).

One World — One Church

In conclusion, I would like to present two more of the greatest signs mentioned in Holy Writ. In Revelation 13:1, 2, John says, "And I stood upon the sand of the sea, and saw a beast rise up out of the sea, having seven heads and ten horns, and upon his horns ten crowns, and upon his heads the name of blasphemy . . . the dragon gave him his power, and his seat, and great authority." This prophecy predicts a period of world government under a world leader. His power will be given to him by Satan, called "the dragon" (Revelation 13:2).

Revelation 13 and Daniel 2 and 7 present identical facts. Nebuchadnezzar, the king of ancient Babylon, had a dream, but forgot it. He immediately requested that his magicians and soothsayers identify the dream and its interpretation. None of his enchanters were able to meet his demands. Only Daniel, God's man, was able to fulfill the stringent request of the king. The report is recorded in Daniel 2:31-36. Verses 31-33 state: "Thou, O king, sawest, and behold a great image. This great image, whose brightness was excellent, stood before thee; and the form thereof was terrible. This image's head was of fine gold, his breast and his arms of silver, his belly and his thighs of brass, His legs of iron, his feet part of iron and part of clay."

The interpretation is located in verses 37-43. Let me give you the jist of the text. Daniel said, "Nebuchadnezzar, you are the head of gold. However, your glory will soon be diminished — the reason being that two arms of silver, representing the nations of Media and Persia, shall flatten your empire. Furthermore, as history continues, the Medes and Persians shall experience defeat at the hands of the Greeks, typified by the stomach of brass. Then, as the years pass, the iron legs of the Roman Empire shall bring Greece from its pedestal of power.''

Every history student realizes that each of the details mentioned thus far occurred in exact accordance with the predictions Daniel uttered. If this is so, then the final prophetical statement concerning the ten toes of iron and clay must also become a reality. Notice carefully that the iron is still in existence at the end time, but in a deteriorated condition. The ten toes have become mixed with clay. Is it not interesting to note that the Roman Empire was never defeated? It fell through corruption. Therefore, since it still exists, it returns to power at the end time in the form of a union of ten Western nations, each of which was a part of the original Roman Empire. We will discuss this prophecy in detail in Part II of this book. Meanwhile, suffice it to say that the Bible also teaches: ''And in the days of these kings [the alignment of the ten Western nations] shall the God of heaven set up a kingdom, which shall never be destroyed . . . '' (Daniel 2:44). Beloved, Christ is coming soon as King of kings and Lord of lords. Be prepared!

The final truth that I would have you see is that a world church is closely associated with this world government. Revelation 17 portrays a woman sitting upon the beast who rules internationally. John says, ''So he carried me away in the spirit into the wilderness: and I saw a woman sit upon a scarlet coloured beast, full of names of blasphemy, having seven heads and ten horns . . . and upon her forehead was a name written, Mystery, Babylon the Great . . . " (Revelation 17:3-5). Who is she? Verse 9 gives the answer: "And here is the mind which hath wisdom. The seven heads are seven mountains, on which the woman sitteth." Rome, the eternal city, is situated, geographically, upon seven hills. Thus, it is likely that the Roman Empire in its gloriously revived state brings the united world church, with headquarters in Rome, into prominence. This church reigns " . . . over the kings of the earth" (Revelation 17:18). It will not be church and state, but church and world unification that then plagues our planet.

As we witness the present ecumenical movement on an international scale, the assembling of the ten toes or ten horns in the form of the European Common Market, the search for a leader to control the lawless dissidents of the world and the promotion of a world number for all humans, we realize that the moment is ripe for the culmination of Bible prophecy.

A Personal Invitation

World history is in its concluding stages for this age. Soon the true bride of Christ will be whisked away to meet the Saviour in the heavenlies. It could happen before a new day dawns. The question, then, is "are YOU ready?"

If you will come to the Lord Jesus today, placing your faith in Him and trusting in His shed blood for the forgiveness of your sins, He will gladly receive you and take control of your life. Here is a prayer to guide you:

"Dear Lord Jesus, I come to You just as I am, a sinner. I turn from my sin and unbelief to You. I now take You by faith as my own Saviour and Lord. I trust You to save me by Your shed blood, and to guide me in the Christian life. In Your name I pray, Amen."

If you receive Christ as your Saviour today, please write to me at the address on the back cover of this book. I will be happy to send you additional literature for successful Christian living.

II

Ten Middle East Prophecies and Christ's Return

1
Science and the Scriptures

Is prophecy accurate? Can one rely on the predictions found within the covers of the Holy Book? You be the judge. Peter Stoner, in his book, *Science Speaks,* shows in a careful consideration of just eleven Bible prophecies that, were they of human origin, their probability of being fulfilled would be one chance in 8 x 10 to the 63rd degree. Think of it! Ten with 63 zeroes behind it, multipled by 8, would equal the possibility that all eleven prophecies could be fulfilled as stated in the Bible. Now, Mr. Stoner is talking about only eleven prophecies. This is nothing in light of the fact that the Bible contains 10,385 predictions, and each one has been or will be fulfilled in the minutest of detail. Amen! " . . . thy word was unto me the joy and rejoicing of mine heart . . . O LORD God of hosts" (Jeremiah 15:16).

What are some of the prophecies which have already been fulfilled? Let's concentrate solely upon the details concerning the birth and life of the Messiah, the Lord Jesus Christ. The Bible states that:

1. He would be the seed of a woman (Genesis 3:15).
2. He would come through the line of Abraham, Isaac and Jacob (Genesis 12:3, 17-19).
3. He would be a descendant of Judah (Genesis 49:10).
4. He would be born in Bethlehem (Micah 5:2).
5. He would be born of a virgin (Isaiah 7:14).
6. He would sojourn into Egypt (Hosea 11:1).
7. He would grow up at Nazareth and be called a Nazarene (Matthew 22:14-16).
8. He would be crucified (Psalm 22:14-16).
9. He would suffer no broken bones at His crucifixion (Psalm 34:20).
10. He would observe men casting lots for His clothing at His crucifixion (Psalm 22:18).
11. He would live again (Job 19:25 & 2:19).

Here we have eleven Bible prophecies — and, humanly speaking, a probability of one chance in 8×10^{63} of their being fulfilled. Yet both the Bible and recorded history prove that each one came to pass! Praise God!

Ten Prophecies and Christ's Return

The Statements of Scientists

Still, there are many prophets of doom among statesmen and scientists of the present hour. Erlich and Felder, Stanford biochemists, have said: "There will be no life left on this earth by the year 2000 because of pollution and over-population." Are they correct?

Between the time that God created man in Genesis 2:7 and the year 1830 A.D., earth's population grew to one billion persons. Then what it took man from the day of his creation until 1830 to accomplish in terms of population, he was able to duplicate in just 100 years — between 1830 and 1930 he produced a second billion. During the period from 1930 to 1960, a third billion appeared, and between 1960 and 1975, a fourth billion. Now we are told that earth's population is going to double to eight billion by the year 2000, and that, should the cycle continue, we will double our population every 30 years following. Thus, in the next century, we'll have sixteen billion, thirty-two billion and sixty-four billion. The century which follows will bring 128 billion, 256 billion and 512 billion. Then, approximately 250 years from now, there should be one trillion human beings upon earth! As a result of this staggering increase in population, scientists predict that the world will soon come to an end because of earth's inability to support such multitudes.

The Promises of Prophecy

I've got good news for you. I care not what the statesmen, scientists, politicians or others have to say. This world is not going to end for at least another 1,000 years, because Jesus Christ must come back and set up His Kingdom. In fact, the Bible says that we who know the Lord are going to rule and reign with Jesus Christ for a millennia or 1,000 years (Revelation 20:4).

We also know that verses such as Isaiah 2:4 have not yet taken place: "They shall beat their swords into plowshears and their spears into pruning hooks." This event *must* come to pass! Again, Isaiah 35:5: "Then the eyes of the blind shall be opened, and the ears of the deaf shall be unstopped. Then shall the lame man leap as an hart, and the tongue of the dumb sing." Yes, there's one day going to be universal utopia upon this earth, under the rulership of Jesus Christ, the King of Kings and Lord of Lords. Thus, I repeat that this world is *not* going to be destroyed for at least another ten centuries!

The Coming Tribulation

I do, however, believe that there is going to be a terrible war. Jeremiah 30:7 says: "Alas! for that day is great, so that none is like it." Daniel 12:1 warns: " . . . there shall be a time of trouble, such as never was since there was a nation," and Jesus Himself said in Matthew 24:21: "For then shall be great tribulation, such as was not since the beginning of the world to this time, no, nor ever shall be.'' Although this event will not be the end of the world, it will bring death to one third of our planet's inhabitants: ''By these three was the third part of men killed, by the fire, and by the smoke, and by the brimstone.'' In fact, when one combines all the facts and figures of the Book of Revelation, he discovers that nearly one half of the earth's population will be destroyed in the greatest fiery conflagration and catastrophic judgment that has ever been known in the history of mankind.

This war has to do with the coming of Jesus Christ to the earth, when He reveals Himself to the entire world. As we learned in Part I, this event is called the Revelation, and is the second phase of the second coming. We also learned that prior to the Revelation, a Rapture — the evacuation of all saints, dead and living, from the earth — takes place (Revelation 4:1). Immediately following the Rapture, the Tribulation Hour, or time of seven years of unprecedented turmoil and trouble begins. Then, at the end of the seven years, Jesus Christ comes back to the earth to set up His Kingdom.

Please remember that all the signs of Matthew 24, Mark 13 and Luke 17 and 21 point to the *second phase* of the second coming, and not to the Rapture. Thus, if there were not one sign in existence anywhere at this moment, we could still go home, because all the signs could occur during the seven-year period, described in chapters 5-19 of the Book of Revelation. Since all the signs point to Christ's return to the earth — not His coming in the clouds (Revelation 4:1) but His coming to the earth (Revelation 19:11) — and since you and I, Christian, return with Him to the earth, then every single sign in Revelation 5-19 points to *our* coming back to the earth as well. Therefore, as we study the signs concerning the Middle East in this particular message, you'll be able to say, "these are the signs that point to *my* return with Jesus Christ. Since I'm still here on earth, I must get to heaven in order to return with Him. So, if the signs say that I am coming back soon *with* Jesus, and I can't come back because I'm still here, then the Lord will certainly have to call me home very, *very* soon in order that I might return with Him!"

2
Three Signs in Israel

Orthodox Jewish Rabbis have, for a number of decades, said: "When three signs appear in the Holy Land, it will be the hour for Messiah to return." What are these three signs? #1: Horseless carriages, or modern automobiles running through the streets of Jerusalem; #2: Jerusalem being defended by airplanes; #3: The desert of Israel blossoming as a rose. Have these things come to pass?

Rexella and I recently visited the Holy Land. We even had the wonderful opportunity to preach in Jerusalem. Thus, I am able to say to you in this message that the signs I shall present and discuss are not just signs that I have read about. They are things I have seen with my own eyes. As I observed them I said: "Rexella, these are the signs that point to *our* return with Jesus Christ." Since they're already in progress, already beginning to be fulfilled, Jesus must be coming soon for His church in that glorious event called the Rapture. Let's investigate these three signs that the Rabbis have so long awaited.

Nahum 2:3, 4 state: " . . . the chariots shall be with flaming torches in the day of his [Messiah's] preparation . . . The chariots shall rage in the streets, they shall jostle one against another [accidents] in the broad ways: they shall seem like torches [headlights and taillights], they shall run like the lightnings [the speed of these vehicles running through the streets of Jerusalem]." This phenomenon is presently occurring!

Secondly, Isaiah 31:5 tells us: "As birds flying, so will the Lord of hosts defend Jerusalem." Since 70 A.D., this city has passed from one Gentile power to another. In 1517, the Turks took control and maintained their authority for exactly 400 years. Then, in 1917, General Allenby of England marched into Jerusalem with his troops. The British also had airplanes, and as they flew overhead, the Turks, never having seen such machines, became frightened, dropped their guns and fled the city. Britain's conquest of Jerusalem was one of the few battles in history won without weapons. Why? Because the Turks saw men flying as birds over Jerusalem. This event was also the beginning of the fulfillment of Isaiah's prophecy. Today, as one stands in the Holy Land, he sees jets flying overhead daily. There is no end to it. The prophecy is here.

Thirdly, Isaiah 35:1 promises: " . . . the desert shall rejoice, and blossom as the rose." During our first visit to the Holy Land in the late 1950s, Rexella and I noticed that area was practically all dry, barren, rocky, mountainous country. Today, this scene has been wonderously transformed into miles of fertile, productive desert. Truly, Isaiah's promise has become a reality!

The Sign of Israel

A fourth sign is the Jew himself, for he is God's timepiece, and the key that unlocks every door of prophecy. This is because God has a special love for Israel. Deuteronomy 7:6-8 declare: "For thou art an holy people unto the Lord thy God: the Lord thy God hath chosen thee to be a special people unto himself, above all people that are upon the face of the earth. The Lord did not set his love upon you, nor choose you, because ye were more in number than any people; for ye were the fewest of all people: But because the Lord loved you." Yes, God chose Israel to be "a peculiar people unto himself, above all the nations that are upon the earth" (Deuteronomy 14:2). David was so enraptured with the truth of God's love for Israel that he excitedly exclaimed in I Chronicles 17:22: "For thy people Israel didst thou make thine own people for ever; and thou, Lord, becamest their God."

The Lord God Jehovah told Israel that their country was to be located in the midst of the land, or more literally, in the "navel of the earth" (Ezekiel 38:12). It's capital city, Jerusalem, was to be situated "in the midst of the nations" (Ezekiel 5:5), and in that capital city the Lord was to put His name "forever, and forever," declaring that His eye and His heart would be there perpetually (I Kings 9:3). There the Lord promised to establish the Throne of David forever (II Samuel 7:16) and to finally give that throne to His own divine and eternal Son. That is why Luke 1:31-33 state: " . . . behold, thou shalt conceive in thy womb, and bring forth a son, and shalt call his name JESUS. He shall be great, and shall be called the Son of the Highest: and the Lord God shall give unto him the throne of his father David: And he shall reign over the house of Jacob forever; and of his kingdom there shall be no end.'' However, God warned Israel of their worldwide dispersion if they were disobedient. He told them that His Son would delay His rulership if their hearts became wicked. Let's look at the prophetical utterances and see if they really took place.

Israel was driven out of her land and scattered among the nations of the earth because of her disobedience (Deuteronomy 28:63-68). During this worldwide dispersion, God visited the Gentiles to take out of them a people for His name, (Acts 15:14). In the meantime, Israel abode many days " . . . without a king, and without a prince, and without a sacrifice, and without an image, and without an ephod, and without a teraphim'' (Hosea 3:4).

In fact, one of the reasons devoted religious Jews cry so vehemently at the Wailing Wall is because they have been without all of these things for centuries — just as God declared.

Since all of these prophecies have come to pass exactly according to prophetical utterance, and since God has shown His mighty power in bringing each utterance into fulfillment, let's now consider the predictions pointing to the return of the Lord Jesus Christ and see if His coming is near.

The Regathering of Israel

Scores of Bible passages clearly indicate that the reestablishment of Israel in her ancient homeland occurs when Messiah is ready to return to earth. Amen! The Messiah is none other than the Lord Jesus Christ of Luke 1:32. Deuteronomy 30:3 states: " . . . the Lord thy God will . . . return and gather thee from all the nations, whither the Lord thy God hath scattered thee." Likewise, Isaiah 11:12 tells us: "And he shall set up an ensign for the nations, and shall assemble the outcasts of Israel, and gather together the dispersed of Judah from the four corners of the earth." Again, Acts 15:16 declares: "After this . . . " After what? Look at verse 14: "God . . . did visit the Gentiles, to take out of them a people for his name." This has been occurring ever since Cornelius, the first Gentile convert, received Christ in Acts 10. God says: "After this [after the Gentiles have had their opportunity] I will return, and will build again the tabernacle of David, which is fallen down; and I will build again the ruins thereof, and I will set it up."

In 70 A.D., Titus, the Roman General, smashed Jerusalem and drove the Jews into all the world. This is called "the diaspora," or worldwide dispersion of the Jews. From that hour until 1948, the Jews had no homeland. Instead, the nations of the world hated them, mistreated them and labeled them "wandering Jews." God, however, said that He would bring His people back to their own land, and that this regathering would be in close proximity to the time when Messiah would set up His Kingdom on earth: "And I will plant them [Israel] upon their land, and they shall no more be pulled up out of their land which I have given them, saith the Lord thy God" (Amos 9:15). Friend, God has put the Jew in his land to stay forever. Is it not interesting that the Arab nations refused to recognize Israel when she became a nation in 1948? They were determined to drive her into the sea and obliterate her memory from the face of the earth, but God had other plans. He said in the verse just quoted that Israel would remain in her land forever once He planted her there. Thus, in 1974 the Egyptians, Syrians and others negotiated with Israel, recognizing for the first time that she was indeed a nation and in her land to stay.

Study Ezekiel the 37th chapter concerning the valley of the vision of the dry bones. Remember the spiritual, "Dry Bones?" There's a message in that song. What's it all about? Ezekiel 37:1-12: "The hand of the Lord was upon me, and carried me out in the spirit of the Lord, and set me down in the midst of the valley which was full of bones, And caused me to pass by them round about: and, behold, there were very many in the open valley; and, lo, they were very dry. And he said unto me, Son of man, can these bones live? And I answered, O Lord God, thou knowest. Again he said unto me, Prophesy upon these bones, and say unto them, O ye dry bones, hear the word of the Lord. Thus saith the Lord God unto these dry bones; Behold, I will cause breath to enter into you, and ye shall live: And I will lay sinews upon you, and will bring up flesh upon you, and cover you with skin, and put breath in you, and ye shall live; and ye shall know that I am the Lord. So I prophesied as I was commanded: and as I prophesied, there was a noise, and behold a shaking, and the bones came together, bone to his bone. And when I beheld, lo, the sinews and the flesh came up upon them, and the skin covered them above: but there was no breath in them. Then said he unto me, Prophesy into the wind, prophesy, son of man, and say to the wind, Thus saith the Lord God; Come from the four winds, O breath, and breathe upon these slain, that they may live. So I prophesied as he commanded me, and the breath came into them, and they lived, and stood up upon their feet, an exceeding great army. Then he said unto me, Son of man, these bones are the whole house of Israel: behold, they say, Our bones are dried, and our hope is lost: we are cut off for our parts. Therefore prophesy and say unto them, Thus saith the Lord God; Behold, O my people, [get this] I will open your graves [Gentile nations], and cause you to come up out of [the Gentile nations], and bring you into the land of Israel." There's no secret about it, for verse 11 proclaims: "These bones are the house of Israel."

Hallelujah, it happened! In 1948 the Jews put up a flag — the six-pointed star of David. After being dispersed for nearly 1,900 years, they had become a nation!

Presently, the population of Israel is four million. One million are Arabs and three million are Jews who have come back from 120 nations of the world, speaking 83 languages. Let me repeat that. They have returned from 120 Gentile nations, and speak 83 languages. I even spoke to a Jew who had returned from Spanish Morocco. As I sat with him on a bus going from Arab Israel to another part of the country I said: "Have the black Jews also returned from Ethiopia?" He said, "Yes. We have come from all nations." When they left Jerusalem 1,900 years ago, the Israelites said, "We will never go back until it is time for Messiah to come." Now the Jews are returning, and I say with all the conviction I have within me, "Jesus Christ's coming back to this earth must be near!" Since you and I come back with Him, and we have to get to heaven first, then that glorious event called the Rapture must be very, *very* near so that we can be in His presence to return with Him.

Yes, the Jews are returning to Israel from all nations. The prophecy of Ezekiel 36:24 is being fulfilled before our very eyes! It's real and it has come to life: "For I will take you from among the heathen [Gentiles], and gather you out of all countries, and will bring you into your own land." We also know that it is only when these bones live (Ezekiel 37:11) that the next prophecy can take place.

3
Russia Invades Israel

The fifth prophecy concerns Russia's invasion of Israel. The important fact about the last prophecy discussed is that Israel has become a nation. Why? Because seventeen times in Ezekiel, chapters 38 and 39, the prophet states that Russia will march on *Israel*. For nearly 1,900 years, there was no Israel as far as a nation with a government is concerned. Now you and I have lived to see Israel becoming this mighty nation. Thus, when we see God's Word foretelling a Russian invasion of Israel, and we know that this nation now exists, we can only say within our hearts, "the coming of the Lord must be near!"

Ezekiel 38:1 states: "And the word of the Lord came unto me, saying, Son of man, set thy face against Gog, the land of Magog, the chief prince of Meshech and Tubal, and prophesy against him." Since we will study these names in detail in Part III, I will not spend time proving that this is Russia. The fact I want you to see presently is that this is a northern enemy, for they come from the north (Ezekiel 38:15; 39:2) — and Russia is due north of Israel!

As the invasion begins, they come "against the mountains of Israel" (Ezekiel 38:8). Verse 16 says: " . . . thou shalt come up against my people of Israel." Verse 19: "Surely in that day there shall be a great shaking in the land of Israel." Ezekiel 39:2: " . . . I will turn thee back, and leave but the sixth part of thee, and will cause thee to come up from the north parts, and will bring thee upon the mountains of Israel." Verse

4: "Thou shalt fall upon the mountains of Israel." Verse 12: "And seven months shall the house of Israel be burying of them."

Let me repeat that Russia could not march until Israel became a nation, and there was no Israel until 1948. Thus, this event could not have taken place in past history. Because Israel now exists as a nation, and because Russia moves against Israel when she is a nation, I want you to follow a thrilling outline with me.

Ezekiel chapters 36 and 37 describe the Jew coming back to his own land and setting up his government. This happened in 1948. In Ezekiel, chapter 40, Messiah is back on earth — and that's when you and I have returned with Him. Between Israel becoming a nation — which you and I have lived to see — and Messiah returning to earth, a war with Russia takes place in the Middle East (chapters 38 & 39). Oh, hear me. The Jews are home. They have their own nation, government, monetary system and armed forces. Russia marches when Israel is a nation, and then Messiah comes back. There is no doubt that we are living right at the hour when the sign concerning Russia's march to the Middle East is about to be fulfilled. It could happen at any time, and then Christ will return to earth. Before that, however, the first state of the second coming takes place, and we Christians are evacuated from the earth. We are called home in the twinkling of an eye so that seven years later, when this war is finished, we can return with the King of Kings and Lord of Lords.

Ten Prophecies and Christ's Return

The Jews Take Jerusalem

Since 400 B.C., the city of Jerusalem has passed from one Gentile power to another. Let me quickly give you the dates since 70 A.D. alone, for the transition of power in Jerusalem fulfills the sixth Middle East prophecy: 70 A.D., the Romans; 614, the Persians; 637 A.D., Caliph Omar; 1099, the Crusaders; 1187, Salidan; 1250, the Egyptian Mamalukes; 1517, the Turks; 1917, the British; and finally in 1967, the Jews captured Jerusalem. The event took place during the Six Day War, June 5 through 10 of that year.

The Jews regaining control of Jerusalem is the most important sign in this message. Why? Because of Jesus' statement in Luke 21:24. The disciples had asked Him, "When are you going to return to this earth?" Jesus replied: "[Jerusalem] shall fall by the edge of the sword, and shall be led away captive into all nations: and Jerusalem shall be trodden down of the Gentiles, until the times of the Gentiles be fulfilled." What was the Saviour saying? Simply that the Jews would be scattered throughout the world and the city of Jerusalem controlled by Gentile powers until the time of His return. All the various Gentile groups — the Romans, the Persians, the Crusaders, the Egyptians, the Turks and the English — controlled Jerusalem until May 1967. Then, in June 1967 — during your lifetime and mine — the Jews took control of Jerusalem for the first time in over 2,000 years! Tie this in with the bones coming to life, the Jews returning from the Gentile nations, and the three prophecies outlined in chapter one, and there is only one conclusion — Christ is coming to earth soon! Seven years prior to this momentous event, however, He comes to get His Church. Are you ready?

4
The Coming World Ruler

The seventh of the ten Middle East prophecies concerns the Antichrist who will rule the entire world from the Middle East. In Revelation 13:1 the apostle John states: "And I stood upon the sand of the sea, and saw a beast rise up out of the sea, having seven heads and ten horns, and upon his horns ten crowns, and upon his heads the name of blasphemy." The ten horns of John's vision correspond with the ten toes of Daniel's image in chapters two and seven of the Book of Daniel. Let's investigate this account.

Nebuchadnezzar, the king of ancient Babylon, had a dream. However, he forgot what the dream was, so he called in all of his magicians, astrologers and soothsayers, saying: "Tell me what I dreamed, or I'll kill you." (I would like to see some of these modern prophets get out of this situation.) The king's advisers couldn't fulfill this request, but Daniel, a man of prayer, fell on his knees three times a day before Jehovah God and got the answer. He came to Nebuchadnezzar and said: "The secret which the king hath demanded cannot the wise men, the astrologers, the magicians, the soothsayers, shew unto the king; But there is a God in heaven that revealeth secrets, and maketh known to the king Nebuchadnezzar what shall be in the latter days.

"Thy dream, and the visions of thy head upon thy bed, are these . . . Thou, O king, sawest, and behold a great image. This great image, whose brightness was excellent, stood before thee; and the form thereof was terrible. This image's head was of fine gold, his breast and his arms of silver, his belly and his thighs of brass, His legs of iron, his feet part of iron and part of clay. Thou sawest till that a stone was cut out without hands, which smote the image upon his feet that were of iron and clay, and brake them to pieces. Then was the iron, the clay, the brass, the silver, and the gold, broken to pieces together, and became like the chaff of the summer threshing floors; and the wind carried them away, that no place was found for them: and the stone that smote the image became a great mountain, and filled the whole earth . . .

"Thou, O king, art a king of kings: for the God of heaven hath given thee a kingdom, power, and strength, and glory . . . Thou art this head of gold. And after thee shall arise another kingdom inferior to thee, and another third kingdom of brass, which shall bear rule over all the earth. And the fourth kingdom shall be strong as iron: forasmuch as iron breaketh in pieces and subdueth all things: and as iron that breaketh all these, shall it break in pieces and bruise. And whereas thou sawest the feet and toes, part of potters' clay, and part of iron, the kingdom shall be divided; but there shall be in it of the strength of the iron, forasmuch as thou sawest the iron mixed with miry clay" (Daniel 2:27-41).

Those who scoff, ridicule, malign and slander the Bible ought to get out their history books and discover the reliability of the Word of the Living God. Daniel gave King Nebuchadnezzar an outline of world history right down to the last days — and it has happened exactly as God said it would! Daniel said, "You, King Nebuchadnezzar, are the head of gold (Babylon), but there will be two nations pictured by the arms of silver (the Medes and the Persians) who will destroy you. Then there will be a kingdom of brass (Greece), pictured by the stomach, which will destroy the Medes and the Persians. Next, the kingdom of iron (Rome), pictured by two legs, will smash Greece." Why two legs: Because at one time in history, the Roman Empire was divided, having headquarters both at Rome and Constantinople.

Notice carefully that the only power not destroyed or put out of existence is the Roman Empire. At the end time, the iron manifests itself in the toes of the image. It is a deteriorated form mingled with clay, but still in existence nevertheless. Is it not interesting to discover in Edward Gibbon's great book, *The History of the Rise and Fall of the Roman Empire*, that Rome was never destroyed but rather lost it's prominence because of degradation and sin? This fact fits the clay of deterioration. Nevertheless, the Empire is revived in the last days through an alignment of ten Western nations, pictured by the ten toes of Daniel's image and the ten horns in John's Book of Revelation.

In verse 44 of chapter two, Daniel says: "And in the days of these kings [the confederacy of ten Western nations] shall the God of heaven set up a kingdom, which shall never be destroyed: and the kingdom shall not be left to other people, but it shall break in pieces and consume all these kingdoms, and it shall stand forever." This, of course, is the return of Messiah, the Lord Jesus Christ, which we believe to be very near. Consider Daniel 2:34 again: "Thou sawest till that a stone wás cut out without hands, which smote the image upon his feet that were of iron and clay, and brake them to pieces." Who is the stone who smashes the image when the ten Western nations have aligned themselves? Acts 4:11: "[Christ] is the stone which was set at naught of you builders . . . " I Corinthians 10:4: " . . . and that rock [or stone] was Christ."

Since 1957, we have witnessed an amalgamation of Western nations in the form of the European Economic Community or "Common Market." The movement began when Belgium, France, Italy, Luxembourg, the Netherlands and West Germany joined together in economic alliance. In 1972, three additional members — Denmark, England and Ireland — were received. Then, January 1, 1981, Greece became the ratified tenth member. Wow! How many toes? How many horns? How many kingdoms represented by the ten horns? How many nations now holding membership in the Common Market?

Wait! There is more! Ireland and Denmark were never part of the old Roman Empire. What about them? The answer is simple. Daniel 7:8 states: "I considered the horns [at the end time], and, behold, there came up among them [the ten] another little horn [number 11!] before whom there were three of the first horns plucked up by the roots." Yes, once a ten-nation Western confederacy has been formed, number 11 comes to power, plucks up three of the first ten and replaces them with his own and two others. This leader will be the world dictator and infamous Antichrist!

At this time, Spain, Portugal and Austria have made formal application for membership in the EEC. Of these three, Spain is the closest to membership. In fact, in August 1979, her Congress of Deputies passed a resolution supporting the nation's entrance into the Common Market. The point I want you to get is that number 11 could not arise, uproot three nations and replace them until there were ten. In all the annals of history since Genesis 1:1 — since God created the heaven and the earth — there has never been a ten-nation Western confederacy until our day — beginning in 1981! We don't know how many months remain before the final phase comes to pass, but again I say that this is a great day to be alive — and SAVED!

The organization of the European Economic Community is important because the first beast, or Antichrist of the Book of Revelation, comes out of such an alignment of Western nations. In Revelation 13:1, John says: "I stood upon the sand of the sea and saw a beast rise up out of the sea . . . " The sea speaks of nations, and the ten toes of Daniel's image and the ten horns of Revelation 13:1 depict a grouping of ten nations. Because of the beginning of the fulfillment of this prophecy, we see the stage being set for a powerful world leader who works through the grouping of Western nations. We know that he comes from out of the west because Daniel 9:26 states that he is of the people that come and destroy the city of the sanctuary. Who are these people?

In 70 A.D., Titus, the Roman General from the Western nations of the old Roman Empire, went down to Jerusalem, smashed the Temple and drove a million of God's people, the Jews, to every part of the earth — and the prophet says that it is of this people that the Antichrist shall come! Therefore, we believe he comes out of the amalgamation of the ten Western nations.

The Rebuilding of the Temple

The next point is important. Watch it. It's so important you can't afford to miss it. The Antichrist comes into prominence and power by signing a seven-year peace contract with Israel (Daniel 9:27). Immediately upon its signing, he proclaims himself as God, the true Messiah, and situates himself in a temple in Jerusalem. This is the eighth prophesy.

Carefully study II Thessalonians 2:4: "Who opposeth and exalteth himself above all that is called God, or that is worshipped; so that he as God sitteth in the temple of God, shewing himself that he is God." During our visit to the Holy Land, I stood by the Wailing Wall in Jerusalem, walked through an arch at the end of the wall, and looked into a great hole in the earth. There the Jews are excavating, attempting to find, as they approach areas of the Dome of the Rock, the Holy of Holies of the old Temple. (Some have indicated through news reports that the Holy of Holies has already been discovered.) They know that the Wailing Wall is part of the old Temple area, and they say, "As soon as we find the Holy of Holies, we will try to build."

Currently, court action is pending on the formation of an organization entitled "The Association for Progress in the Rebuilding of the Holy Temple." The objectives of the organization are as follows: (1) to rebuild the Temple in Jerusalem, (2) to enlist scholars to research laws and traditions relating to Temple worship, (3) to set up a fund to receive contributions from Jews in all nations for rebuilding, and (4) to enlist architects, builders, and designers to draw up the plans. What's holding them back? According to the Jewish press, the status of the organization is being held up in court because the Israeli government does not want to incite further Arab hatred at this point. Meanwhile, Israel continues to go about making preparations for her rebuilding of the Temple in her own way. Excavations around the Wailing Wall and the old boundaries are resulting in the outlining of the boundaries of the old Temple site, and they also constitute important foundational work. Believe it! I was there and saw it.

A thrilling parallel to the rebuilding of the Temple concerns the $14 million Jerusalem

Great Synagogue which was dedicated August 4, 1982. Built adjoining the "Hechal Schlomo" near the intersection of King George V and Ramban streets in the new part of Jerusalem, the edifice is but a mile and a quarter west of the old Temple site. The synagogue is intended as a rallying point for world Jewry and as a house of prayer. (The Lord Jesus referred to the old Temple as "a house of prayer" in Matthew 21:13.)

Interestingly, construction of the Jerusalem Great Synagogue took seven years, plus eleven months of delays, to complete. Students of the Bible will recall that King Solomon's original Temple also took seven years to construct — with an additional eleven month delay! In addition, consider the facts that (1) a symbolic "half shekel" offering was received from Jews around the world to finance construction costs; (2) the number of $50,000 donors were limited to 12 as was the number of $25,000 donors. These figures equal the number of the tribes of Israel, and, combined equal the 24 elders seated around Christ's Throne in Revelation 4:4; (3) the Synagogue Presidents are limited to 70, the number of elders who once comprised the Sanhedrin.

Although the Jews prefer to call this building a synagogue rather than a temple — indeed, one of the chief rabbis insists, "we must never believe that this is a substitute for the temple" — observers note that the Great Synagogue could well serve as the Tribulation Temple. The building contains a symbolic Ark of the Covenant (which could be replaced by the actual Ark if and when it is discovered in the old Temple excavation), a Bema seat, and is constructed of the same Jerusalem limestone as Solomon's Temple. Although there is no sacrificial altar at present, one could easily be constructed and made ready for use.

The Coming World Church

Revelation 13:11 introduces us to a second beast who will serve as an ally to the Antichrist. This second beast is known as the false prophet or leader of the world church of Revelation 17. He will be closely identified with the religion of the Roman Empire, and will influence the nations to worship the Antichrist — even to the point of setting up an image in the Jewish Temple in Jerusalem. The Lord Jesus referred to this image as "the abomination of desolation" (Matthew 24:15).

When it comes to pass, the true Jewish heart will be broken, because idolatry contradicts the Ten Commandments found in Exodus 20. The second Commandment states: "Thou shalt not make unto thee any graven image or statue or likeness of anything that is in heaven above or that is in the earth beneath, or that is in the water under the earth." (verse 4). The false prophet's religion, however, will have no qualms or conscience with respect to idols and statues. Thus, the second beast will set up an idol in honor of the Antichrist and the world forced to bow to it.

Anyone who remains true to the Lord Jesus Christ, His blood and the inspiration of the Scriptures will be killed: " . . . I saw the souls of them that were beheaded for the witness of Jesus and for the Word of God, and which had not worshipped the beast, neither his image, neither had received his mark upon their foreheads or in their hands; and they lived and reigned with Christ a thousand years" (Revelation 20:4).

The Coming World Number

The false prophet will also issue an international identification number. This is the ninth prophecy: "And he had power to give life unto the image of the beast, that the image of the beast should both speak, and cause that as many as would not worship the image of the beast should be killed. And he causeth all, both small and great, rich and poor, free and bond, to receive a mark in their right hand, or in their foreheads: And that no man might buy or sell, save he that had the mark or the name of the beast, or the number of his name. Here is wisdom. Let him that hath understanding count the number of the beast: for it is the number of a man; and his number is six hundred threescore and six [or 666]" (Revelation 13:15-18).

As I stood in Jerusalem, I saw buses, taxicabs, and other public vehicles displaying a triple digit prefix on their license plates — 666. This identifies them as being Arab owned. The requirement has been in effect since 1973, but no one seems to know the reason for using that particular number — just as no one has been able to explain the use of 666 in more than 50 prominent locations internationally at the present time. Yet the Bible says that a man will sit in a temple in Jerusalem saying, *"I'm God.* You must receive my number and worship my image if you want to eat. If you won't worship me, you'll be killed!" The number started in Jerusalem in 1973, and has appeared in more and more places throughout the world since that time. It will become an international requirement after we Christians are taken.

Who is the Antichrist? Where is he? I have no doubt that he is alive and on the scene presently — awaiting the moment of his ascendency to the world throne. Since the international bankers have set the 1980's as the period during which their one-world government will be established, this Antichrist may soon be revealed. When he is, he will set up a world computer system which will keep track of every person on earth, giving them a number — "666" according to Revelation 13:16-18. What is the relationship between this number and the Antichrist? Revelation 13:17 states that "666" is " . . . the number of his name . . . " Verse 18 adds: "Here is wisdom. Let him that hath understanding count the number of the beast: for it is the number of a man . . . "

"666" and Gematria

The Rev. Jerry R. Church, founder and director of the Prophecy in the News Ministry in Oklahoma City, Oklahoma, has spent many hours researching the development of the number "666" as it relates to modern society. He tells us that the word "count" in Revelation 13:18 comes from the Greek word meaning "to compute." Thus, the verse literally states: " . . . let him that hath understanding compute the number of the beast . . . " Now, in order to compute a number from a name, one must devise a system of ascribing numerical values to letters of the alphabet. This procedure is known as "gematria."

In attempting to find a gematria for the English alphabet, Rev. Church discovered that the ancient Samarian civilization of modern-day southern Iraq used a sexagesimal system of numerics. The Samarians lived in the days of Noah, and constitute the earliest civilization known to archaeologists. Their numbering system was based on a root of six as opposed to our ten. Thus, the common fractions $\frac{1}{2}$, $\frac{1}{3}$, $\frac{1}{4}$ and $\frac{1}{5}$ would be written as $\frac{30}{60}$, $\frac{20}{60}$, $\frac{15}{60}$ and $\frac{12}{60}$. In fact, the Zondervan Pictorial Enclyclopedia of the Bible, Volume 4, implies the likelihood that the number "6" was the base of civilization's first system of computation!

Rev. Church also learned that the English alphabet is basically the same as that of every other language of the world since all languages found their origin in a common source prior to the tower of Babel. Thus we have "A," "B," "C" in English; "Alpha," "Beta," "Gamma" in the Greek and "Aleph," "Beth," "Gimel" in the Hebrew. Reasoning that the Antichrist may have an English name, Rev. Church used a gematria formed by adding the number "6" to each letter of the alphabet. Thus, A = 6, B = 12, C = 18, D = 24, E = 30, F = 36, etc. He then proceeded to compute the numerical values of various words associated with scripture. For example, the ancient idolatry of Babel involved the worship of the sun and moon. Computing the numerical values of these words (S = 114, U = 126, N = 84 / M = 78, O = 90, O = 90, N = 84) he was shocked to discover that the two words totaled "666." Identical values were found for the following: LUCIFER (444) + HELL (222) = 666; LUCIFER + HADES = 666; DEVIL + SHEOL = 666; DEVIL + DRAGON = 666; MARK + OF + BEAST = 666; PEOPLE + SIN = 666.

Since the image of the beast (Revelation 13:14, 15) is undoubtedly a sophisticated computer, Rev. Church decided to find the numerical value of the word, "computer" (C = 18, O = 90, M = 78, P = 96, U = 126, T = 120, E = 30, R = 108). The total: 666! Wow! His finding is given ominous credence by a statement contained in the November, 1981 issue of *Science Digest*. On page 39, Harvard theologian Harvey Cox states: "The true successors of the [ancient] sorcerers and the alchemists are not the priests and theologians but the physicists and the computer engineers." Certainly this will be true in the case of the Antichrist.

Next, Rev. Church began searching for a city whose numerical value would indicate it as a possible location from which the Antichrist will arise. Since Rome plays a central role in Bible prophecy, he began there. However, Rome's gematria totaled only 306. Likewise, the ancient city of Babylon (currently being rebuilt) equals 426 and Jerusalem comes to just 624. Continuing on through the other major cities of the world — London, Paris, Brussels, Moscow, Peking, Tokyo and even Washington, D.C. — each effort proved fruitless — until he came to New York City (N = 84, E = 30, W = 138, Y = 150, O = 90, R = 108, K = 66, TOTAL: 666)! Although one cannot conclusively prove that New York is the city which will produce the Antichrist, it is spine-tingling to note that it serves as the home of the current world parliament (The United Nations) and is also a base for the international bankers. Incidentally, just outside New York City is a suburb named "Babylon."

Topping off Rev. Church's research was a telephone call from a computer programmer who had been studying the numbering systems of the great empires of world history — Rome, Greece and Babylon (along with the Medo-Persian empire which had the same numbering system as Babylon). The programmer had discovered that a modern-day name could be formed from the letter values of the number "6" as taken from these three ancient numbering systems.

The number "6" in Roman numerals is made up of the letters "VI." The ancient Greek number "6" was taken from the 6th letter of their alphabet, the letter "stigma" which looks like the English letter "S." Returning to the Babylonian empire and their sexagesimal system of numbers, the programmer considered the possibility that their letter "A" equaled 6. Thus, from the three great world empires of history, he found that the composition of the number "666" spells the word "VISA" — the exact name of today's most accepted and popular credit card! (Dr. Emil Gaverluk, noted scientist and President of Caleb Communications U.S.A., has personally informed me that he and a group of his fellow scientists will reject the successor to VISA. He states: "The next card beyond VISA's stage will be a universal card, and will probably be issued out of Europe. It will be issued to all the industrialized nations and they'll tell you this is the best card you've ever had in your life. Some of us, as a group of scientists, are prepared to reject that card because the next stage after that is the number on the forehead or hand.")

Just what relationship Rev. Church's unusual finding might have to the fulfillment of Bible prophecy remains to be seen. I do not set dates or make predictions. Personally, I am convinced that Christians will not know who the Antichrist is (or from what city he comes) because we will be gone (via the Rapture) before he is revealed. Still, it is both interesting and exciting to see the number "666" exposed in so many ways through gematria.

The Image of the Beast

With respect to the Antichrist's image, this may well be the computer of computers — the masterpiece of the knowledge explosion! Envision it with me. It is awe-inspiring. It staggers the imagination. Its ability to know practically everything about everyone is astonishing. Does this sound farfetched? Let's look at Revelation 13:15 and see: "And he had power to give life unto the image of the beast, that the image of the beast should both speak, and cause that as many as would not worship the image of the beast should be killed."

Quit laughing, scoffing and mocking and take note of the facts. Speaking computers already exist! The Phil Donahue Show hosted a talking computer called "Leachum." Millions of Americans saw this robot seated on a desk. He had eyes, arms, legs — and a voice that spoke as clearly as I could speak to you! He also had unbelievable knowledge, for he answered any question asked him in a moment of time. Are you shocked? This is but one example. Lt. Colonel Vernon Walters states that he has created a computer with a 4,000-word vocabulary and is using it at international conferences. Likewise, George Bullard, Detroit News higher education writer, tells us about a computer he saw at Michigan State University. He reports: "It has a heavy accent and lisps slightly, but speaks." Scientists and engineers saw and heard it at a conference in Detroit. These specialists heard the robot speak any sentence typed into it, along with foreign languages as well. It did all this and was only one year old!

Where will it all end? I now present the most chilling report which has ever come to my attention. It is taken from the December 1981, issue of *Omni* magazine and an article entitled, "Biochip Revolution." The author, Kathleen McAuliffe, states: "While microchip architects race to squeeze more and more information onto wafer-thin silicon, a few pioneering biochemists are plotting a computer revolution that could make obsolete the most advanced circuits dreamed up in the back rooms at Intel and Motorola. Almost unnoticed, the ultimate biological computer has reached the drawing boards. The prototype is taking shape . . . at EMV Associates, Inc., . . . in Rockville, Maryland. [Dr. James McAlear], EMV's president and co-founder [says]: 'Our aim is to build a computer than can design and assemble itself by using the same mechanism common to all living things. This mechanism is the coding of genetic information in the self-replicating DNA double helix and the translation of this chemical code into the structure of protein.'

"The gemlike biocomputer of McAlear's dreams, implanted in the brain, will sprout nerve projections from its tiny protein facets. The host's neurons will link up with these spindly outgrowths, sending out electrochemical pulses in the brain's own language. The implant . . . would ideally combine the brain's ability to relate incoming data — to reason — with electronic speed and efficiency. [Dr. McAlear further states:] . . . 'we are looking at conductive velocities about a million times faster than nerve cells, circuit switches one hundred million times faster than neuronal junctions, or synapses, and packing densities of the functional circuit elements a million times greater than are formed in the brain. This factor of ten to the twentieth power is truly incomprehensible in terms of any present concept of intelligence. It would be expected that the "being" of an individual so equipped would live in the computer part, not in the central nervous system. It is also possible that when the corpus perishes, its implant would survive and could be transmitted to a fresh host. Well, that pretty much fits the specifications for an immortal soul. And if you have something that has intelligence and the ability to communicate at high speed, it might well become a single consciousness — a superior, an omnipotent being.' " Asked if he believes in God, Dr. McAlear replied, " . . . not only do I believe in an almighty God, but I'm probably the only one here that has any idea how to build it."

According to Kevin Ulmer of Genex Corporation, "The ultimate scenario is to develop a complete genetic code for the computer." He believes that such research and experimentation will offer a large market for the gene-tampering industry!

Wow! Dr. McAlear's project and Mr. Ulmer's observation are of unprecedented prophetic significance in light of Revelation 13:15 which states: "And he [the Antichrist] had power to give life unto the image [a computerized clone?] of the beast, that the image of the beast should both speak, and cause that as many as would not worship the image of the beast should be killed."

Yes, the days of laughing at God's Word are forever finished. Only atheistic pagans, unlearned ignoramuses and hardened sinners could do so in the light of such an array of facts. When the Apostle John was given the message from God 1,900 years ago that the end times would produce an image that spoke, I imagine even he was flabbergasted. Now, you and I have witnessed its beginning! Let's quit laughing at the prophecies of the Word of God in days when we're seeing such wonders developing before our very eyes.

The Tribulation and Armageddon

After the church of Jesus Christ has been evacuated from the earth via the Rapture — phase one of the second coming — the Antichrist will reveal himself to those left behind and the Tribulation Hour will begin. This seven-year period of time is known as Daniel's 70th week (Daniel 9:24-26). The church is taken in Revelation 4:1, and the judgments begin in chapter six.

121

The events of the Tribulation are terrifying as the following sampling of verses proves: Revelation 6:4: "And there went out another horse that was red; and power was given to him that sat thereon to take peace from the earth, and that they should kill one another: and there was given onto him a great sword." Verse 8: "And I looked, and behold a pale horse: and his name that sat on him was Death, and Hell followed with him. And Power was given unto them over the fourth part of the earth, to kill with sword, and with hunger, and with death, and with the beasts of the earth." Verse 12: "And I beheld when he had opened the sixth seal, and lo, there was a great earthquake; and the sun became black as sackcloth of hair, and the moon became as blood." Chapter 8, verse 7: "The first angel sounded, and there followed hail and fire mingled with blood, and they were cast upon the earth: and the third part of trees was burnt up, and all green grass was burnt up." Chapter 9, verse 2: "And he opened the bottomless pit; and there arose a smoke out of the pit, as the smoke of a great furnace; and the sun and the air were darkened by reason of the smoke of the pit." Verse 18: "By these three was the third part of men killed, by the fire, by the smoke and by the brimstone . . . " (the exact effects of a nuclear blast!) Chapter 11, verse 2: " . . . the holy city shall they tread under foot forty and two months." Chapter 16, verse 2: " . . . there fell a noisome and grievous sore upon the men which had the mark of the beast." Verses 3, 4: "And the second angel poured out his vial upon the sea; and it became as the blood of a dead man: and every living soul died in the sea. And the third angel poured out his vial upon the rivers and fountains of waters; and they became blood." Verse 16: "And he gathered them together into a place called in the Hebrew tongue Armageddon."

Rexella and I visited the Valley of Megiddo and watched bombers flying overhead toward the Golan Heights, Syria and Egypt. As we stood in that very place where the greatest military confrontation in history will occur, we couldn't help but wonder how long it will be before this final prophecy is fulfilled. What is Armageddon? It is the closing scene of three and one half years of skirmish in the Middle East. It begins with Russia's invasion of Israel after the peace contract of Daniel 9:27 is broken in the midst of the Tribulation Hour. At that time, Rosh, or Russia, moves from the north against Israel (Ezekiel 38:15, 16).

Additional participants in this holocaust include the ten kings under the dictatorship of the Antichrist (Daniel 7:24 and Revelation 13:1); the kings of the east (Daniel 11:44) under China; and the king of the south (Daniel 11:11), which would involve much of Africa. So here we have the west (the kings of the ten-nation confederacy), the north (Russia and her European hordes), the east (China and her Oriental allies who will cross the Euphrates River to join in the battle), and the south (Africa and her armies) engaged in the bloodiest battle in the history of the world. Armageddon itself climaxes the campaign as the Lord and His armies appear from heaven. At this point, the militarists from the four corners of the earth battle Almighty God and the hosts of heaven (Psalm 2:2; Isaiah 34:2; Zechariah 14:3; Revelation 16:14; 17:14; 19:11; 19:14, 15).

So great and complete will be the destruction resulting from this battle that the blood of those killed will form a river 200 miles long, rising " . . . even unto the horse bridles . . . " (Revelation 14:20). Seven months will be required to bury the dead (Ezekiel 39:12).

In Revelation 19:11-16, John says: "And I saw heaven opened, and behold a white horse; and he that sat upon him was called Faithful and True, and in righteousness he doth judge and make war. His eyes were as a flame of fire, and on his head were many crowns; and he had a name written, that no man knew, but he himself. And he was clothed with a vesture dipped in blood: and his name is called The Word of God [that's Jesus Christ's name — John 1:14]. And the armies which were in heaven follow him upon white horses [that's you and me Christian] clothed in fine linen, white and clean. And out of his mouth goeth a sharp sword, that with it he should smite the nations: and he shall rule them with a rod of iron: and he treadeth the winepress of the fierceness and wrath of Almighty God. And he hath on his vesture and on his thigh a name written, KING OF KINGS, AND LORD OF LORDS."

Verses 19-21 state: "And I saw the beast, and the kings of the earth, and their armies, gathered together to make war against him [the Lord Jesus Christ] that sat on the horse, and against his army. And the beast was taken, and with him the false prophet that wrought miracles before him, with which he deceived them that had received the mark of the beast, and them that worshipped his image. These both were cast alive into a lake of fire burning with brimstone. And the remnant were slain with the sword of him that sat upon the horse, which sword proceeded out of his mouth: and all the fowls were filled with their flesh." Thus ends Armageddon.

When Christ returns and puts away all rebellion, then there is utopia, a millennia, a thousand years of true peace upon earth. The signs surround us. Christ is coming back to this earth soon — and if you're saved, you and I will return with Him. First, however, we must be called into His presence through the Rapture. Again I say that if the signs indicating that He's coming to the earth are near, how very near must be His coming in the air for His bloodbought children. Are you ready? Is your entire family circle united in Christ?

There is only one way to be saved. "For I delivered unto you first of all that which I also received, how that Christ died for our sins according to the scriptures; and that he was buried, and that he rose again the third day according to the scriptures" (I Corinthians 15:3-4). He shed His blood for your sin, but you must *receive* Him today. There is no other way. Then, just as a magnet draws metal to itself, so you and I will be drawn to Christ at the Rapture when the three words, "Come up hither," are sounded in the heavenlies, oh glorious day!

PART

III

The Coming War With Russia

1
Russia in Review

The materials for this message have come from such mighty prophetical giants as Dr. L. Sayle Harrison, Dr. M.R. DeHaan, Dr. Gabeline, Dr. C.I. Scofield, Dr. Marmion Lowe, Dr. Charles Pont, Dr. Louis Talbot, Dr. Raymond Edmond, Dr. Clarence Larkin, Dr. Herbert Lockyer, Dr. J. Dwight Pentecost, Dr. John F. Walvoord, and Dr. Wilbur Smith. Additional sources include the *International Standard Bible Encyclopedia, The New Schaeffer's Encyclopeia of Religious Knowledge,* historians Flavius Josephus, Edward Gibbon and others. I might also explain that I will be using Ezekiel, chapters 38 and 39, so often in this message that I'm not going to repetitiously name the Book. Thus, if I simply say "38:6," you will know that I am referring to Ezekiel, chapter 38, verse 6. When I use other books, I'll name them, but when I'm in Ezekiel,

I'll simply state the chapter and verse.

There are always those who are skeptical when a message such as this is presented. They reason: "These preachers see what's going on in the world and try to be sensational by finding something in the Bible to fit the situation of the hour." Let me disprove such conjecture immediately. All one has to do is get a Scofield edition of the Bible, turn to Ezekiel 38:39 and read the footnotes. Dr. Scofield states that the text describes Russia, Moscow and Tobolsk marching to the Middle East. When did he say it? Turn to the front of the Bible. You'll discover that the notes were copyrighted in 1909. Likewise, Dr. Gabeline, whose book on Ezekiel was written in 1890, declares that the 38th and 39th chapters concern Russia, Moscow and Tobolsk marching to the Middle East.

How did these men know this nearly 100 years ago? How could Bishop Lowth of London, England, preach it more than 200 years ago? They traced the names found in these two chapters through the encyclopedias and history books to cities in modern-day Russia. Here is a thrilling excerpt from the sermon of one Anglican priest: "[Ezekiel's] prophecy, without question, relates the latter ages of the world when Israel shall return to their own land. Rosh signifies those inhabitants of Scythia from whence the Russians derive their name. This formidable invasion of the land of Israel, God will defeat. The Persians, Iran, Iraq and Afghanistan from the east, the Ethiopians from the south, and the Moors (Libyans) from the west shall join

The Coming War With Russia

with Rosh in this invasion toward the end of the world — after the general restoration of the Jewish nation." Let me follow the pattern established by these prophetical scholars and begin my message by identifying the men and nations.

In chapter 38, verses 1 and 2, Ezekiel states: "And the Word of the Lord came unto me, saying, Son of man, set thy face against Gog, the land of Magog, the chief prince of Meshech and Tubal, and prophesy against him." Here, as well as in verses 5 and 13, we see the names of various tribes and nations listed. As our study progresses, I will prove beyond any shadow of a doubt that these tribes and nations are in existence today.

Notice also that all the names, details and events of these two chapters are for one time and only one time in history — the latter years (38:6). Now if all the names, details and events of these chapters are for the latter years and latter days, then it is only reasonable to assume that these names must be in existence during the latter years and latter days. If this be so, where are they? Who are they?

Of Persons and Places

We begin our investigation in the book of beginnings, Genesis 10:1, 2: "Now these are the generations of the sons of Noah, Shem, Ham and Japheth: and unto them were sons born after the flood. The sons of Japheth; Gomer, and

Magog, and Madai, and Javan, and Tubal, and Meshech, and Tiras.'' Immediately, we see that the individuals named here are the sons of Japheth (who fathered the Gentile people) and grandsons of Noah. After the experience of the flood, they settled in Asia Minor, became dissatisfied with that part of the world, and set out to locate other areas of the globe in which to live.

The first name in our text is *Gog*, and it means nothing more or less than "end time ruler." However, there are two interesting sidelights. The Caucasus Mountains running throughout Russia, in the oriental tongue, mean, "Fort of Gog or Gog's Last Stand." If one were to stand in Russia and say to a Russian, "What do you call the tips, the tops, the heights of the Caucasus Mountains?" he would reply, "The Gogh" — G-O-G with an H added to it. That fact is interesting, but it really doesn't tell us much. The names *Magog, Meshech* and *Tubal* — which we have just traced to Genesis chapter 10 where they originated — do!

Magog, with his tribe, left Asia Minor and went to the southern part of the land we now call *Russia,* settling in an area with the Caucasus Mountains as its southern boundary. Proof? Josephus Book 1, chapter 6. This historian, who lived almost 2,000 years ago, stated that the Scythians were called "Magog" or "Magogites" by the Greeks. What's important about that? The fact that the Scythians are given the credit for populating Russia, and that these Scythians are repeatedly called "Magog" or "Magogites" by the Greeks.

Meshech and his tribe left Asia Minor and went to the western part of the land we now call *Russia,* settling in what is presently called Moscow. The city's original name was *Meshech,* then *Mosach,* then *Moscovi* and now *Moscow.* That's why Dr. Gabeline, back in 1890, said "Moscow" or "Meshech."

Tubal, with his tribe, left Asia Minor, went to the eastern part of the land we now call *Russia,* and settled in the region of Siberia. This is the area where Gary Powers, the U2 Pilot, was shot down. The name *Tubal* also makes it easy to prove that Russia is definitely going to play a part in the great war in the Middle East prior to the Battle of Armageddon. Why? Put your finger on a world map, run it over to the U.S.S.R., and then find Siberia. Now notice that southwest of Siberia on the map is the city of Tobolsk. In the Bible it's *Tubal,* on the map it's *Tobolsk.* Why? Because the *sk,* a Russian suffix, has been added to the ending of the names of the cities in the Siberian area. *Tubal* is also the Greek spelling. Nevertheless, it's the identical tribe that settled right there more than 2,000 years ago. Tobolsk is the eastern capital of the U.S.S.R., while Moscow is the western capital.

Now do you see why Dr. Scofield and Dr. Gabeline identified these names as "Moscow" and "Tobolsk," and said there would be a great conflagration in the Middle East in the last days? Oh my friend, we're living in tremendous times.

We can recognize these actual cities in Russia. We know from God's word that in the last days, Russia will march to the Middle East. Presently, almost everything concerning Russia has to do with the Middle East. Yes, Christ is coming soon.

The next name is *Rosh*. Our English version of the Bible says "chief prince" (38:2, 5 and 39:1). The Bible, however, was originally written in Hebrew (Old Testament) and Greek (New Testament). If we had a Jewish version of the Bible — written in Hebrew — we would find the name Rosh instead of "chief prince." Why? Because the English translators translated the *meaning* of the name (chief prince) rather than the name itself.

Perhaps the best way to illustrate this action is through my own name, *Jack*. I, Jack Van Impe, am a person. I'm *Jack*. However, a jack also holds up a car when one is changing a tire. Now, take the sentence, "Jack is strong," and translate it into a foreign language but instead of making "Jack" a person, make it the device which holds up a car. The translation would then read: "That which holds up a car is strong." That's exactly what happened in our text. The translators put the meaning of *Rosh* rather than the name itself. This is important, because Rosh was the tribe dwelling in the area of the Volga. The Greeks, as we have learned, called the Scythians "Magog" or "Magogites." The Orientals, however, called these same Scythians "Rosh." American newspaper headlines often use the abbreviation, "RUS." In Belgium and Holland they use "RIS." Both, however, are from the root word *Rosh*.

Conclusive proof concerning this name comes from Dr. Wilbur Smith, the great prophetical scholar. He obtained from the Soviets themselves, information concerning the derivation of their modern name, *Russia*. The story goes back to the eleventh century when the northern barbarian hordes were attacking Constantinople. The emperor said, "Who are these northerners? They seem to have no name." As he searched for information concerning them, he came to Ezekiel 38:2 and the name, "Rosh." Checking out the geography which I am about to present, he concluded that these people from the uttermost north (which we presently identify as *Russia*) had to be the *Rosh* of this verse. Consequently, for the next 700 years of history, the nations of the world called these people Rosh, or the Greek, *Rucia*. The name was changed to the modern *Russia* just a little over 200 years ago. What a God! What a Book, giving us the very names of those who will be involved in the Middle East conflagration — and presenting them over 2,000 years in advance! Man could never have done this. Only an omniscient God could make such statements. That's why we know that the Bible is the Word of the Living God.

Of Names and Nations

If you do not consider the foregoing information proof enough, then study the geography. This enemy comes against Israel from the north: "And thou shalt come from thy place out of the north . . . " (38:15) again: "And I will turn thee back, and leave but the sixth part of thee, and will cause thee to come up from the north . . . " (39:2). The prophet Jeremiah also foresaw trouble at the end time, and said in chapter 1:13: "The Word of the Lord came unto me the second time, saying, What seest thou? And I said, I see a seething [or boiling] pot; and the face thereof is toward the north." In addition, Daniel speaks of "the King of the North" (11:40). Verse 44 states: "But tidings out of the east [the Orient], and out of the north [Russia] shall trouble him . . . " Trouble whom? The Antichrist who sits in the temple in Jerusalem during this time of war!

Dr. M.R. DeHaan also taught that there would be an invasion of Israel from the north. In fact, on one of his worldwide radio programs, he said: "I challenge any man on the verse I am about to give, because the only nation on earth that can meet the geographical requirements of this verse happens to be Russia." What verse is it? A most important one which I'll be mentioning a few times myself in this message — Joel 2:20: "But I will remove far off from you the northern army, and will drive him into a land barren and desolate [Siberia], with his face toward the east sea, and his hinder part toward the utmost sea . . . " The only land north of Israel with a barren area and bordered by two oceans or seas is the U.S.S.R. Thus, when one sees so much happening in the Middle East, realizes that the Bible predicts Russia to play a major role in it all, and knows that God has revealed these activities for the last days, he says within his heart, "Jesus Christ's coming must be very near."

Who will unite with the communist bloc against Israel? "Persia, Ethiopia, and Libya with them; all of them with shield and helmet: Gomer, and all his bands; the house of Togarmah of the north quarters, and all his bands: and many people with thee" (38:5, 6).

Persia is easily identified, for this nation changed it's name to Iran in 1932. Thus, *Persia* includes Iran and Iraq. We also see the names "Ethiopia and Libya" — parts of Africa. This is interesting because Daniel 11:40-44 also mentions these two nations, but couples them with Egypt. That's right, **Egypt!** Many Bible teachers believe that Russia will come to the aid of Egypt and the English-speaking nations to the aid of Israel, as we'll see.

The next name we discover is "Gomer and all his bands." Edward Biggon, in his great book, *The History of the Decline and Fall of the Roman Empire*, volume 1, page 204, says that Gomer is modern Germany. Mr. Gibbon, incidentally, is praised by the *Encyclopedia Brittanica* for his reliable reporting of historical facts. Interestingly, the oldest maps of the world show "Gomer," "Gomerlunt," "Gomeria" and "Ashkenez," his son, listed in the area of modern-day Germany. I believe that since Germany was divided following World War II, these verses give us the exact alignment of the nations for the coming war — with the possible exception of a few nations moving over one way or the other.

Next, we see "Togarmah of the north quarters." Dr. Edmond of Wheaton College spent many hours researching this name, and concluded that *Togarmah* is the nation of Turkey. Turkey is north of Israel. The name *Togarmah* would also include Syria, because Haik came down from Togarmah and fathered the people of Syria.

Have you ever heard the expression, "the great northern bear?" The reasoning behind it is this: *Magog, Meshech, Tubal* and *Rosh* form the Soviet Union, *Persia* takes in Iran and Iraq and *Togarmah* includes both Turkey and Syria. Thus, there is a great northern bloc of nations, or "great northern bear," moving to the Middle East in the last days.

Who will be involved in this war of wars as far as the Oriental world is concerned? The Bible states that armies from both the north (Russia) and from the east (China) are going to move into the Middle East. I don't know whether they'll be unified or if they are going to march separately — each to get what he can get — but both will definitely be there: "But tidings out of the east and out of the north shall trouble him . . . " (Daniel 11:44). Again: "And the sixth angel poured his vial upon the great river Euphrates; and the water thereof was dried up, that the way of the kings of the east [Orient] might be prepared" (Revelation 16:12). In fact, the Bible pictures the armies of the Orient as an incredible multitude, "And the number of the army of the horsemen were two hundred thousand thousand [or two hundred million!]" (Revelation 9:16).

Presently the Chinese are constructing a highway through Manchuria, Mongolia, Nepal, Tibet, West Pakistan and Afghanistan. The superhighway leads to the Euphrates river and Israel! Previously, this body of water presented the only obstacle in reaching the Middle East via expressways. Now Russia has constructed a dam in Tabqua, Syria, on the Euphrates River, which can dry up the entire area from Syria to the Persian Gulf when the gates are closed. Two more dams are being built in Turkey and Iraq. All the preparatory invasion routes predicted in the Bible are nearly ready, and soon the eastern and northern armies of the Orient and Russia will advance against Israel.

What nations are going to raise a voice of opposition? Ezekiel 38:13: "Sheba, and Dedan, and the merchants of Tarshish, with all the young lions thereof . . . " According to the *International Standard Bible Encyclopedia, Sheba* and *Dedan* are Arab nations who do not support a unified Arab pact. We also see the name *Tarshish*. It is found twenty times in the Bible, and always refers to the land farthest west of Israel, or Great Britain. Notice that our text says, "merchants of Tarshish," for they traded goods around the world. When this portion of Scripture was written, there was only one way to trade goods, and that was through ships. Do you remember the slogans of history? "Britannia rules the waves." "England the mistress of the seas." The ancient Phoenicians and others got all of their tin from Tarshish. In fact, Britain means, "land of tin."

Our text says, "Tarshish with all the young lions." The symbol on top of the American flag is the eagle and the symbol on top of the English flag is the lion. Thus, "Tarshish with all the young lions" refers to the English-speaking nations of the world. There will also be the union of Western nations as depicted prophetically in Daniel, chapters 2 and 7. Oh, my friend, all these nations are already binding together. They're preparing for the great conflict. What hour do you think it is? Jesus *must* be coming soon!

The Mounting Sounds of Battle

As I have already proved in Part II, the battlefield for this great war will be the Middle East. Seventeen times in Ezekiel 38 and 39, the text points to this area, and Israel in particular. Why will Russia invade Israel? "To take a spoil, and to take a prey . . . " (38:12). Yes, the motive is pure greed.

What does Israel have to offer? First of all, there is the thousand-mile oil line. CIA reports presently predict a Soviet oil shortage beginning in the mid-1980s. Such a shortage would force the U.S.S.R. to import up to 3.5 million barrels of oil per day, thus increasing the possibility of a Russian move against the Middle East oil fields. According to the *Miami Herald*, Saudi Arabia's oil minister has already warned that such a move "would mean World War III." He further stated that he is personally convinced that Russia's invasion of Afghanistan was "to get closer" to Middle East Oil.

Secondly, there is the Dead Sea which is worth two trillion dollars in rich mineral deposits. Shlomo Drorry, Chief Engineer for the construction of Israel's Mediterranean-Dead Sea Canal, told Rexella and me that, when completed, the project will give Israel an enviable position in both the Middle East and throughout the world. He stated that the canal will not only enable Israel to produce inexpensive hydroelectric energy — possibly via a single power plant — but that the Dead Sea itself will allow the production of fertilizers and pesticides for a hungry world. In addition, it will provide a new source of minerals for the aeronautic industries. The main element in the Dead Sea is magnesium, and this is considered to be the metal of the future because it has only half the weight of aluminum. Summarizing Israel's potential for the future, he said, "There is no technology in the world like the one we have developed here."

Thirdly — and this is the most important reason — the era during which this war takes place is going to be the greatest time of anti-Semitism in world history. In fact, it will be the devil's last attempt to liquidate, obliterate and blot out the Jew: "And thou shalt come up against my people of Israel . . . " (38:16).

The devil hates the Jew because God has set His love upon Israel (Deuteronomy 7:7). Although there have been times when God was disappointed with His people, even times when His judgment has fallen on them, the love in His heart for Israel has never diminished. He allowed Jews to write both the Old and the New Testaments, and in the process many were converted out of Judaism to Christianity. He also chose a Jewish virgin as the vehicle through which He brought His Son, the Lord Jesus Christ, into the world. Oh, how Jehovah God loves the Jew! Still, He will permit Satan one last attempt to murder every Jew upon the face of the earth.

Interestingly, even as these words are being written, an *Associated Press* release out of Moscow reports that a Kremlin-backed Soviet group has launched an anti-Zionist campaign. Specifically, the release states: "A group of Soviets with apparent official backing on Thursday urged their countrymen to join a movement to fight Zionism, branding the ideology embraced by many Jews as an imperialist 'strike force' against communism. The appeal came two weeks after an international conference on Soviet Jewry in Jerusalem accused the Soviet government of 'pervasive and virulent anti-Semitism.' "

Whether or not this attack is the beginning of the final onslaught, let me be quick to point out that Satan's attempt will ultimately fail. Even though Israel will experience a time of severe trial and persecution (the time of Jacob's trouble — Jeremiah 30:7), God will remain on the side of His ancient people. He still loves them.

2
World War III
And Israel's Final Holocaust

Most prophetical Bible teachers believe that Russia marches to the Middle East during the Tribulation Hour. Therefore, in discussing Russia's invasion of Israel, the ensuing conflict and the final Battle of Armageddon, I will be using many Tribulation texts.

The Bible clearly depicts the coming conflagration as a totally devastating event. In comparison, World War I, World War II, Korea, Viet Nam and any other war which might precede it will look like a Sunday school picnic. This is so for several reasons.

Fantastic Military Might

First of all, we notice the magnitude of the armies involved: "And thou shalt come up against my people of Israel, as a cloud . . . " (38:16). John, who was given a glimpse of this coming day in Revelation 9:16, states: "And the number of the army . . . [was] two hundred thousand thousand [or two hundred million!]." That's the population of the United States of America!

Does such a number of military men coming out of the Orient sound impossible? Read carefully. The *Associated Press* reports that the U.S. Department of Defense has estimated that one out of every five Chinese has been trained for warfare. Furthermore, because China's population has now reached the one billion mark, one out of-five equals a total of two hundred thousand thousand, or two hundred million — *the exact figure of the Book of Revelation!* What a God! What a Bible, to give us the exact details hundreds of years in advance.

Incredible Weaponry

Second, we see the deadliest weapons in the history of mankind. I'm talking to skeptics now — those who have mocked the Bible. They continually argue that such things can never happen. Well, get out the oldest Bible you can find and look up II Peter 3:10. There you will find as clear a definition of atomic warfare as is contained in any library. The text states: "But the day of the Lord will come as a thief in the night; in the which the heavens shall pass away with a great noise, and the elements shall melt with fervent heat. The earth also and the works that are therein shall be burned up."

Nearly everyone is familiar with the basic effects of a nuclear explosion. First, there is the tremendous mushrooming effect as the blast takes place and ascends into the heavenlies. Nineteen hundred years ago, the Apostle Peter had this very occurrence in mind when he wrote: "The heavens pass away with the noise thereof." Next, as the force of the explosion moves in a downward direction, the tremendous heat disintegrates everything in its path. In fact, during one of America's early atomic tests, a 500-foot steel tower melted to the ground.

Likewise, Peter also said: "The elements shall

melt with fervent heat." Now that wasn't Peter's imagination working overtime — it was God Almighty telling him what to write nineteen centuries ahead of time! Notice, in particular, the word *elements*: "the elements shall melt . . . " If you went to the library and said to the librarian, "I want to study the Atomic or Hydrogen Bomb, she would take you to the letter *E* and the word *element*. Why? Because scientists have classified these weapons under that term. How did Peter come to have the *exact word* hundreds of years in advance? The answer is not that he was a great intellect or a genius. In fact, Acts 4:13 says: "When they saw the boldness of Peter and John, [they] perceived that they were unlearned . . . " The answer is that God wrote the Bible. Proof? " . . . holy men spake as they were moved by the Holy Ghost" (II Peter 1:21).

Finally, the scientists who observed our nation's atomic tests at Alamorgordo, New Mexico, tell us that the desert became a sea of blazing, burning gas or gases. Again, the Apostle Peter states: "the earth and the works therein shall be burned up."

I want to emphasize that II Peter 3:10 is for a later hour — the end of the world — and not the Tribulation Hour. As I said earlier, mankind will continue on for at least another 1,000 years under the rulership of Jesus Christ, the King of kings and Lord of lords. We Christians are going to rule with the Lord during that time: " . . . and they lived and reigned with Jesus Christ one thousand years" (Revelation 20:4).

Then II Peter 3:10-12 constitute the final culmination. However, I do foresee atomic warfare as I study other parts of the Scripture.

What other verses have to do with a war of fire? Psalm 97:3: "A fire goeth before him . . . " Isaiah 66:15: "For, behold, the Lord will come with fire . . . " Ezekiel 20:47: " . . . the flaming flame shall not be quenched . . . " Joel 2:3: "A fire devoureth before them . . . " Earlier in the message we discovered the northern army being driven back to Siberia (verse 20). In verse 3, however, they are en route to Israel and the Middle East. Then, as they're being pushed back, Joel sees "blood, fire and pillars of smoke" — the exact effects of a nuclear blast — in verse 31. In fact, Zephaniah 1:18 states: " . . . the whole land shall be devoured by the fire of his jealousy . . . " Malachi 4:1: " . . . the day cometh, that shall burn as an oven . . . " and Revelation 8:7 tells us: " . . . and the third part of the trees was burnt up, and all green grass was burnt up." Once again, I direct your attention to the *Life Pictorial Atlas* information quoted on page 41 of Part I.

Devastating Warfare

Third, we see the bloodiest battle in military history. I am fully aware of the fact that there are those who believe this war has already been fought — that it took place hundreds of years ago. However, as we consider the verses to follow, notice that every one of them is saying that there never will have been anything like this war in the past, nor shall there ever be a war like it again in the future. The coming war with Russia will be the culmination: "Alas! for that day is great, so that none is like it . . . " (Jeremiah 30:7). " . . . there shall be a time of trouble, such as never was since there was a nation . . . " (Daniel 12:1).

Those who think that this event has already transpired are mistaken. The prophet Joel, in chapter two, verses one and two, cries out: " . . . let all the inhabitants of the land tremble: for the day of the Lord cometh . . . A day of darkness and of gloominess, a day of clouds and of thick darkness." Then, in verse 10, he states that the earth shall quake before them. Whom? The enemy! Who is the enemy? Verse 20: " . . . the northern army [which will be driven] into a land barren and desolate, with his face toward the east sea, and his hinder part toward the utmost sea [Siberia]." The world does what? "[Quakes] before them."

Oh, we have been so duped here in America. We have been told that the communists are now a great people, and that we have nothing to fear. Many of our leaders believe that they'll keep all their treaties, and so we sign every kind of pact and agreement with them. Let me tell you very frankly friend, they haven't honored most of their treaties in the past, and they're not going to honor them in the future.

During the past 38 years, the Russian communists have relentlessly pursued their announced objective of world domination. With each passing year, they have enlarged their control over land area and population. Count the countries: Poland, Czechoslovakia, Romania, Hungary, Austria, Yugoslavia, Bulgaria, Albania, all of China, East Germany, most of Southeast Asia, one half of Korea, Mozambique, Angola, Ethiopia, Somalia, West Pakistan, Afghanistan, South Yemen and Cuba. According to Alec de Montmorency, the communists' world conquest has thus far cost more than 145 million human lives.

In the *U.S. News and World Report,* July 14, 1975, Aleksandr Solzhenitsyn warned the West of its "senseless process of endless concession to aggressors" in the Kremlin. He stated "Nikita Krushchev came to America and said, 'We will bury you.' People did not believe that — they took it as a joke. [But] nothing has changed in communist ideology. The goals are the same as they were."

The 45-Point Goal of the Communist Party

1. U.S. acceptance of coexistence as the only alternative to nuclear war.
2. U.S. willingness to capitulate in preference to engaging in atomic war.
3. Develop the illusion that total disarmament by the United States would be a demonstration of moral strength.
4. Permit free trade between all nations

regardless of communist affiliation, and regardless of whether or not items could be used for war.

5. Extension of long-term loans to Russia and Soviet satellites.

6. Provide American aid to all nations, regardless of communist domination.

7. Grant recognition to Red China, and admit Red China to the United Nations assembly.

8. Set up East and West Germany as separate states in spite of Krushchev's promise in 1955 to settle the German question by free elections under the supervision of the United Nations.

9. Prolong the conferences to ban atomic tests, because the United States has agreed to suspend tests as long as negotiations are in progress.

10. Allow all Soviet satellites an individual representation in the United Nations.

11. Promote the United Nations assembly as the only hope for mankind. If its charter is rewritten, demand that it be set up as a one-world government with its own independent armed forces.

12. Resist any attempt to outlaw the Communist Party.

13. Do away with all loyalty oaths.

14. Continue giving Russia access to the U.S. Patent Office.

15. Capture one or both of the U.S. political parties.

16. Use technical decisions of the courts to

weaken basic American institutions by claiming that their activities violate civil rights.

17. Get control of the schools. Use them as transmission belts for socialism and current communist propaganda. Soften the curriculum. Get control of teacher's associations. Put the Party line in the textbooks.

18. Gain control of all student newspapers.

19. Use student riots to foment public protests against programs or organizations which are under communist attack.

20. Infiltrate the press. Get control of book-review assignments, editorial writing and policy-making positions.

21. Gain control of key positions in radio, television and motion pictures.

22. Continue discrediting American culture by degrading all forms of artistic expression.

23. Control art critics and directors of art museums. Promote ugliness, repulsiveness and meaningless art.

24. Eliminate all laws governing obscenity by calling them "censorship" and "a violation of free speech and free press."

25. Break down cultural standards of morality by promoting pornography and obscenity in books, magazines, motion pictures, radio and television.

26. Present homosexuality, degeneracy and promiscuity as "normal, natural and healthy."

27. Infiltrate the churches and replace revealed religion with "social" religion. Discredit the Bible and emphasize the need for "intellec-

tual maturity" which does not need a "religious crutch."

28. Eliminate prayer or any phase of religious expression in the schools on the ground that it violates the principle of "separation of church and state."

29. Discredit the American Constitution by calling it "inadequate, old-fashioned, out-of-step with modern needs and a hindrance to cooperation between nations on a worldwide basis."

30. Discredit the American founding fathers. Present them as selfish aristocrats who had no concern for the "common man."

31. Belittle all forms of American culture and discourage the teaching of American history on the ground that is was only a minor part of the "big picture." Give more emphasis to Russian history since the communists took over.

32. Support any socialist movement to give centralized control over any part of the culture, education, social agencies, welfare programs, mental health clinics and et cetera.

33. Eliminate all laws or procedures which interfere with the operation of the communist apparatus.

34. Eliminate the House Committee on Un-American Activities.

35. Discredit and eventually dismantle the FBI.

36. Infiltrate and gain control of more unions.

37. Infiltrate and gain control of big business.

38. Transfer some of the powers of arrest from

the police to social agencies. Treat all behavioral problems as psychiatric disorders which no one but psychiatrists can understand or treat.

39. Dominate the psychiatric profession and use mental health laws as a means of gaining coercive control over those who oppose communist goals.

40. Discredit the family as an institution. Encourage promiscuity and easy divorce.

41. Emphasize the need to raise children away from the negative influence of parents. Attribute prejudices, mental blocks and the retarding of children to the suppressive influence of parents.

42. Create the impression that violence and insurrection are legitimate aspects of the American tradition; that students and special-interest groups should rise up and use united force to solve economic, political and social problems.

43. Overthrow all colonial governments before native populations are ready for self-government.

44. Internationalize the Panama Canal.

45. Repeal the Connally Reservation so the United States cannot prevent the World Court from seizing jurisdiction over nations and individuals.

Russia's insatiable quest for power and dominion is far from being complete. Presently we see stirrings in numerous nations as the communists gain control of labor unions, educational systems and governments. The chaos and confusion will lead to something drastic sooner than most of us think. Yes, there is coming a day when the whole world will quake before them! The Lord Jesus Christ said in Matthew 24:21: "For then shall be great tribulation, such as was not since the beginning of the world to this time, no, nor ever shall be." This will not be the end of the world, but one third of the earth's population will perish in the conflict. Revelation 14:20 tells us that "the blood came out of the winepress to the horses bridles, by the space of a thousand and six hundred furlongs." In American calculations, that's a river of blood two hundred miles long! Actually, this passage is telling us that the entire nation of Israel will be soaked in blood from one end to the other, for Israel is two hundred miles long from north to south.

Miraculous Deliverance

Fourth and finally, the Bible informs us that this war will result in the greatest defeat and funeral any nation has ever experienced (39:1-12). Praise God, communism is going to be smashed by the power of God Almighty!

As we examine verses 1 and 2, I am going to quote them exactly as they were interpreted in chapter 38, for they contain the same names. "Behold, I am against thee, O Gog, [The Rosh, Rucia, Russian prince of Moscow and Tobolsk]: And I will turn thee back, and leave but the sixth part of thee." Yes, five sixths of Russia's army will fall in the march against Israel. So great is the number of casualties that: "Seven months shall the house of Israel be burying of them, that they may cleanse the land." Every available worker will do nothing but bury the dead for seven solid months. The remaining one sixth of the army will be driven back to Siberia. Here again is Joel 2:20: "I will remove far off from you the northern army, and will drive him into a land barren and desolate, with his face toward the east sea, and his hinder part toward the utmost sea." Hallelujah! Communism will be defeated, and defeated forever!

For years, the communists have raised clenched fists toward heaven and mocked God. Sometimes they've said, "We don't believe there is such a being," and at other times they have contradicted their own statements. They've even gone so far as to say, "We're going to drag this bearded villian from the heavens." What a strange statement if He doesn't exist. Such conduct is typical of atheists. Throughout life, they say, "there is no God." Then, when they reach 75 or 80 years of age, and begin to think about death, they change their attitude. I'm here to tell you that there *is* a God and *all* will meet Him. Communism is going to meet God in the Middle East, and the confrontation will be their Waterloo.

When will it all begin? " . . . in the latter years" and "the latter days." (38:8, 16). God says that in the latter years and the latter days Russia will become a great military power. She has! In the latter years and latter days these nations will align themselves. They have! What hour do you think it is, then? God also says that in the latter years and latter days, Israel will become a nation, will be hated, and that these nations will march against the Jew in his own land. Since we have lived to see the Jew establish his land (1948), what hour do you think it is?

Now I want to show you something very interesting. Take chapters 36-40 and study them. Chapter 36, verse 24 is a picture of the Jews coming from all nations: "I will take you from among the heathen, [Gentiles] and gather you out of all countries, and will bring you into your own land." They've come from 120 nations, speaking 83 languages — and all in our lifetime. What are you going to do, God? "I'm going to bring them from all the lands of the world to their own land." Chapter 37 presents the vision of the valley of the dry bones. Remember the spiritual, "Dry Bones?" There's a message in that song — and in chapter 37. Both picture the Jews returning to their homeland from the nations of the world — the nations where they have been scattered for nearly 2,000 years, where they have practically died, where they've almost become non-existent and where they almost lost their identity. In chapter 37 God says that in the last days there will be a stirring among these bones. Skin will come on them. They'll come back to life. Then, so that no one misses the point, God tells us what He means in verse 11: "These bones are the whole house of Israel [becoming a nation]!''

Remember that in 1948 the Jew pulled up his flag — the six pointed star of David. Thus, one can write the date *1948* above chapters 36 and 37, for that's when Israel started to live after being dead as a nation for 2,000 years. Now chapter 40 presents Messiah (the Lord Jesus Christ) on earth, ruling over His millennial Kingdom. Therefore, between chapters 36 and 37 (the Jews returning to their home land) and chapter 40 (Messiah returning to earth), we have chapters 38 and 39 where Russia marches to the Middle East. Remember what I said earlier? Egypt sides with Russia (Daniel 11: 40-44), and the English speaking people support Israel. Today we can see these events beginning to take place through the alignment of nations.

I believe that when this war is ready to break, we Christians will be gone. Why? Consider the fact that every Israeli school child studies the Bible for 11 years in the Hebrew educational system. He knows that there is going to be an invasion from the north. He knows that it will take place in the latter years and latter days (38:8, 16), and he knows that it will be just before Messiah comes. Now, just as the Jewish people look for Messiah to come and establish His Kingdom upon earth, we Christians look for the coming of Jesus in the clouds (the Rapture), seven years prior to His coming to the earth (the Revelation). Then, after we are gone, the Tribulation Hour begins, the war with Russia takes place, and the Lord Jesus returns to earth.

11:59 and Counting

I'm not discussing eschatology at this point, and I'm not arguing pre-millennialism versus post or amillennialism. What I am saying is that even the Jewish people believe that the coming of their Messiah ties in closely with an invasion of Israel from the north. Thus, if we see Russia making preparations and realize that the Jews believe this ties in with the coming of their Messiah — and we Christians believe that it ties in with the coming of our Saviour to call us away *first* (I repeat that we're gone when it happens) — just how much time do you really think we have left? An article in the *Jerusalem Post* stated: "When you see Russia getting ready to cross the Dardanelles [the straight between Greece and Turkey which joins the Aegean Sea with the Sea of Marmara], put on your Sabbath garments and get ready for the coming of Messiah." Ready or not, we're living right in the last hours of history. Jesus Christ is coming soon!

In conclusion, I want to point out that in the closing moments of this present age, just as World War III appears inevitable, a great leader will come to international prominence proclaiming, "Peace! Peace!" He will jet from one nation to another negotiating his proposals, and ultimately establish contracts between Israel and other countries (Daniel 9). The world will say, "This is it! Utopia! Peace! No more of that which we've known — heartache and war." Unfortunately, this world-charmer will keep his agreement for only 42 months. Then, in the middle of Daniel's 70th week (the seven year period of Tribulation), he will break the contract (Daniel 9:27) — and at that time Russia will begin her march to Israel!

Wait! Before this one can come to power, before he can exercise full sway in bringing this false 3½-year peace, we Christians must be gone. How do I know? Because this Antichrist will sit in a temple in Jerusalem (II Thessalonians 2:4). Yes, he will make blasphemy out of the Jewish people's temple. II Thessalonians 2:7 tells us: "For the mystery of iniquity doth already work: only he who now letteth [that's the old English word for 'hindereth'] will [hinder], until he be taken out of the way [removed]." Who is hindering the coming of the Antichrist? The Holy Spirit. However, He is to be removed before this world leader comes into prominence over the Middle East situation.

Now the thrilling fact is that that Spirit lives in the hearts of Christians: "For if any man have not the spirit of Christ, he is none of [Christ's]" (Romans 8:9). Look up all these verses: I Corinthians 3:16, I Corinthians 6:19-20. He lives in us. Therefore, if He is to be removed, He can't be removed unless we Christians are also taken because He is part of us. That's why I believe one of the next events on planet earth will be Revelation 4:1: " . . . come up hither . . . " At that moment, in the twinkling of an eye the Spirit will be removed and we Christians will be taken: "For the Lord Himself shall descend from heaven with a shout, with the voice of the archangel, and with the trump of God; and the dead in Christ shall rise first; Then we which are alive and remain shall be caught up together with them [the dead] in the clouds to meet the Lord in the air; and so shall we ever be with the Lord'' (I Thessalonians 4:16-17).

Are you ready? Is the Holy Spirit living in *your* heart? Have *you* received Jesus Christ? Get saved today. You folks who are backslidden — away from God — come home. Be ready! Tomorrow may be too late.

IV

America in Prophecy

1
The Decline and Fall
of the American Dream

"**M**y country tis of thee, Sweet land of liberty, Of thee I sing . . . Long may our land be bright With freedom's holy light; Protect us by Thy might, Great God our King."

Millions of Americans have heartily echoed this refrain and petition down through the annals of our history. In past days God was willing to grant this request because our foundations and roots were anchored in God and the Bible. For instance, the Mayflower Compact, signed November 11, 1620, began: "In the name of God, Amen. We, whose names are underwritten . . . have undertaken, for the glory of God, the advancement of the Christian faith." Again the final sentence of the Declaration of Independence contains a declaration of dependence upon the Almighty God. George Washington, in his first inaugural address, given on April 30th, 1789, directed supplications to God for His continued blessings upon the formation of our new government. America's education system used the McGuffey Reader for nearly one hundred years. The series was loaded with the Word of God. In fact, one story in every four was a biblical narration. Some of the lessons with religious instructions were: "The Hour of Prayer," "Religion, the Only Basis of Society," "Control Your Temper," "The Bible and the Best of Classics," "The Baptism," "The Folly of Intoxication," and "Beware of the first drink." Today, through the influence of one loud-mouthed atheist, the Bible has been extricated and virtually eliminated from the curriculum of the educational system in America. The result — righteousness has been been replaced by debasing and debauching trash.

Perhaps we had better begin fighting at the grass roots level and clean up our filthy educational system. Through multitudinous illustrations, I will endeavor to prove that America, the land I love, the land of which I am a citizen, is on the decline, and may soon suffer horrendous judgment. Does the Bible predict such calamities? Is America literally found in Bible prophecy? Let's look and see.

America Depicted

There are a number of chapters within the

pages of God's Word that certainly seem to picture the USA. I will not dogmatically say that the
facts I am about to present demand this conclusion. However, I will emphatically declare that
no other nation throughout the pages of history
can so convincingly fulfill all of the requirements
of the prophesied texts. Immediately someone
mentally argues: "Well, the USA is not mentioned by name in the Bible." True. However, it is
equally true that America must be included in
texts prophesying that "all nations" suffer judgment. Micah 5:15 states: " . . . I will execute
vengeance in anger and fury upon the nations [all
of them], such as they have not heard." Again
Ezekiel 39:21 declares that " . . . all the nations
shall see my judgment . . . " America is certainly included in the blitzkrieg upon all nations.
Though we are not specifically named, logical
deduction makes us know that we too shall suffer. The main reason the name "America" is not
found in the Scriptures is obviously because the
nation was not in existence when the prophecies
were penned. Therefore, we must move ahead to
the study of characteristics and traits involving
nations to see which country fulfills the prophetical predictions. When this is accomplished,
the USA alone meets the requirements. She
seems to be the political Babylon of the hour.
God's Word mentions three Babylons: a city
(Genesis 11), a church (Revelation 17), and a
country (Revelation 18). Don't confuse the three
by intermingling these chapters. The context of
each text identifies "Who's Who" to the careful

student. Isaiah, Jeremiah and John graphically describe this nation. Who is she? Let's begin with Isaiah, chapter 18:1-2.

Isaiah's Depiction of America

"Woe to the land shadowing with wings, which is beyond the rivers of Ethiopia: That sendeth ambassadors by the sea, even in vessels of bulrushes upon the waters, saying, Go, ye swift messengers, to a nation scattered and peeled, to a people terrible from their beginning hitherto; a nation meted out and trodden down, whose land the rivers have spoiled!" The nation described in this text is in dire difficulty with God because the opening word is judgmental. God says, "Woe," and the term always connotes judgment. This nation:

1. has the insignia of wings — similar to our national emblem, the bald eagle, with extended wings.

2. is a land that is beyond the sea. Israel is always the focal point in the Bible. So, the message of warning is directed to a far country beyond Ethiopia and across the sea from Israel. This designation eliminates Europe, Asia and Africa. Instead it is directed to a nation with outstretched wings across the sea from Israel — and America qualifies.

3. is scattered and peeled. Scattered means widely spread out or having great land areas.

4. is measured. This certainly describes our beloved country with its counties, cities and

states. One is amazed as he traverses America by air and sees the staked out acres from the heavens — tens of thousands of miles completely measured and marked.

5. is a land whose rivers are spoiled. Ecological experts vouch that this significant prophecy has occurred in our waterways. Isaiah simply tells us that dreadful judgment will come upon a nation with outstretched wings, beyond the seas of Israel — a nation with vast measured land areas and polluted waters.

Jeremiah's Depiction

Jeremiah also pinpoints America's characteristics with even greater detail. In chapter 30, verse 11, God states: " . . . I make a full end of all nations . . . " It is evident that unprecedented judgment shall sweep the world. However, the prophet singles out a specific nation for judgment. Who is this "Babylon" mentioned by the Holy Spirit in Jeremiah, chapters 50 and 51? She is a country . . .

1. who is destroyed by an assembly of nations from the north. This certainly was not fulfilled when the Medes and Persians from the east attacked Babylon. Neither could these two small nations fulfill the latter-day prophecy concerning an assembly of great nations moving against Babylon from the north. Thus, the prophecy, presently unfulfilled, must be futuristic.

2. whose mother is sorely confounded (Jeremiah 50, verse 12). Again we see that an-

cient Babylon had no mother — only a father and founder named Nimrod. Prophetical and futuristic Babylon has a mother who exists at the same time as Babylon, but in a confounded, deteriorated condition. Surely Britain is this modern-day mother if America is in view. The recent shrinking of the English pound to the lowest point in history confirms that "mama" is confounded and troubled.

3. who is the youngest among the great world powers for she is the "hindermost of the nations" or last to become internationally prominent (Jeremiah 50:12). America celebrated its bicentennial July 4th, 1976. However, two hundred years of age makes our country but a teenager among the nations of earth, comparatively speaking.

4. who is an end-time nation, for she exists when Israel is back in her land. Jeremiah 50:19 declares: " . . . I will bring Israel again to his habitation . . . " This began in 1948 when the Jews of the world returned to their homeland, hoisted their flag, the six pointed star of David, and named the country ISRAEL. What tremendous proof that God had an end-time Babylon in mind when Jeremiah penned the prophecies 25 centuries ago.

5. who "hath been proud against the Lord." This situation exists presently in America. The Supreme Court ruled Bible reading and prayer *out* of the educational system, and constantly votes on the side of hell-bent schemes. Regular judges set criminals free more quickly

than police can apprehend them. Filthiness also floods the land as pornography, obscenity and depravity hold sway. Surely haughtiness against God reigns in modern Babylon.

6. of mingled people. Have we not been called the "melting pot" of the world? Millions have come from every nation and tongue to the land of milk and honey. My own Belgian parents were part of the immigration to America in 1929, and became part of the mingled multitude (Jeremiah 50:37).

7. of wealth, for "Babylon hath been a golden cup in the Lord's hand . . . " In fact, the nations who have tasted of her delicacies " . . . are mad" (Jeremiah 51:7). Even now the "third world" nations, whose income levels produce mass starvation, have tasted of America's dainties via movies and television and are becoming insane in their quest to partake of its reality. Who but America could fulfill their dreams? Babylon could, for she is "abundant in treasures" (Jeremiah 51:13).

8. who " . . . dwellest upon many waters . . . " (Jeremiah 51:13). This could not be ancient Babylon, a desert country, but must be a nation similar to ours, bordered on each side by the world's two largest oceans and having the longest river in the world — the mighty Mississippi — some 4,200 miles long.

9. who, like ancient Babylon, tries to " . . . mount up to heaven . . ." (Jeremiah 51:53). We have already arrived on the moon, sent spaceships to Mars and have become the

preeminent leader in space technology. Certainly the type is cast, the sign fulfilled and the future calamitous. God sent confusion of tongues to ancient Babylon because they tried to reach heaven without God and failed — so will America.

John the Revelator's Depiction

John, in the book of Revelation, also gives us insight into modern Babylon. Chapter 17 deals with religious Babylon located upon the seven hills of Rome (verse 9), while chapter 18 deals with Political Babylon, which probably is the United States of America. What does John depict?

1. A nation through whom " . . . the merchants of the earth [have] waxed rich through the abundance of her delicacies [or luxuries]" (Revelation 18:3).

2. A nation laden with sins (verse 5).

3. A nation which " . . . hath glorified herself, and lived deliciously . . . " (verse 7). That's us! We spend 173 billion dollars annually for food, alcohol, tobacco, recreation and gambling. This is "living high on the hog."

America's Decapitation

The present enjoyment will not last forever. America's decapitation and destruction may come in jet-speed fashion. If we do not have an old-fashioned, Holy Ghost revival, we could in all probability be the nation God has in mind.

We could become the brutalized, battered and beaten Babylon of the following texts. God says: "For, lo, I will raise and cause to come against Babylon an assembly of great nations from the north country: and they shall set themselves in array against her . . . " (Jeremiah 50:9). Revelation 18 pictures the kings of the earth, who have lived scandalously in the arms of Babylon, weeping as her disintegrating smoke ascends heavenward. They are standing afar off and crying: " . . . Alas, alas that great city Babylon, that mighty city! for in one hour is thy judgment come" (Revelation 18:10). They continue in verses 16-19: " . . . Alas, alas that great city, that was clothed in fine linen, and purple, and scarlet, and decked with gold, and precious stones, and pearls! For in one hour so great riches is come to nought. And every shipmaster, and all the company in ships, and sailors, and as many as trade by sea, stood afar off, and cried when they saw the smoke of her burning, saying, What city is like unto this great city! And they cast dust on their heads, and cried weeping and wailing, saying, Alas, alas that great city, wherein were made rich all that had ships in the sea by reason of her costliness! for in one hour is she made desolate." Today a devastating atomic attack could, in one hour's time, obliterate everything a nation took two centuries to build. If God has America in mind — and it certainly looks that way — then what? *Are you prepared* for the judgment that may soon hit our nation like a bolt of lightning? Have *you* anchored your soul to the Lord Jesus Christ? There is no other way to be saved and ready for the coming hour of woe. Should it occur before the Rapture, one can, by trusting Christ, say goodnight here and good morning up there. However, I believe that the saved will be evacuated first. Nevertheless, death is not a sad ending but a glorious beginning for the saved. " . . . to be absent from the body [is] to be present with the Lord" (II Corinthians 5:8). If you desire to prepare, accept the Lord Jesus Christ as your Saviour today.

2
The Moral Decay of America

Is America in prophecy? If so, what prophetical predictions allude to the United States of America? Is the destruction of the USA portrayed in Holy Writ? These and other vital questions are discussed in this chapter.

America's Deception

The present discussion among the superpowers concerning harmony and peace is but superficial window dressing. Communism still plans the eventual overthrow of America and its Western allies. The plans perpetrated over sixty years ago are still moving according to schedule. At that time Lenin, who imported communism into Russia by murder, said: "First, we will take eastern Europe, then the masses of Asia, then we will encircle the United States, the last bastian of capitalism. We will not have to attack. She will fall into our hands like overripe fruit." The plan is presently in its final stages. In spite of it, Americans are so duped and deceived that tomorrow's concentration camps are never discussed. The information could ruin one's pleasurable pursuits! It could affect one's golf score, batting average or amusement schedule! The rotten, overripe fruit — a symbol of leisure-mad Americans — is beginning to fall and the end may be imminent.

The British historian Arnold Toynbee stated that of the 21 civilizations throughout world history, nineteen fell through atheism, alcoholism, materialism, and socialism. The handwriting is on the wall, America. Our decline along these same lines may bring sudden destruction if there is not a movement toward God within our nation — soon!

America's Decline

Is decline already visible in America? Definitely! We, like other civilizations, have allowed atheists, agnostics, skeptics and weirdos to set our standards. PhD's told our college students that there was no creation by an Almighty God. Instead, a lot of "monkey business" took place. These irresponsible, irreligious, God-deniers never found the "missing link" of their evolutionary hypothesis and never scientifically proved their allegations — nevertheless, an entire generation of "brainwashed" graduates listened, and accepted their unverified theories. From this beginning the schools eventually banned the "creation theory," the Bible, and then God Himself. What nonsensical pagans some mortals be. This degenerative process led to immorality, impropriety and immobility as they experimented and died from drinks and drugs. Today every conceivable act of vice and violence is the practice of the hour — the result of atheistic, yea communistic, influence through the educational system and entertainment media.

America's Defilement

The result? Our nation has been defiled morally. Today Americans spend approximately 31 billion dollars per year for alcoholic beverages. This amounts to 3-½ million dollars *per hour!* The disease has reached epidemic proportions, and child alcoholism is part of the menace. The Federal Government's National Institute on Alcoholic Abuse and Alcoholism states: "By the time students reach the twelfth grade, 50% drink regularly and 25% have been drunk." Millions more are drug addicts. Both sins destroy a nation and send unrepentant addicts and drunkards to hell. I Corinthians 6:9-10 state: "Know ye not that the unrighteous shall not inherit the kingdom of God? Be not deceived: neither fornicators, nor idolaters, nor adulterers, nor effeminate, nor abusers of themselves with mankind, nor thieves, nor covetous, nor DRUNKARDS, nor revilers, nor extortioners, shall inherit the kingdom of God." Galatians 5:19-21 lists seventeen sins. Number sixteen is DRUNKENNESS. After naming these practiced abominations, including drunkenness, the Bible says, " . . . they which do such things shall not inherit the kingdom of God." Concerning drugs, the Bible declares in Revelation 21:8 that " . . . the fearful, and unbelieving, and the abominable, and murderers, and whoremongers, and sorcerers, and idolaters, and all liars, shall have their part in the lake which burneth with fire and brimstone: which is the second death."

171

The term "sorcerer" is the English transliteration from the Greek, "Pharmakeia" and means "pharmacy" or "drug store." The original idea is to use drugs for a "high," a "lift," or a "kick" — not a medication! God plainly states that those who use drugs promiscuously are in the "lake of fire."

The defilement extends into the sexual area as well. Dr. Murray Kappleman states: "The sex revolution is over and sex has won." Sexual experimentation is now occurring at 13 and 14 years of age. "The pressure from the peer group and the media to be sexually active is enormous. Today if a girl is a virgin at 17 she is made to feel she is in need of therapy — just the opposite of 20 years ago." Dr. Kappleman indicts the media for much of this immorality. Is there any validity to his claim? Let's see.

This filthy "brainwashing" is having its effect. It contributes to sexual intercourse on the part of 35 percent of the girls in the nation who are 15-19 years of age, according to Patricia McCormack in a *United Press International* release. Surely this makes 1,300,000 sinners who shack up without a marriage license in our nation feel comfortable in their adulterous condition. After all, if the heroes of the silver screen can do it and make it look decent — why not try it! The problem is that God, yea the God of holiness, is still against any act of sex that takes place outside the bonds of holy matrimony. If one does not have a marriage license and plays sex games, he will end up in a Devil's hell. God's Holy Commandment in Exodus 20:14 is: "Thou shalt not commit adultery." What makes one think he can flaunt God's rules and end up in eternal bliss? Just who do we think we are? God is no respecter of persons (Romans 2:11) and one day " . . . God shall judge the secrets of men by Jesus Christ . . . " (Romans 2:16). Then our brazen disregard of God's laws will be judged. God's law declares: "Marriage is honorable in all and the bed undefiled [in marriage]: but whoremongers and adulterers [the swingers and the one-night flingers], God will judge" (Hebrews 13:4). Revelation 22:15 declares: "For without [of heaven] are dogs, and sorcerers, and whoremongers [woman-chasers and men-seducers], and murderers, and idolaters, and whosoever loveth and maketh a lie."

Can America sink any lower in the mud of depravity? Wicked, satanically controlled purveyors of smut — the publishers, printers and sellers of pornography — are the guilty culprits behind this filth. However, the *educational system* of the United States *also shares* some of the blame for the deteriorated debacle in which the nation finds itself. Recently, a 13-year-old girl in Austin, Texas came home in a distraught condition because a sex education film entitled, "All About Sex," had been shown in her Home Economics class. It showed a nude couple in the actual act! America needs an investigation into the morals of its teaching staff! Many of them bring their barnyard manners into the classroom and present them as rationally acceptable. Now, since the "intellectually elite" accept such depravity, no questions should, therefore, be asked. The problem is that a corrupt mind, educated or uneducated, is still rotten to the core. God says: " . . . their mind and conscience is defiled" (Titus 1:15). This deterioration of standards has led to one million abortions within the last year. Think of it! The "brainwashed" victims — monkey see, monkey do — whom instructors with evolutionary "monkey" tendencies indoctrinated, now do what *monkeys* would never do — kill their babies! Where will it end? The next step, undoubtedly, is related to Nazism and communism. Why? Because both maniacal organizations murdered millions. Hitler believed in genocide and practiced it. Babies and adults with physical blemishes were liquidated. The communists murdered millions more than the Nazis for political reasons. Likewise, our educated "morons" are now advocating "mercy killing" as the next step in America's defiling decline. Dr. Francis Crick, Nobel Prize winner, advocates that newborn babies should not be considered alive until they are two days old and have been certified as healthy by medical examiners. He also advocates compulsory death for all at age eighty. Dr. Gallop said: "If a doctor takes money for killing an innocent babe in the womb, he will kill you with a needle, when paid by your children." "This," he said, "is the terrible nightmare we are creating for the future."

Murderers

It is plain to see that callousness is sweeping the nation. Kill the unborn, kill the aged, kill anyone who stands in the way of one's selfish aspirations. This callousness produces sadistic and violent murderers. In past history rare instances of torture and mutilation occurred. Today, it is the rage of the hour.

I don't know about you, but God and the Bible are for capital punishment and vicious killers such as these should pay with their lives! Exodus 21:12 says: "He that smiteth a man, so that he die, shall be surely put to death." Again: ' . . . he that killeth any man shall surely be put to death" (Leviticus 24:17). Many of today's criminals escape earthly judgment because of lenient judges. Still, *eternal judgment* will come because " . . . murderers . . . shall have their part in the lake which burneth with fire and brimstone . . . " (Revelation 21:8).

This same callousness also produces merciless robbers, looters and plunderers. A few lights go out in a city and the "animals" stalk their victims. They cry: "We are hungry" and most of them look like stuffed sausages. Their obesity speaks louder than their lament. Many of these thieves had previously robbed, raped and plundered when the lights were on and scores more had top-paying jobs. Their "Uncle Sam owed it to me" attitude prevailed and crime reigned. Our dependency from cradle to grave on governmental funds will undoubtedly produce a socialistically controlled nation. This same situation destroyed civilization after civilization as creeping socialism grasped power. *How different from God's instructions!* He states through Paul in II Thessalonians 3:10-12: " . . . if any would not work, neither should he eat. For we hear that there are some which walk among you disorderly, working not at all, but are busybodies [or troublemakers]. Now them that are such we command and exhort by our Lord Jesus Christ, that with quietness they WORK, and eat their own bread." Laziness and idleness produce robbers, rapers, looters, troublemakers, and murderers who have nothing to do but daydream and carry out their "fairy tale" hallucinations. *God help us!*

America's Ministerial Defilement

To further aggravate the situation, we have *doctrinally defiled* clergymen who mock everything that is right. They know more than God. He wrote the Bible and they knock its precepts, standards and teachings. For instance, a London *(AP)* release stated: "The divinity of Jesus is being challenged by a panel of British Protestant theologians who say He should be regarded as a great teacher, not a supernatural miracle worker." In a new book entitled, *The Myth of God Incarnate,* the seven theologians argue that Jesus was not God in human form but "a man approved by God" for a special role. The authors state that Jesus did not claim to be divine but was promoted to divinity by early Christians who were still under pagan influences. *What blasphemy!* This kind of dedication to the destruction of God and His Word is common. Our pulpits are full of ordained hypocrites who spouted fundamental Bible principles at their ministerial induction services and then slid back into religious anarchy as the years progressed. God, speaking about this crop of apostates, says in Jude verse 8: " . . . these filthy dreamers defile the flesh, despise dominion, and speak evil of dignities" (including the God-man, the Lord Jesus Christ). The apostle Peter states, " . . . there shall be false teachers among you, who privily shall bring in damnable heresies, *even denying the Lord that bought them . . .* " (II Peter 2:1). No doubt about the teachings of the Bible — Jesus is God: " . . . God was manifest in the flesh . . . " (I Timothy 3:16).

Every precious doctrine held by Christians throughout the centuries is being attacked by ministerial antichrists. Pollution and defilement permeate every area of America's populous, including the ministry. *Judgment is on the way:* "The wicked shall be turned into hell, and all the nations that forget God" (Psalm 9:17). Though it may be too late to save America nationally, we can *individually* prepare to meet the Lord. How? Christ shed His precious blood for the remission of mankind's sin. He died for *you,* for *your* sin, for *your* defilement. If you call on His name now, He will save you.

3
America's Coming Judgment

America is on the road to judgment, and it does not take the Babylonian prophecies to grasp this biblical fact. God's Word speaks of an hour when all nations shall be involved in a horrendous international conflict, undoubtedly World War III. Isaiah gives witness to this fact in chapter 14. He speaks of a war in which Babylon will be involved and declares in verse 26: "This is the purpose that is purposed upon the *whole earth:* and this is the hand that is stretched out upon *all the nations."* In Jeremiah 30:11, God says: "I make a full end of *all nations* whither I have scattered thee [Israel] . . . " This would of necessity include America because five million scattered Israelites abide in the USA. Our end is predicted in this text even without a Babylonian connection. No nation is exempt — including the United States — from the universal judgment described in these texts. Again, " . . . I will execute vengeance in anger and fury upon *the nations,* such as they have not heard!" (Micah 5:15). " . . . I will destroy the strength of the kingdoms of *the nations . . .* " (Haggai 2:22). " . . . he shall bring forth judgment to *the nations . . .* " (Isaiah 42:1). "The lion is come up from his thicket, and the destroyer of *the [nations]* is on his way . . . " (Jeremiah 4:7). There is no doubt about the matter — America is part and parcel of this horrendous catastrophe that will envelope the globe. We along with other nations have sinned terribly and must pay the price. The Bible says, "Righteousness exalteth a nation: but sin is a reproach to any people" (Proverbs 14:34). Again, "The wicked shall be turned into hell, and *all* the nations that forget God" (Psalm 9:17). Soon nuclear and neutron blasts shall engulf the world as sin is judged. When it happens the human race will have brought the devastating destruction upon itself, for " . . . they that plow iniquity, and sow wickedness, reap the same" (Job 4:8). Sinner, the judgment will strike in a split second. You, too, are guilty and will experience the devastating damnation of doomsday. "Be not deceived; God is not mocked: for whatsoever a man soweth, that shall he also reap" (Galatians 6:7).

Thus far, we have shown that America is part of the "all nations" experiencing destruction during earth's bloodiest hour. However, there is even stronger evidence to suggest that our nation is specially mentioned and pinpointed for oblivion. What and where is this evidence? First and foremost it is found in the Babylonian prophecies which speak of a nation under judgment. Jeremiah states that Babylon is a desolation among the nations (50:23), that she has cities of her own (51:43) and that she also has a king or leader ruling over her (50:18). This certainly could not depict ancient Babylon which was a *city,* not a nation. Also, *old* Babylon was destroyed by the Medes and Persians from the *East,* while *future* Babylon will be destroyed by *Northern* nations. God says " . . . I will raise and cause to come up against Babylon an assembly of great nations from the north country

[Russia] . . . '' (Jeremiah 50:9). Russia is not only the northern *invader of Israel* (Ezekiel 38:15 and 39:2), but the northern *aggressor of Babylon* as well. In addition, Russia is *north* of America! Then, too, *old Babylon* was a wicked idolatrous nation whereas the final *political Babylon* is called the "heritage" of the Lord who faces judgment because of her backsliding (Jeremiah 50:11). Finally, old Babylon was *not* a city of mingled races, but end-time Babylon *is* a nation of integrated "mingled people" (Jeremiah 50:37). This Babylon is singled out for devastation. We prove this by studying the same inspired writers who were used to depict America as modern Babylon in Chapter One.

Isaiah's Predictions

We begin with the prophet Isaiah in chapter 13 who speaks of the "burden of Babylon" in verse 1. The judgment is upon the entire world (verse 11), and occurs at a time when the stars of heaven and the constellations fail to give their light. Isaiah 13:10 states: " . . . the stars of heaven and the constellations thereof shall not give their light: the sun shall be darkened in his going forth, and the moon shall not cause her light to shine." This is, futuristic. because *Jesus* mentioned the *same signs* in Matthew 24:29 and pinpointed the time. He said: "Immediately *after the tribulation* of those days (the conclusion of the 7-year Tribulation period) shall the sun be darkened, and the moon shall not give her light, and the stars shall fall from heaven, and the powers of the heavens shall be shaken." This did *not* happen to ancient Babylon, but occurs in *future* Babylon during the Tribulation Hour. Is it any wonder, then, that Babylon is burdened as " . . . the weapons of his [God's] indignation, to destroy the whole land" (Isaiah 13:5) are prepared? Isaiah predicts judgment upon the land whose emblem contains outstretched wings; the land located beyond the seas of Israel with large land areas completely measured and whose waters are polluted. In fact, he opens the chapter with a "woe," and "woe" is always associated with judgment. This "woe" is administered in chapter 18, verse 5: " . . . afore the harvest, when the bud is perfect, and the sour grape is ripening in the flower, he shall both cut off the sprigs with pruning hooks, and take away and cut down the branches." In grape-producing nations, the pruning of grape vines is normally severe. It is seldom administered before a harvest. Pruning is done at the conclusion of a season to better prepare the vines for the coming year. Preharvest cutting is damaging to the productivity of the vine. Nevertheless, the text's judgmental pronouncements upon Babylon take place *before the harvest* — at a time when Babylon is abundantly productive. Then, *at that moment,* she is cut off.

Jeremiah's Predictions

The prophet Jeremiah, in chapters 50 and 51,

also presents a clear-cut picture of this destructive way. The gruesome truths portrayed are not the ramblings of a senile prophet, but the very *words of* and *warnings from* Jehovah God. God tells the prophet: " . . . I have put *my* words in thy mouth" (Jeremiah 1:9). In fact, God dictated the message through Jeremiah, for in chapter 30, verse 2, God says: " . . . Write thee all the words that *I have spoken* unto thee in a book." Since God is in command of the situation, speaking the very words penned, the prophecies are worthy of consideration and acceptance. What are they?

In chapter 50, verse 9, an assembly of great nations [superpowers] come up against Babylon from the north country. Russia is north of the USA. The advancing enemies' arrows are shot with reliable accuracy. This could picture an onslaught of missiles which Russia has perfected. The sneak attack which catches Babylon unaware, verse 24, cuts asunder and breaks the nation described as the "hammer of the earth" (verse 23). Is America symbolized by a hammer? A hammer shapes and creates. Blacksmiths have been famous for their creation with hammers and America has created and shaped foreign policy for years. Now, this sneak attack against the hammer of the earth is devastating because the archers (missile loaders) are called together against Babylon to knock her from her haughty pedestal and punish her for rejecting the Lord (verse 29). All this takes place through a nuclear holocaust, for God continues to say, "And the most proud shall stumble and fall, and none shall raise him up: and I will kindle a fire [atomic warfare] in his cities, and it shall devour all round about him" (verse 32). Furthermore, "a sword is upon their horses, and upon their chariots, and upon all the mingled people that are in the midst of her . . . " (verse 37). Then, "As God overthrew Sodom and Gomorrah and the neighbor cities thereof [for homosexuality] . . . so shall no man abide there, neither shall any son of man dwell therein." The reason? "Behold, a people shall come from the north, and a great nation . . . " (verses 40 and 41). "They [the Russians] shall hold the bow and lance: they are CRUEL, and will not show mercy: their voice shall roar like the sea . . . " (verse 42). "At the noise of the taking of Babylon the earth is moved, and the cry is heard among the nations" (verse 46). Chapter 51 continues: "Babylon is suddenly fallen and destroyed: howl for her; take balm for her pain . . . " (verse 8). One of the reasons for this nation's fall lies in the fact that draft dodgers have resisted the call to serve. Yes, "The mighty men of Babylon have forborn to fight, they have remained in their holds: their might hath failed; they became as women . . . " (verse 30). Another reason lies in the fact that terroristic saboteurs cause internal havoc in the nation. Verse 32 declares: " . . . the passages are stopped . . . and the men of war [military leaders] are affrighted [scared to death]." "Passages" may mean "communication lines" and "stopped" is self-explanatory. The traitorous Judases seize the lines of communication and stop all television, telegraph and telephone releases. Radio, too, is cut off. New York City's past power failures give one a descriptive picture of what follows in the wake of sabotage. America is ripe for such terrorism. William P. Hoar, contributing editor for the *Review of the News,* informs America that Capitol Hill is loaded with Soviet K.G.B. agents. Their manpower has increased by 400 percent in recent months and they go as far as monitoring White House communications with electronic devices located on the roof of the Soviet Embassy in Washington. The Soviet Embassy doubles as a K.G.B. headquarters from which the Reds operate on Capitol Hill. God give our leaders some brains and brawn — *brains to see it and brawn to destroy it!* To cite further evidence concerning the rise of terrorism within our borders, the head of the F.B.I. warns: "Communist countries are stepping up efforts to steal U.S. industrial secrets and Americans should be on the alert against such spying." The Red agents "aim to recruit our scientific personnel, steal our research and development technology, and develop information on the economic policies of the United States." The F.B.I. director pleads with Americans "to exercise patriotism and give America support and cooperation in reporting and stopping such saboteurs within our shores." Despite all that "patriots" try to do, it appears that a hopeless situation confronts America. Judgment is coming upon "all nations" (Jeremiah 30:11), and

"Babylon" cannot escape this infamous international conflict. Though she builds a spectacular space program and mounts " . . . up to heaven, and though she should fortify the height of her strength [by creating utterly fantastic, atomic-laden SPACE VEHICLES] . . . " (verse 53), still " . . . the broad walls of Babylon shall be utterly broken, and her high gates shall be burned with fire . . . " (verse 58).

John's Predictions

John, the New Testament expositor of Babylonian destruction, pictures the scene as follows: God is angry with Babylon whose " . . . sins have reached unto heaven . . . " and remembers her iniquities (Revelation 18:5). Babylon must reap what she has sown. Thus, " . . . her plagues come in one day . . . " and consist of the earth [world leaders and statesmen], who have committed ungodly acts with her and lived deliciously off of her unlimited wealth, bewail her, and lament over her, when they see the " . . . smoke of her burning" (verse 9). They cry " . . . Alas, alas that great city Babylon, that mighty city! for in one hour is thy judgment come. And the merchants of the earth [the world's stockbrokers, bankers and salesmen] shall weep and mourn over her; for no man buyeth their merchandise any more: The merchandise of gold, and silver, and precious stones, and of pearls, and fine linen . . . " (verses 10-12). Nuclear blasts end the "covetous" grasping for goods in one hour — yes, " . . . in one hour so great riches is come to nought [or nothingness] . . . " (verse 17). No wonder the Saviour said, " . . . lay up for yourselves treasures in heaven . . . " (Matthew 6:20). Here one's accumulated wealth through giving abides forever in the form of souls won to Christ. Thank God we will not be present, dear Christian, to cry with earth's multitudes when " . . . they cast dust on their heads, and [cry], weeping and wailing, saying, Alas, alas that great city . . . for in one hour is she made desolate" (verse 19).

This is God's message of destruction and doom. *You,* unsaved reader, *are included in the warning!* Soon, everything you possess — your little empire — may crumble in an hour of time. Then what? *You* may perish in the catastrophic and uncontrolled burning of this prophesied time! *The saved,* however, *will escape* this horrible judgment for true believers are called up in Revelation 4:1 — the burning of Babylon takes place fourteen chapters later. Are you ready for the great escape, the coming of the Lord for His "born again" children? The only hope is found in receiving Christ. This makes one a son of God (John 1:12). Receive Him now before Babylon burns!

4
America in Review

This chapter continues our discussion of America in Bible prophecy. The question and answer method will be used to recapitulate the startling truths mentioned in the past three chapters.

Q: Do you think that America's present and future are predicted in the Bible?

A: My answer must be affirmative. After delving into this subject intensely, I cannot come to any other conclusion.

Q: What are these prophecies and where are they located?

A: They are mentioned in the writings of Isaiah, Jeremiah and John. Let's begin with Isaiah. In chapter 18:1-2, the prophet depicts a latter-day nation that amazingly resembles modern America. He says: "Woe to the land shadowing with wings, which is beyond the rivers of Ethiopia: That sendeth ambassadors by the sea, even in vessels of bulrushes upon the waters, saying, Go, ye swift messengers, to a nation scattered and peeled, to a people terrible from their beginning hitherto; a nation meted out and trodden down, whose land the rivers have spoiled!" From this we deduce the following:

1) America's emblem, a bald eagle with outstretched wings, fulfills the prophet's description of a land shadowed with wings.

2) The nation is beyond the sea from Israel.

3) This nation is scattered and peeled, meaning spread out and cultured.

4) She is measured or staked out as well.

5) She has spoiled or polluted waterways that affect the land.

Q: Is there more? What about the description of Babylon itself? Where is she mentioned in God's Word?

A: Political Babylon is mentioned in the writings of Jeremiah and John. However, may I unequivocally state at this point that it was God Almighty Who gave the prophecies through His servants. God spoke and man wrote. That is why God says in Jeremiah 30:2: " . . . Write thee all the words that I have spoken unto thee in a book." This is important to know. Why? It makes one realize that the predictions are not the ramblings of men, but statements from Jehovah God Himself.

Q: What does Jeremiah state?

A: In chapters 50 and 51 of the book bearing his name, Jeremiah presents conclusive evidence that a "latter-day" Babylon shall spring into existence far different from, and superior to, ancient Babylon. As one studies his remarks, it is amazing to see that modern America seems to be the fulfillment of these predictions because:

1) She is a nation of mingled people (Jeremiah 50:37). America and Russia both have intermingles and interracial inhabitants, but Russia is not in mind as we will prove.

2) She is a nation whose " . . . mother shall be sore confounded . . . " (Jeremiah 50:12), coexisting with "mother" at the hour of her decline. Ancient Babylon does not fit the bill since she was founded by a father — Nimrod. However,

America's mother is England who presently is confounded, confused and near collapse, financially. She no longer is considered a superpower and soon mother and daughter shall both be challenged.

3) She " . . . dwellest upon many waters . . . " (Jeremiah 51:13). This typifies America, bordered on each side by the world's two largest oceans and possessing the longest river on the globe — the mighty 4,200-mile-long Mississippi. Surely ancient Babylon, composed of barren deserts, was not in view when Jeremiah penned such prophecies.

4) Her wealth plagues the nations of earth to the point of insane jealousy, for Jeremiah 51:7 declares: "Babylon hath been a golden cup in the Lord's hand . . . therefore the nations are mad."

5) Her space exploits are so utterly fantastic that she tries to " . . . mount up to heaven . . . " (Jeremiah 51:53). America's Echo 1, Echo 2, the Telstar satellites' voyages to the moon and unmanned space flights to Mars are significant in the light of Jeremiah's declarations.

6) Babylon exists when Israel is back in her land. America is only 200 years old, and the newborn babe — Israel — a child. The new land of Israel was established in 1948, meaning that the prophecies could only coexist since that hour. Who but America can fulfill the requirements mentioned to this point and coexist with Israel? The answer is obvious!

Q: It is all so convincing! Can the Apostle John add anything to this discussion?

A: Yes! John, in the book of Revelation, pictures two Babylons. One is portrayed as a world religion, geographically located on seven hills — undoubtedly the seven hills of Rome (Revelation 17:9). The other Babylon is an internationally respected nation (Revelation 18). John describes the nation by saying:

1) " . . . the merchants of the earth are waxed rich through the abundance of her delicacies" (Revelation 18:3).

2) She is laden with sins (Revelation 18:5).

3) " . . . she hath glorified herself, and lived deliciously . . . " (Revelation 18:7). Sadly, her superabundance of material goods produced idleness and sin.

Q: The Apostle John mentions her overabundance of wickedness. What is presently happening in America relating to this "latter-day" prophecy?

A: America has never been in such a state of degradation and hopelessness. Truly America is laden or loaded with iniquity. The pollution inundating our land centers around:

1) **Drunkenness** or culturally identified: "alcoholism." Ten million inebriates drink themselves into insensibility on a continual basis while millions more spend *billions* on booze annually.

2) **Drug addiction** which mars and scars another ten million in our nation.

3) **Tobacco** which pollutes both lungs and land

to the tune of *ten billion dollars* per year.

4) **Gambling** which robs needy millions through governmentally controlled lotteries and mafia-dominated casinos to the amount of *60 billion dollars* each year.

5) **Prostitution and pimping** which spreads disease and shame to *nine million* Americans every twelve months and costs 25 to 100 dollars per act.

6) **Homosexuality** which seeks to arrogantly, egotistically, blatantly and publicly boast about its perverted members. In anger they desire to come out of the closet. Well, the closet is a good place to practice sex. If it is good enough for the married in the privacy of the closet, why should homos receive special privileges to proclaim their perversity. God says, " . . . it is a shame even to speak of those things which are done of them in secret" (Ephesians 5:12).

7) **Smut peddlers** spreading sexual filth via magazine racks also cover the nation. Their satanically inspired garbage is found everywhere including the corner grocery store. Christians should rise up in arms, boycott the devil's hangouts loaded with soul-destroying adulterous materials, and patronize the shops of decent Americans. Since Jesus said that lust through the eyegate amounted to adultery (Matthew 5:28), then why fraternize such soul-damning dealers who bait the young into a life of lustful slavery and eternal hell. Make a decision, *then fulfill it!*

8) **Immoral lepers** also plague the nation. As a result, millions are carrying illegitimate babies.

Thousands of the victims are 11 to 13 years of age. It appears that high school sex education courses have stimulated rather than educated the young. Sex sin, however, is reaping its reward. Presently *nine million persons* with venereal disease have reaped the reward of running sores from eyes, ears, mouth, genitals and other moisture producing areas of the body. That is why the kiss of the V.D. carrier is even obnoxiously unclean. Do not get "tricked" or "trapped." The shame is not worth the brief encounter. Beware, young man and young lady! Beware, Mother and Father! Your fling may sting for " . . . they that plow iniquity, and sow wickedness, reap the same" (Job 4:8).

9) **Abortion,** the murder of "unwanted babies," is also affecting *one million* women annually. These so-called cultured but barbaric sinners think nothing of having their little bundles from God hacked to pieces and flushed. Never mind that God says, "Thou shalt not kill" (Exodus 20:13). Sinners have taken the matter into their own hands, but remember God holds the final trump card — *the Judgment* (Revelation 20:11-15).

10) **"Mercy Killers"** are also on the ascendency in America. They are progressive abortionists who have become hardened to killing and now wish to include the "mommies and daddies" along with the "babies." The "honor thy father and mother" in God's commandments (Exodus 20:12), interferes with their fun. The responsibility is too great. So, the old folks must go.

These sick birds must be related to Hitler. Am I proclaiming fairy tales or does such thinking and planning exist? *You be the judge:* Drs. Watson and Crick, the famous Nobel prize winning discoverers of the DNA molecule, have both recommended such a course. Dr. Crick advocates compulsory death for all at age 80. Presently, pro-abortionists, killing one million babies annually, are involved in brainwashing programs for "euthanasia" or "mercy killing." They cry: "Why let your poor mother or grandfather die in misery? Surely your compassionate nature should make 'Death with Dignity' a consideration." *This is the ultimate of a depraved society, created by humans who have decided to play God!*

11) **Murderers** beyond abortionists and 'Death with Dignity' advocates stalk the country. *Fifty thousand* are savagely slaughtered within the nation annually. The human animals who stalk, torture, brutalize and then slaughter their victims, use hatchets, knives and guns. They then decapitate and dismember the victims and finally burn and bury the remains. My files are flooded with such atrocities.

12) **Robbers and looters** also rear their ugly faces, destroying, plundering and pillaging another man's lifetime accumulations. They call it "fair play" because of their many shortages.

Q: Can a nation continue under such sinful circumstances?

A: Not indefinitely! The Bible says: "Righteousness exalteth a nation, but sin is a reproach to any people" (Proverbs 14:34). Sin can only produce disaster both for individuals and nations. This is why Psalm 9:17 declares: "The wicked shall be turned into hell, and all the nations that forget God." Job 4:8 states: " . . . they that plow iniquity, and sow wickedness, reap the same."

Q: You believe then that judgment may be imminent for our beloved nation?

A: There is no doubt about it! Isaiah describes the judgment of the "later days" as being administered upon *all* nations — including America. One does not have to agree with the interpretation of Babylon to know that America, as a nation, is part of the coming holocaust administered against *all* nations. She then must be included in such texts as Jeremiah 30:11: " . . .I make a full end of all nations . . . " " . . . I will execute vengeance in anger and fury upon the nations such as they have not heard" (Micah 5:15). " . . . [God] shall bring forth judgment to the nations" (Isaiah 42:1), and " . . . the destroyer of the nations is on his way . . . " (Jeremiah 4:7). No doubt about it — America *is part* of the "all nations" package marked for destruction.

Q: Are there any specific judgments administered against Babylon already identified as America?

A: Most assuredly so. A sneak attack, similar to Pearl Harbor, is predicted upon Babylon in Jeremiah 50:24. God says: "I have laid a snare for thee, and thou art also taken, O Babylon, and thou was not aware . . . " John, in Revelation 18, describes the effects of this surprise attack. The bankers, merchants and workmen all wail, saying: " . . . Alas, alas that great city, Babylon, that mighty city! For in one hour is thy judgment come" (Revelation 18:10).

Q: Who will be the ruthless villain who violently strikes without warning?

A: None other than Russia! All her blasphemous negotiations around the detente doctrine add up to lying rhetoric. Her communistic leaders have never known the meaning of truth or honesty — and the future will prove it! In Jeremiah 50:9, an assembly of great nations (superpowers) come up against Israel from the north. This is the same Northern bear that marches on Israel (Ezekiel 38:15). Actually, Russia is north of *both* America and Israel. It is interesting to note that neither the USA nor the Soviet Union wins. Both military giants are crushed. Some biblical scholars believe that Russia starts the sneak nuclear attack against the USA, crippling her, and then moves against Israel where God Almighty smashes this godless communistic monstrosity into oblivion — leaving but one sixth of her armies (Ezekiel 39:2). Whatever the alignment of events, it is clear that *both* nations fall, Christ returns, and world peace begins.

Q: All these signs, then, are directly related to Christ's return?

A: No doubt about it. In fact, it all occurs *after the Rapture* and *just before* Christ returns to earth. The timetable is presented in Isaiah

13:10. In this text, " . . . the stars of heaven and the constellations thereof shall not give their light; the sun shall be darkened in its going forth, and the moon shall not cause her light to shine." This is the *exact* prophecy Christ mentioned in Matthew 24:29, portraying the final scenes of the Tribulation Hour prior to His return to earth. He said: "Immediately AFTER THE TRIBULATION of those days shall the sun be darkened, and the moon shall not give her light, and the stars shall fall from heaven, and the powers of the heavens shall be shaken." The sneak attack, then, is *definitely* a final Tribulation occurrence.

Q: What hope is there for the world in the light of these facts?

A: " . . . Salvation is of the Lord" (Jonah 2:9). Trust in Christ. He died at Calvary to save sinners for time and eternity. By receiving Him and the merits of His shed blood, one can be prepared for the future, yea for eternity. Do not delay! The events mentioned in this lesson are at hand. Tomorrow may be too late!

V

The '80s, the Antichrist and Your Startling Future!

1
What In The World Is Happening?

With good reason, humanity is concerned about the future. People ask, "Is world peace a realistic goal? What about America's future? Will civilization be destroyed soon?" Students of the Bible have no difficulty in answering these searching inquiries, for God allows His children to preview coming events through prophecy.

The Knowledge Explosion

Daniel 12:4 declares: *"But thou, O Daniel, shut up the words, and seal the book, even to the time of the end: many shall run to and fro, and knowledge shall be increased."* This prophecy has been and is being fulfilled before our very eyes with meticulous accuracy. Notice that the Book of Daniel was to be sealed — its contents kept incomprehensible — until *"the time of the end."* Is it not strange that one is unable to find expositions of this book until recent times? No attempts were ever made to explain Daniel verse by verse until the twentieth century. Then, again, this *"time of the end"* would also witness tremendous strides in international travel and knowledge. This is happening. In fact, the two predictions are interrelated. Because of mankind's prolific explosion of knowledge, tourists are able to hop from continent to continent and astronauts whiz through the universe. *U.S. News & World Report*, July 20, 1981, states: "As Americans head for vacations, they will realize just how fast the world is shrinking. Consider as the travel season gets into high gear . . . You can fly to Europe in 3¼ hours. It took 13 hours in 1950, 17½ in 1947. More than 8 million Americans are going abroad, an increase of 1,093 percent since 1950. About 7.7 million foreigners are coming here, up 3,084 percent."

Adam and Eve traveled at the rate of 30 m.p.h., for a limited period of time, on horseback. Centuries passed and the human race continued to cry, "Giddy-up!" Then, in 1913, Henry Ford built his first Model T. This vehicle attained the fantastic speed of 25 m.p.h. — slower than a horse, but able to run for hours.

Soon the genius of man increased automobile speeds to 120 m.p.h. Today, race car enthusiasts have smashed records, hitting at the astronomical rate of more than 600 m.p.h. at the Bonneville Salt Flats. "Bullet" trains in Japan have also fulfilled the *"to and fro"* prediction of Daniel for the end times. In addition, the French Concorde Jet is presently crossing the Atlantic at more than 2,000 m.p.h. and spaceships rocket along at 24,000 m.p.h.

There is no end to mankind's stupendous search for and increase in knowledge. Library shelves authentically display it. In fact, the *Encyclopedia Britannica* must print a volume of newly accumulated information annually. Medical men presently own special transmitters which keep them up to date with the latest international reports concerning recent discoveries. Scientists state that knowledge is *doubling* every two and one half years! Dr. Tim LaHaye, in his book, *The Beginning of the End,* reports: "It has been estimated that 70% of the medicines in use today were developed after World War II. More than 90% of the scientists who ever lived are alive today! Knowledge has increased so rapidly that the Sperry Rand Corporation has developed a memory bank which can assimilate the 850,000 words in the Bible five times per second!" Computers are so highly developed that when the Apollo 13 mission was nearly aborted because the ship became crippled in space, a mere 84 minutes were required to discover the problem. A man with pencil and paper would have needed

1,000,000 **years** to solve the same difficulty!

As fantastic as all this may seem, we must also remember that one can now cross the ocean within a period of 55 seconds by direct dialing. I have talked with loved ones in Belgium, and Rexella and I called home from the Philippines to instantaneously converse with other family members. Imagine! Thousands of miles covered in seconds. In fact, *U.S. News & World Report* informs us that, "The number of overseas telephone calls has jumped from 900,000 to 191 million in 30 years." In addition, by simply pushing a television button, one can view a live sports event in California as he sits in his home in Connecticut, or he can watch a boxing match in Africa over his TV set in Arizona. Again, *U.S. News & World Report* states that, "The hours of international television traffic via satellite have soared from zero in 1950 to 80 in 1965 to 7,887 in 1975 to 28,393 in 1980." This latter point is especially interesting in light of one of the greatest prophecies contained in the book of Revelation. During the Tribulation Hour, God's two witnesses are killed and the entire world views their bodies: *"And they of the people and kindreds and tongues and nations shall see their dead bodies* [the two witnesses] *three days and an half, and shall not suffer their dead bodies to be put in graves"* (Revelation 11:9). For centuries, Bible scoffers ridiculed such an idea. Today, television has silenced these simpletons who mock God's Word. In fact, one is now able to comprehend how *"every eye shall see him"* [the

Lord] when He returns to earth (Revelation 1:7). Since His return is to the Mount of Olives near Jerusalem, and since Middle East developments are being shown nightly via TV news, who can question the accuracy and reliability of God's Holy Word? Prophecy is being fulfilled, and skeptics must forever admit their short-sightedness. *" . . . yea, let God be true, but every man a liar"* (Romans 3:4). Through his scientific accomplishments, man has made it possible for Christ's return to be witnessed internationally. The equipment is ready for the greatest event of the ages. **Are you?**

Wonders in Space

Meanwhile, other unbelievable activities are either happening or being planned for the heavenlies. For instance, in August and September of 1977, two Voyager spacecraft were launched into the great beyond. Before they finish their journey, they will have traveled billions of miles. They carry sounds of laughter, music by Beethoven and greetings from celebrities, all tucked away on copper phonograph records. Their course has taken them past Jupiter and Saturn, and they are continuing on to Uranus. Space experts inform us that never in the history of the world have scientists had an opportunity for such close examination of the moons of the two planets. This is a "first," because no spacecraft from earth had ever made the billion-mile flight to Saturn.

However, it has happened in our day! By 1986, the vehicles will pass Uranus and then, by 1989, hurl themselves into outer space. If all goes well, the Voyagers will pass a star in 40,000 years — and 107,000 years later, a second star! All this is incredible in light of the fact that Jesus prophesied that the space age would signal His return to earth. **This event of the ages must be at hand!** The predictions uttered by Christ 1,900 years ago never took place until the present day — beginning with the launching of Sputnik I in 1957. Since then, more than 175 scientific probes have been rocketed into space. Soon, the LST, or Large Space Telescope, will be placed into orbit. It will enable scientists to gaze deep into space — possibly to the edge of the cosmos or universe. This proposed project sends chills up my spine because God's heavenly throne is at the edge of the universe or beyond the cosmos! The location is called *"the third heaven"* in II Corinthians 12:2.

Living in Space

Ladies and gentlemen, keep your eyes on the heavens. Soon men will be living in space colonies. What? That's right. You read correctly. Humans will live in space cities within another 13 to 14 years! This information comes from the lips of University of Michigan scientist James Loudon. He states: "Space colonies could become reality by the 1990s. I am not trying to be sensational or feed science fiction fantasies to the public. Instead, I am reporting what reputable and recognized scientists already consider feasible." Professor Loudon said that the colonization of space with artificial worlds "which would be miles in size and have tens of thousands of people at first and then escalate into millions, could be the consequence of the first space shuttle flights." When asked if this really could happen he replied: "It is the consensus of the best scientists alive. Apollo explorations proved that materials found on the moon could be used in the construction of space colonies. They would be hollow, doughnut-shaped or cylindrical, and glass enclosed." He added that these self-sustaining colonies could eventually solve the earth energy crisis.

Such statements should silence the skeptics. Twenty years ago, the Bible account of a space city was derided as the writing of a deranged mind. Today, the scoffers of God's Word have become the simpletons. Why? Intelligent, educated scientists with doctorates predict space cities similar to the one John envisioned 1,900 years ago in Revelation 21:2: "... *I John saw the holy city, new Jerusalem, coming down from God out of heaven, prepared as a bride adorned for her husband.*" Verses 10 through 23 provide a detailed description of this celestial wonder. If men are presently designing such cities that will accommodate thousands and eventually millions, is there a reader who thinks that Almighty God cannot keep a promise He gave to John nineteen centuries ago? Perish the thought! This **will** happen, and it looks as if we may be in the last roundup as humans because Jesus, in prophesying His return, said that there would be signs in space.

War in Space

Wait! There is still more, for Jesus also said: *" . . . there shall be signs in the sun, and in the moon, and in the stars; and upon the earth distress of nations, with perplexity; the sea and the waves roaring; Men's hearts failing them for fear, and for looking after those things which are coming on the earth: for the powers of heaven shall be shaken"* (Luke 21:25, 26). What is it that causes men to panic as they watch the heavens? Could it be a space war just preceding Christ's return to earth? Let's examine the present-day Buck Rogers scenario further and prove that this, too, is now a distinct possibility.

In a *Detroit News* article entitled, "**U.S.-Soviets Gear Up For Outerspace Wars:**" Edwin G. Pipp states: "Russia and the U.S. are moving toward fighting future wars in space. The two superpowers now have the potential to wage space battles between unmanned satellites hundreds of miles above earth. Everything will be ready in the early 1980s. The possibility of conflict in space is real enough to convince the Air Force to seek 10.8 million dollars to protect America's satellite systems from possible Soviet efforts to destroy or disable them. And the Air Force is spending even more millions for U.S. offensive space systems.''

U.S. News & World Report, July 27, 1981, stated: '' **'Star Wars' Weapons May Come True.''** ''Satellite killers, laser artillery, space cruisers — the stuff of today's science fiction could revolutionize tomorrow's battlefield. American and Soviet scientists are racing to perfect ray guns and killer satellites that may turn outer space into the kind of battleground once thought possible only in science fiction movies. Two recent events underscore the urgency of the battle for military dominance in space. On March 14, the Soviet Union reportedly succeeded for the 11th time with a test-firing of a killer-satellite space weapon. Early in June, the U.S. Air Force started experiments with a new airborne laser weapon, but with only mixed results. Both missions are described by intelligence experts as highly significant developments in the multibillion-dollar race for mastery of what may be the ultimate ''high ground'' in warfare. A growing number of military planners believe that whoever dominates space will have an overwhelming strategic advantage on earth.''

Another *U.S. News & World Report* article, published June 1, 1981, described military spy satellites already in use. The report states: ''Some satellites now aloft are so sophisticated that, from 100 miles out in space they can identify an object as small as a grenade in the hand of a Russian soldier. [In addition], a whole new generation of satellites is now being developed. If present plans work out, the space shuttle will begin carrying them aloft during the latter part of the decade. The new generation . . . will enable the United States not only to keep track of every ship at sea, but to monitor the movements of all aircraft as well.''

Concluding my observations on this subject is an article from the Jackson, Mississippi, *Clarion Ledger* newspaper, August 16, 1981: ''The world is moving into the bewildering age of space warfare faster than most Americans realize. The development of this awesome new dimension in military tactics has been kept largely hidden from the public by the liberal use of 'Top Secret' classification stamps. An ultra-secret directive from the Joint Chiefs of Staff listed the priorities the Pentagon has laid out for the elimination of Soviet satellites. For what small comfort it may offer, the Pentagon's plans for destruction of Soviet spy satellites do not involve lobbing nuclear warheads into the stratosphere. The reason is that nuclear missiles launched against Russian satellites might well damage American satellites that are also orbiting the earth. According to the secret directive, there is a maximum of 45 Soviet satellites that will pose a threat to the United States by 1985 and must therefore be destroyed quickly in the event of war.''

No wonder Jesus said that men's hearts would fail them for fear for looking after those things which would come on the earth, and that the powers of heaven would be shaken! In the light of all these articles, is it not interesting that the

Bible, 1,900 years ago, predicted a space war for the end time? Revelation 12:7 states " . . . *and there was war in heaven . . .* " No longer is it intelligent to scoff at God's Word. By doing so, one only shows his ignorance of current events!

Information and World Control

Where will all this knowledge eventually and inevitably take us? What lies ahead for civilization? What does the Bible predict? Guided by the Holy Spirit, Daniel states in chapters 8 and 11 that knowledge and scientific advancement will be used by an **international despot** to control the nations of the world. After the Rapture of the Church of Jesus Christ, this leader — called the Antichrist — will take control of a newly built Jewish temple in the Holy Land. He will proclaim himself as the awaited Messiah and claim that he is God! II Thessalonians 2:4 describes his action by stating that the Antichrist, " . . . *opposeth and exalteth himself above all that is called God, or that is worshipped; so that he as God sitteth in the temple of God, shewing himself that he is God.*" The world accepts his proclamations out of **fear**. Yes, as world war is about to be unleashed upon the earth, this global charmer convinces humanity that he has the answers to the world's ills — that he alone can bring peace. Thus, on the basis of peace negotiations between Israel and many nations (Daniel 9:27), he is accepted.

As I stated in Part II, I believe that the Antichrist will enslave and control earth's billions through a sophisticated computer fashioned in his likeness. Thus, he will be able to have all the facts on every member of the human race at his fingertips and, with unerring precision, know who receives his orders, obeys his commands and honors his laws. Present-day computers are already storing information on members of the human race. Mr. Paul Peterson, in his book, *Sinister World Computerization,* reports: "I saw the computer in Luxembourg that can computerize facts and figures on everyone in the world. The building that houses it is over a half-block square. The main floor contains all the computerization." One of the things that intrigued Mr. Peterson was a micro tape approximately one half inch wide on a reel two feet in diameter. This reel had the capability of storing 20 pages of documentation on every person living in the United States of America! Think of it! A single reel carried the potential of 20 pages of information on more than 210 million persons — **and there were 7,000 reels on location!** *Europe,* the magazine of the Common Market, reported in the September/October, 1979 issue: "European researchers will soon be linked through a unique system for computerized data — the Direct Information Access Network for Europe (called DIANE). DIANE is to interconnect numerous nations through the most advanced computer and telecommunications devices. The system will include data networks from Community countries with the future possibility of incorporating networks of non-Community countries.'' In a related article, *Europe* stated: ''We will have access to 100 computer banks around the world. The name and data relating to every individual in the Western world is stored in computer banks everywhere. All this information can be fed into the Euronet computer that the European Community locates at Brussels, Belgium.'' (Read carefully the following statement to avoid the recent confusion over the Belgian computer:) Only the computer **LINKS** are in Brussels. The actual Euronet computer is located in LUXEMBOURG, housed in the building described by Mr. Peterson.

What is the speed of such computers? *Computer Digest* states: ''In one half second, today's computers can: Debit 2,000 checks to 300 different bank accounts, or can examine 1,000 electrocardiograms, or score 150,000 answers on 3,000 exams, or figure the company payroll for 1,000 employees.'' The international dictator will use such a computer, fashioned after his likeness (Revelation 13:14), to enslave the inhabitants of planet earth. He will effectively do this through commerce — the buying and selling of products. Revelation 13:16, 17 state: *''And he causeth all, both small and great, rich and poor, free and bond, to receive a mark in their right hand, or in their foreheads: And that no man might buy or sell, save he that had the mark, or the name of the beast, or the number of his name.''* This forthcoming computer of the ages will give the Antichrist all the information necessary for him to govern the world. Its memory bank will know the number, record and history of every living person! This number will definitely include ''666'' in one manner or another (Revelation 13:18).

I believe it will be a prefix, such as 666-7, 666-300, etc. Every individual credit card number must have some differentiation to distinguish one person from another. If all credit cards were identical, there would be mass confusion. Similarly, there will be some variance along with the ''666'' marking.

Some students of Bible prophecy theorize that this number will actually be composed of the international, national and area computer codes presently in use (or being implemented) plus an individual number such as one's Social Security number. The present international computer code is ''6,'' and is anticipated to expand to ''666.'' The national computer identification code for the United States is ''110,'' and within our nation are many area codes presently used for telephone communication. Thus, by using each of these codes in sequence, ending with the Social Security or other assigned number, every man, woman and child within our borders could be individually identified. Such a number might be: 666-110-212-419-27-2738.

Now I want to report a startling mathematical equation which was worked out on current computers by Colonel Henry C. MacQueen, Sr., of Saratoga, California. He took the three six-digit units, which with their permutations of numbers, came out to N = 60, and multipled them by three. I don't expect you to understand the depth of the statement which I am about to make because I personally can only repeat what the computers revealed. I, too, am unable to grasp the enormity of the following figures. I state them to show you that each of earth's four billion inhabitants could possess his own personal number through the permutations of the figures described as "666." In fact, the computers arrived at the conclusion that 46,834,995,519,212,567,931,529,902,559,-000 (forty-six nonillion, eight hundred thirty-four octillion, nine hundred ninety-five septillion, five hundred nineteen sextillion, two hundred twelve quintillion, five hundred sixty-seven quadrillion, nine-hundred thirty-one trillion, five hundred twenty-nine billion, nine hundred two million, five hundred fifty-nine thousand) human beings could each have his own number. Six hundred sixty-six, with its permutations, fits the bill, regardless if trillions more were born!

As a final note on computer development — and an interesting sequel to Colonel MacQueen's equation — I quote an article which appeared in the December 8, 1981 edition of the *St. Louis Post Dispatch:* " . . . mathematicians at the Weizmann Institute of Science in Israel and the Massachusetts Institute of Technology are working on a new cryptographic system and microcomputer chip **that may be able to provide everyone in the world with a personal, unbreakable code.** The goal is to ensure for privileged **government, business** and **personal** communications the confidentiality threatened as never before by espionage of all sorts . . . The new cryptographic technique . . . is 'one of the surest means of concealment ever devised.' "

World computerization is so near that the international bankers, through "SWIFT" (Society For Worldwide Interbank Financial Telecommunications), are already preparing the way for the world leader to take control. Mr. Henry Spaak, one of the organizational leaders in Brussels, has stated: "We do not want another committee. We have too many already. What we want is a man of sufficient stature to hold the allegiance of the people, and to lift us out of the economic morass into which we are sinking. **Send us such a man, and be he God or the devil, we will receive him**." Mr. Spaak, as a fellow Belgian and a believer in Christ, may I say that your wish will soon be granted! A new "Hitler" with a monstrous computer to enslave millions may soon take over the earth. All these events signal the imminent return of the Lord Jesus Christ. Before this year — or even this **day** — ends, He may come!

Are you ready? The good news is that Christ died for our sins by shedding His precious blood, was buried and then rose again (I Corinthians 15:3, 4). He did this to save you. Now **YOU** must decide to make Him your Saviour by receiving him as your own. **Do it today!**

2
A New World Order

Will a gigantic, computerized robot eventually run the world's affairs? If so, is there any proof that earth's four billion inhabitants are headed for such an hour? Read and understand the facts as we discover **why** mankind needs, wants and ultimately receives a computer number for commercial purposes.

$$$ versus 666

The world's current monetary system is creating havoc among bankers. In America alone, the annual check processing cost is $10 million! What a waste. Cash causes even greater problems as graft, bribery, corruption and crime sweep the world. Leaders are crying, "Away with cash and eliminate crime!" The *American Bar Magazine* reports: "Crime would be virtually eliminated if cash became obsolete. Cash is the only real motive for 90% of the robberies. Hence its liquidation would create miracles in ridding earth's citizens of muggings and holdups." This approach to the problem is spawning national experimentation. The *Los Angeles Herald Examiner* printed the following statement: "Cashless buying [has been] approved for twelve states by the Comptroller of the currency." The *Associated Press* also stated: "Supermarkets, gasoline stations and department stores in numerous cities are testing the cashless bank account deduction plan for their customers. This is a portion of the Electronic Funds Transfer

System which takes care of all one's needs through a number." In connection with a cashless society, plans are being laid internationally to make a numbers system feasible. This explains the strange lines and figures known as the "Universal Product Code" on virtually every item of merchandise in today's market. The metric system is also being promoted and installed at a cost of billions of dollars by the international bankers. Their aim is the establishment of a one-world government during the decade of the '80s! This government will control human beings through computerized numbers for all people. Presently, no one knows how each of us spends our cash. Once every transaction is credited to one's number, however, "BIG BROTHER" will know everything about everyone through computers!

U.S. News & World Report, in April of 1978, reported: **"Uncle Sam's Computer Has Got You.** Chances are your personal life is all on tape somewhere in the government's data banks. Now Americans want more assurance that Washington will not use modern technology to harass or intimidate ordinary citizens. Available in government computers is a vast array of data on virtually every American, including personal finances, health, family status and employment. For those who have ever had a brush with the law or been suspected of illegal activity, had a driver's license lifted, travelled abroad or even hunted certain species of animals, the chances are that somebody, somewhere in the government has a record of this information. David F. Linowes, who headed the Privacy Protection Study Commission, asks: 'What happens if this data that is being collected gets into the wrong hands? There is no reason to believe that someone won't come along at some point in the future to abuse it.' " **What a profound statement in the light of Bible prophecy!** The new system is on the way, and its equipment is being built at breakneck speed. *Computer World's* Nancy French reports: "The Society for Worldwide Interbank Financial Telecommunications (called "SWIFT" and referenced in chapter 1) has completed its principal hardware and software selection for a communications network linking 240 members worldwide. This system is so designed that any (ANY!) type of computer system in the world can become a participant." Think of it! Any computer system in the world can be hooked into the mother computer in Luxembourg (whose major links are located in Brussels, Belgium). This information is doubly interesting when one realizes that Brussels is the headquarters of the Common Market nations and NATO. In all probability the present preparations may be part of the formation of the final ten-kingdom federation of nations prophesied in Daniel, chapter 2 and Revelation, chapter 13. I will have more to say about this in chapter 4.

Let us now consider how the number "666" could become functional in such a mechanized society. Supposing every person in the world were assigned a single credit card and individual identification number. Do you think this is impossible? The *Knight News Service* of Miami, Florida, reports: "[During the 1980s], many bankers predict, most shoppers will exchange the wallet full of credit cards they now carry for a single, all-purpose card and number." Another article, by Gerald L. Nelson, *Detroit News* special writer, states: "The American dollar is under attack again, but not from Arab oil sheiks or Japanese car manufacturers or inflation or any of the dollar's usual enemies. The dollar is being threatened by, of all things, the computer. Why? Well, picture this: It is 1985 and you are checking out at your neighborhood grocery. By then your food bill might come to something like $99.50. That is irritating, but take heart. You may not have to fumble around with checkbooks or cash. 'Your debit card, please,' the cashier will say, and you will hand her a thin piece of plastic — a credit card look-alike. Then you will punch in a code number, your own **secret** number, and, presto, you've paid for your groceries." We see, then, that a world number is feasible in the near future. However, this is a problem. One could be kidnapped or killed for the numbered card. Because of this fact, some are advocating **the insertion of a number on one's body!** The suggested method propagated thus far has been one that would not mar, scar or detract from one's features. It would be a laser beam tattoo, invisible to the human eye but clearly seen under an infra-red light. You don't believe that such ideas are presently being suggested? Then read carefully, Mr. Skeptic. *Senior Scholastic*, a news-magazine used in American high schools, pictured a group of young people with numbers on their foreheads. The photo was captioned, "The Future." Again, William B. Saxbe said: "The growing economic problem of our expanding society has difficulties. How do we solve them? Some have suggested national computerization . . . but we just can't put a number on people and say, 'Step up and put your head in a computer.' " **Mr. Saxbe, how in heaven's name did you ever make such a statement? Do you know that you are quoting God's Holy Word? What seems impossible to you is actually going to happen!** Revelation 13:15-18 state: " *. . . he* [the world ruler] *had power to give life unto the image of the beast* [undoubtedly a monstrous computer], *that the image of the beast should both speak, and cause that as many as would not worship the image of the beast should be killed. And he causeth all, both small and great, rich and poor, free and bond, to receive a mark in their right hand, or in their foreheads: And that no man might buy or sell, save he that had the mark, or the name of the beast, or the number of his name. Here is wisdom. Let him that hath understanding count the number of the beast: for it is the number of a man; and his number is Six hundred threescore and six"* — "666!"

Neighbor, it looks as if it is later than you think. Horrible events are just around the corner, but hope abounds for those who are saved because the Lord Jesus Christ is coming soon to snatch away all His own!

The Foundations of World Government

At this point, you are probably inquisitive as to what may bring such a system into immediate existence. I personally have no doubt that the spiraling inflationary trend will be the culprit. In fact, I think that a worldwide economic crisis is just ahead of us. This crisis may lead all of us into a world government under a Satan-dominated one-world despot who manipulates humanity with his international computers. How close are we to such a government? The scene has been set in your lifetime and mine through the creation of the following international agencies:

1. **International Atomic Energy Agency (IAEA)** The published aim of this agency is to promote peaceful use of atomic energy. The inevitable result will be to disseminate among foreign nations vital information on American atomic resources.

2. **International Labor Organization (ILO)** The purpose of this arm of the one-world government is to coordinate labor demands throughout the world. It provides an ideal vehicle for the promotion of socialism and the one-world philosophy.

3. **Food and Agricultural Organization (FAO)** This organization has been established to standardize food qualities and levels of nutrition internationally. It is the model instrument for im-

plementing the Antichrist's law that no man might buy or sell except he receive the mark of the beast (Revelation 13:17).

4. **International Bank for Reconstruction and Development (World Bank)** This international bureaucracy is designed to internationalize money standards. Ultimately, it will place all the money power of the world in the hands of one giant agency. Already there is talk of issuing international currency under the direction of the United Nations.

5. **International Development Association (IDA)** This one-world financing organization is responsible for establishing international control of natural resources.

6. **United Nations Educational, Scientific and Cultural Organization (UNESCO)** The purpose of this agency is to promote collaboration among nations through education, science and culture. The ultimate aim is the complete integration, miscegenation and mongrelization of the races, plus leveling all world religions to a common plateau — thus making paganism, Christianity and communism bosom bedfellows.

7. **World Health Organization (WHO)** The internationalization of medicine, surgery and the treatment of disease is the goal of this organization. It also gives political advantage to the world dictator in that it provides a logical instrument for committing political opponents to hospitals for the mentally ill, thousands of miles from friends and supporters.

8. **International Finance Corporation (IFC)**

This organization is responsible for implementing a plan to take over the poorly developed areas of the world in order to bring smaller nations into subjection to a one-world government.

9. **International Monetary Fund (IMF)** This fund will promote and expand international trade, standardize commerce and industry and make it a very simple matter for the Antichrist to issue his decree that no man can buy or sell except he receive the mark of the beast.

10. **International Civil Aviation Organization (ICAO)** This group has been established to standardize aviation laws, procedures, patterns and practices throughout the world.

11. **Universal Postal Union (UPU)** This agency is designed to promote uniformity in postal services and the development of international collaboration — **openly to promote the reciprocal exchange of mail.** This is the first step toward the international control of communications and censorship.

12. **International Telecommunications Union (ITU)** The purpose of this organization is to provide international regulations for radio, telegraph and telephone services, thereby making the worldwide preaching of the Gospel of Jesus Christ by means of radio and television a practical impossibility.

13. **World Meteorological Association (WMA)** The aim of this agency is to standardize and coordinate all meteorological work — weather information and forecasts — of the world. Weather control and climate modification is a

sinister possibility.

14. **Intergovernmental Maritime Consultive Organization (IMCO)** This group promotes the coordination of international shipping and aims to remove all discrimination by governments and all restrictive practices by shippers. Thus, international transportation will be under the control of another giant bureau which can dictate **who** and **what** can and cannot be served.

15. **International Trade Organization (ITO)** By tightening the terms of commerce and promoting the free flow of goods from one country to another under international agreement, the **ITO** will break down national boundaries and pave the way for Satan's emperor, the Antichrist, to take control of the entire world.

16. **General Agreement on Tariffs and Trades (GATT)** The goal of this agency is the subject of current battles in the United States Congress. The fight centers on the lowering, or complete abolition, of all tariffs on foreign imports, the leveling of national boundaries and the destruction of national loyalties. Such actions would set the whole world up for allegiance to the beast from perdition.

The formation of these organizations has led outstanding thinkers, such as Mr. William P. Hoar, to state that a new world order is on the horizon!

3
The International
Bankers Have A Plan

Dr. Saul H. Mendlovitz declares: "There is no longer a question of whether or not there will be a world government, for the declaration of interdependence is a part of the continuing drive to dilute, then dissolve, the sovereignty of the United States of America for the new world order, a new international economic order.

"In 1960, there were virtually no courses being taught along the lines of world order in our universities. Today, there are between 500 and 1,000 colleges and universities teaching the new international order, all sponsored by the Rockefeller Foundation. All this planning does not come from the lips of impotent, powerless Utopians. Instead, the perpetrators of the world order are moving ahead by planning a new economic order."

Paul Scott had this group in mind when he reported the following in the *Washington News Intelligence Syndicate:* "The one-world perpetrators are calling for the development of a global policy on food and oil within the framework of the United Nations. It is their belief that by controlling food they can control people, and by controlling energy — especially oil — they can control nations and their financial systems. By placing food and oil under world control, along with the monetary system, they believe that they can have a world government operating [in the 1980s]." It is happening before our very eyes! These statements are tremendous

The '80s, the Antichrist and Your Future!

in the light of Bible prophecy!

The Energy Controversy

Now it is easy to see why the energy crunch ideology has been crammed down the throats of Americans and others in the world. It is a plan to destroy paper money through an inflationary spiral that will make the nations submissive to a new and carefully planned economic system.

The *Washington Post* reports: "The American public . . . never has taken the 'energy crisis' as seriously as do the politicians and technocrats of Washington, who periodically scold the nation for its ignorance or greed. The public skepticism is encouraged, if not fully confirmed, by the optimistic revisions in recent forecasts. Meanwhile, the world markets are glutted with oil, particularly on the West Coast of the United States . . . "

I predicted these results five years ago! Yet, there is no doubt in the thinking man's mind that the oil embargo and promoted "crisis" thinking has affected the entire Western world and Eastern bloc of nations. Gasoline, coffee, doughnuts and all staples are approximately double the cost they were five years ago. Each additional "crisis" adds to the vicious cycle of catastrophic events. In fact, we are on the same spiral Germany experienced from 1914 to 1922. It took eight short years for their economic system to fail. Read the following firsthand report by C.M. Ripley who was on the scene at

223

the time:

"The collapse of German finance changed the nation into an economic madhouse. Gas bills were thirty times as high as rent costs. Prices were unbelievable. A pound of lard cost 20 million marks. A menu in a local restaurant offered the following: Two orders of roast goose, 160,000,000 marks; vegetables, 39,000,000 marks; tax 69,000,000 marks, plus 20 million marks for service. This would have been $131,432,000 American dollars before the war, including beverages. In stores, a box of matches cost 3 million marks, one raw egg 12 million marks and a quart of milk ran 30 million marks on Tuesday and changed to 40 million on Wednesday. The bill at Adlon Hotel for six nights totaled two billion, 336 million marks. This again would have been one half million American dollars.

"Everything was normal in 1914. Butter sold for one and one half marks per pound. However, by 1918 it had jumped to three marks — a 100% increase in four short years. (This is the exact pattern in America since 1974.) Then the real problem began. By the spring of 1922, butter had risen to 2,400 marks per pound, by summer to 150,000 marks per pound and by fall it had reached the astronomical figure of six million marks per pound, or the equivalent of one and one half million American dollars."

We are on the same dangerous treadmill presently. Supposing the results are the same! This catastrophy would certainly usher in a new world system.

The Dollar's Demise

Economic experts agree that America's monetary system is in grave danger. In fact, in January of 1978, the United States intervened on a massive scale to prop the dollar abroad by announcing a plan to back the battered currency through a $20 billion swap arrangement with foreign central banks and a special $4.7 billion currency stabilization fund. Previously, in order to bolster the sagging dollar, Japan and West Germany came to the rescue. The following year they refused to do so and the U.S. Treasury and Federal Reserve System had to trade the more stable foreign currency on hand to purchase foreign-held U.S. dollars. The next step is that the United States will be forced to use its remaining gold to buy back Eurodollars and Petrodollars. When the last of this gold has been used to prop up these dollars, the day of the dollar is finished and a new system will become a matter of necessity.

Another thorn in America's economic side is the $80 billion we have loaned to Russia through the years. In all, communist nations have borrowed **one trillion** dollars from the United States, and if they default or refuse to repay these loans we are quite simply finished, economically. In fact, economic magazines written by the experts are for the first time in agreement concerning the fact that the dollar could become obsolete within 18 months! Leonard K. Ruse, president of the St. Louis Federal Reserve Bank, stated in the *Journal of Commerce:* "The American economy may finally be running out of steam." Douglas R. Casey, in a *Detroit News* article, said: "The United States — in fact, the entire world — now faces a massive depression. The effects . . . will persist well into and even beyond the 1980s. As wonderful as recent technological advances have been, they will not postpone the inevitable . . . Nor will the government."

In *International Money Line,* Julian Snyder says: "The U.S. is trying to solve its problems through currency depreciation. It never worked throughout history and will not work now." Mr. Snyder further stated that the "crash" could well occur **this year!** Meanwhile, the *Holt Investment Advisory* reports: "The efforts of government to solve problems by printing more paper money are making things worse. This is adding to the worldwide mistrust in paper money and strengthening the demand for gold." In the *Zweig Forecast,* Martin Zweig states: "Stock prices are perched on a precipice and there is a fair chance of an outright crash."

The Memphis, Tennessee *Commercial Appeal* newspaper looked at the future and stated: "The average worker retiring at age 65 in 2050 would draw retirement checks of nearly $259,000 while some individuals would get the maximum of $405,000. If the Social Security projections hold true, wages will increase roughly 62-fold over the next 72 years. If prices followed suit, today's 60-cent loaf of bread would cost $37.50; a $25 tab at the grocery store would run $1,562; a 15-cent phone call or newspaper would cost $9.40; a medium sized $4,500 auto would retail for $281,000; a $55,000 home would sell for $3.4 million, and that average $656,000 wage earner would be paying more than $50,000 annually in Social Security taxes. The maximum tax would be $114,000 on income up to $1.5 million.''

Personally, I believe that the *Commercial Appeal's* predictions will become reality long before the year 2050. If the Lord Jesus Christ tarries, I think we will see such hyper-inflation sweep our nation and the world within the next ten years. I am not a prophet, nor am I the son of a prophet. I may be wrong, but the economic experts believe that financial destruction is just ahead of us. Meanwhile, in order to replace the downgraded dollar, the nations of the European Economic Community have created a new currency — the ECU — which fulfills both the role of international denominator and world reserve tender — the two key functions previously reserved for the dollar. The ECU will be backed in gold and hard-currency reserves by the strongest European nations and firmly insulated against any fluctuations or disturbances caused by the instability of the dollar. To further eliminate U.S. economic leadership and the influence of dollar transactions, the European nations have agreed to replace the American-dominated International Monetary Fund with a European Monetary Fund endowed with over $50 billion in liquid assets — almost a third more than the IMF now commands. Under the control of this new anti-dollar money union, European currencies will be stabilized without — in fact, against — a U.S. presence!

The international bankers indeed have a plan, and according to *The Fact Finder* of Phoenix, Arizona: "The international bankers, most of whom are located in the United States, have no basic loyalty toward this country and not a vestige of patriotism for America. Their aim is to change our monetary system to make it easier for them to control all monetary systems, worldwide. President James Garfield said: 'Whoever controls the volume of money in any country is absolute master of all industry and commerce.' "

4
Your Startling Future

Is a new world economic order about to appear? Is it possible that the present inflationary trend signals such a moment in our history? Here are the facts:

Bill Neukirk, reporting for the *Associated Press,* said: "A new world exchange system which will dominate the economies of nations for the next 25 years is but months away. This is so because top finance ministers at the Annual International Monetary Fund meeting came close to an agreement on such a system." Now for a real shockeroo! Remember the Watergate tapes? Here is a quote from one of them as reported in the *Daily Oklahoman:* "Nixon brushed aside an offer from his top aide, Halderman, to brief him on the devaluation of the British currency. Nixon said, 'I don't care about it. There is nothing we can do about it.' Halderman said: 'You want a rundown, Mr. President?' Nixon: 'No, I don't.' Halderman observed that the British action [concerning convertibility] reveals the wisdom of not considering convertibility **until we get a new system.**" Think of it! Years ago, plans were already being laid. Today we are moving ahead with alarming velocity!

Willard Cantelon, author of *The New World Monetary System,* says: "I have been in conversation with men chosen to advise the President of the United States. I have weighed their deductions and examined all their saying. It is one message. We are moving toward a new system, a number system run by computers. There is not a conversant person in the world with whom I have spoken who would argue that the world is presently beyond the point of no return. No longer is the question, 'Is a new system coming,' the question is '**WHEN?**' "

Shadows of "666"

The question indeed is "WHEN?" Another question is "**WHO?**" Yes, who will be the Antichrist? A world ruler **must** arise with the new system. This beast is described in Revelation 13:7, 8, 16 and 17: " . . . *power was given him over **all** kindreds, and tongues and nations. And **all** that dwell upon the earth shall worship him . . . And he causeth **all**, both small and great, rich and poor, free and bond, to receive a mark in their right hand, or in their foreheads: And that **no man** might buy or sell, save he that had the mark, or the name of the beast, or the number of his name.*"

At our ministry headquarters, we have watched with awe the increasing use of "666" throughout the world. The proliferation of this number since its initial assignment to all Arab owned vehicles in Jerusalem in 1973 is astounding. In fact, I believe the nations are currently being brainwashed into accepting this code as normal and necessary in order to pave the way for its becoming an absolute requirement during the reign of the Antichrist. Following is a list of 35 different places the number "666" has either appeared in the past or is currently appearing:

#1: The Hollywood film productions, "The Omen I and II" plus "The Final Conflict" concerned themselves with the world dictator. The number "666" appeared in the advertisements for these movies.

#2: Since 1973, the license plate numbers of all Arab-owned vehicles in the city of Jerusalem have been prefixed with "666."

#3: The first ship to pass through the reopened Suez Canal in 1975 displayed "666" on its side.

#4: Beginning in 1977, the IRS Circular E (supplement) Employer's Tax Guide W-2P form required a "666" prefix.

#5: Beginning in 1979, the IRS W-2 form for nonprofit corporation employees required the "666" prefix. (**NOTE:** I understand that the IRS is changing its requirements as a result of public pressure.)

#6: The IRS Alcohol, Tobacco and Firearms Division employee badges display the number "666."

#7: Metric rulers distributed throughout America in 1979 contained the number "666."

#8: Since August, 1980, MasterCard has used "66" on its statements.

#9: The design of Australia's national bank card incorporates a configuration of the number "666."

#10: Shoes produced in Italy display a "666" label.

#11: An introduction-to-algebra book for children, released by the Thomas Corwell Co.,

New York, is entitled, *666 Jellybeans.*

#12: South Central Bell Telephone Co.'s Telco Credit Union card requires a "666" prefix plus the holder's Social Security number.

#13: Parent/Teacher training books offered by the Channing L. Bete Co., Inc., Greenfield, Massachusetts, are catalog coded "C-666."

#14: The universal computer code for international communication is "6" and is anticipated to expand to "666."

#15: Central computers for Sears, Belks, J.C. Penney and Montgomery Ward stores around the world prefix transactions with "666."

#16: Various computer receipts across the U.S. now contain a "666" number.

#17: The formula for the NCR Model 304 supermarket computer is 6-06-6 or "666."

#18: U.S. Selective Service cards contain a "666" code.

#19: Financial institutions in Florida use the "666" number.

#20: The overseas telephone operator number from Israel is "666."

#21: Israel's national lottery tickets and advertisements prominently feature the number "666."

#22: The Federal Government Medicaid Service Employees Division number is "666."

#23: State governments are now using "666" on paperwork for office purchases.

#24: The Koehring and Clark equipment companies now use "666" as part of their product identification on certain models.

#25: Armstrong "Sundial" floor tile is coded "666-13."

#26: Shirts produced in mainland China contain a "666" label.

#27: Work gloves manufactured by the Boss Glove Co. prominently display the number "666."

#28: Crow's Hybrid Corn Company of Nevada, Iowa, has developed a "666" hybrid.

#29: The McGregor Clothing Company has advertised a "666 Collection" for men.

#30: The IBM equipment in America's supermarkets displays the number "3X666."

#31: The identification tags on Japanese parts received by the Caterpillar Co., Peoria, Illinois, contain the number "666."

#32: Stickers distributed at DuPont Company plants state: "To be in the know, call 'MOM' (666)."

#33: Materials produced by the Bliss-Hastings Co. contain the number "666."

#34: "Performer Q," a little-known, semi-secret list of show business personalities used by programmers, production studios, advertising agencies and others, contains the names of 666 individuals.

#35: The 85th annual Frontier Days festival in Cheyenne, Wyoming, featured July 23, 1981 as "666 Rodeo Day."

As if the foregoing were not evidence enough of the fact that a brainwashing movement, designed to acquaint the public with the "new system," is in progress, the October 1980 issue of *Advertising Age* magazine carried a full-page advertisement featuring the supermarket computer scanner offered by TeleResearch Item Movement, Inc. (called TRIM). This advertisement featured the picture of a man with a Universal Product Code imprinted on his forehead! Whether or not anyone in the TRIM organization was aware of the prophetic implication of this advertisement is beside the point. One day soon, **all** buyers and sellers — the consumer and the producer alike — will be required to *"receive a mark in their right hand, or in their foreheads"* (Revelation 13:16). This requirement can only be initiated and enforced by the Antichrist himself!

As I stated earlier, I believe that when the Antichrist makes his debut and officially institutes the number "666" internationally, we Christians will be gone. Paul makes this fact emphatically clear in II Thessalonians 2:3-8. In verses 6-8, he informs the saints that the Antichrist cannot mount his throne until the hinderer — the Holy Spirit — is removed: *"And now ye know what withholdeth* [or what holds back the Antichrist's coming to power] *that he might be revealed in his time . . . only he who now letteth* [hindereth] *will let* [hinder], *until he be taken out of the way."*

After the restrainer's removal, then shall that wicked one be revealed. Antichrist cannot reign until the Holy Spirit's restraining influence is removed. This restraining influence consists of believers in whose hearts the Spirit dwells. Christ must come to call His own out of this world **before** the leader of the one-world government assumes power. **Are you saved?** Christian, are you ready?

Closing Out World History

Remember that the signs of God's Word point to Christ's return to the earth. They point to our return with Him when He comes as Lord of Lords and King of Kings. Yes, every sign in the Bible presently indicates that Christians are coming back soon with Jesus — but we can't do it at the moment because we are still here on planet earth. Thus, we have to get up and out in order to come back. I am not a prophet, nor am I the son of a prophet. I'm not the seventh son of a seventh son. Yet, I know that everything about us says that Jesus Christ is coming soon. Never before in history have we had a confederacy of ten Western nations. Never in 25 centuries has there been an Israel who can sign a world peace contract with the one — number 11 — who comes to power, whoever he is and whenever it is. The signs are with us and Dr. John F. Walvoord, President of Dallas Theological Seminary, has said: "From the hour that this world leader signs the peace contract with Israel, one can count down on the calendar — seven years to the day — to the return of Christ as King." Why?

The Antichrist's peace contract lasts only 42 months. Daniel 9:27: *"And he shall confirm the covenant with many for one week: and in the midst of the week he shall cause the sacrifice and oblation to cease, and . . . that determined shall be poured upon the desolate.''* Although he signs a peace contract of seven years' (or 84 months) duration, he breaks it at the halfway point (42 months). Then Russia marches to the Middle East, for she says: '' *. . . I will go up to the land of unwalled villages; I will go to them that are at rest that dwell safely . . .* '' (Ezekiel 38:11).

World Leaders Voice Concern

More and more, well-informed people are concerned that Moscow will succeed in its ultimate goal of world conquest. ''What kind of a world are we leaving to our children?'' they ask. Eugene V. Debs Rostow, the former Under Secretary of State for Political Affairs, is convinced that ''we are living in a **pre-war** and not a post-war period.'' Frank Barnett, head of the prestigious National Strategy Information Center, has told leading Americans: ''You are fully aware, of course, that in terms of the shifting military balance, the U.S. today is about where Britain was in 1938, with the shadow of Hitler's Germany darkening all of Europe.'' Dr. Edward Luttwak of the Georgetown Center for Strategic and International Studies in Washington states that the United States ''hasn't carried out a single major successful military operation in the last 30 years.'' In specific, he cites the failure of the American rescue mission in Iran: " . . . the abandonment of the dead, of secret documents and intact helicopters is contrary to all the customs of war and the usages of the service. This has a powerful effect in intensifying the great loss of prestige that the country has suffered as a result of this debacle."

Another embarrassment for U.S. intelligence forces came as a result of the 1981 Israeli raid on the Iraqi nuclear facility in Bagdad. *U.S. News & World Report*, June 22, 1981, stated: "Even with its extensive intelligence assets in the region, the Pentagon said that news of the June 7 raid arrived as a 'thunderous surprise.' The Israeli jets evidently were never spotted by the four AWACS radar planes that the U.S. flies over Saudi Arabia. One Pentagon official said the sophisticated radar did not pick up 'one single, solitary blip.' America's supersensitive satellites were no help, either. Analysts explain that spy-in-the-sky devices, though able to observe tiny stationary targets, remain virtually blind to such moving objects as a jet in flight. The satellites' intelligence-gathering activities, said one defense expert, are good at measuring damage after an attack, but not in warning of one."

In an interview with *U.S. News & World Report,* February 16, 1981, Senator John Tower, Chairman of the Armed Services Committee stated that the U.S. faces "nothing less than military inferiority" in light of the present Soviet military buildup. He reports that, "Our longstanding technological supremacy in aircraft and other weapons could be wiped out. With the accuracy of the new ICBM's they're building, we can't count on our present missiles surviving too much longer.'' The following weapons statistics and projections serve to confirm Senator Tower's statements and provide a comparison of U.S. and Soviet power:

Total Strategic Nuclear Launchers
(missiles & bombers)

	1981	1985	1990
U.S.	2,058	2,014	1,935
U.S.S.R.	2,582	2,600	2,850

Total Warheads

	1981	1985	1990
U.S.	9,000	10,000	12,800
U.S.S.R.	7,000	12,700	21,000

Estimated Megatonnage of Warheads

	1981	1985	1990
U.S.	3,300	4,000	5,000
U.S.S.R.	5,500	9,000	10,000

Source: *U.S. News & World Report*
February 16, 1981

In an article entitled, ''The Defense Gap That Worries The President,'' *U.S. News & World Report* states that: ''What has created this situation is a massive, sustained Soviet military buildup at a time when the U.S. effort was declining throughout the 1970s. In sheer numbers, Moscow has caught up with and may soon surpass the U.S. in strategic power. Vast improvements in the accuracy and power of Soviet missiles could give the Kremlin the means — at least in theory — to wipe out all 1,054 of America's land-based missiles in a first strike. **That, according to one recent defense survey, could confront an American President with 'a choice between surrender and Armageddon.' "**

Russia is indeed preparing for war, and Armageddon it will be as the conflict grows to finally include the turning of **all** nations against Israel at Jerusalem, according to Zechariah 14:2.

God's Word reveals the outcome: *"Then shall the Lord go forth, and fight against those nations, as when he fought in the day of battle. And his feet shall stand in that day upon the mount of Olives, which is before Jerusalem on the east . . . "* (Zechariah 14:3, 4). This is the glorious return of the Lord Jesus Christ and His saints (the Christians who were raptured seven years earlier) to earth. The scene is also described in Revelation 19:11-21. When Christ returns, He, as the *"stone cut out without hands"* (Daniel 2:34 and 45), smashes all existing powers and sets up His Kingdom. Then Daniel's interpretation of King Nebuchadnezzar's dream will have been fulfilled in every detail.

11:59 and Counting

Summary

When the Lord Jesus Christ returns to earth in Revelation, chapter 19, **how** does He return? As King of Kings! **When** is He coming as King? Daniel 2:44 " . . . *in the days of these kings* [the ten-nation Western confederacy] *shall the God of heaven set up a kingdom, which shall never be destroyed.* " We have prayed it through the ages . . . we pray it so often in our churches on Sunday morning. Matthew 6:10: *"Thy kingdom come. Thy will be done on earth, as it is in heaven."* When is He coming? When the Roman Empire has been revived in the form of a ten-nation confederacy. There are now ten nations bound together in such a confederacy, but number 11 will uproot and replace three of them. Then each member nation will have been a part of the old Roman Empire — and in the days of **these** ten kings shall God set up **His** kingdom. **Hallelujah!** That's the return of the Lord Jesus Christ with you and me if you're saved. **Are you ready for the exciting climax of world history?** *" . . . prepare to meet thy God . . . "* (Amos 4:12).

VI

The Great Escape

1
The Coming Tribulation

A number of recently published books have ridiculed the thought of a pre-Tribulation rapture. One author, Dave MacPherson, entitles his book, "The Unbelievable Pre-Trib Origin." After reading it twice I decided the only thing unbelievable about the presentation is its lack of scriptural authority. It quotes scores of men, but omits the God-breathed Word (2 Timothy 3:16). The few scripture-related portions I saw were quotations of Irving, Darby and Margaret — the ones Mr. MacPherson castigates. Personally, I am unimpressed with the quotations of men because they are all fallible. Only as fallen man rests his case upon the infallible Word of God is there any semblance of authority. *". . . let God be true, but every man a liar . . . "* (Romans 3:4).

The Tribulation Defined

First, let's define the Tribulation. It is a definite period of unparalleled trouble and sorrow upon the earth. Daniel 12:1 states: " . . . there shall be a time of trouble, such as never was since there was a nation even to that same time . . . " Jesus said in Matthew 24:21: "For then shall be great tribulation, such as was not since the beginning of the world to this time, no, nor ever shall be." Revelation 3:10 speaks of it as "the hour of temptation, which shall come upon all the world, to try them that dwell upon the earth."

Tribulation Versus Tribulations

This unprecedented period of tribulation is not to be confused with daily tribulations which all of God's people experience. Jesus said: " . . . In the world ye shall have tribulation: but be of good cheer; I have overcome the world" (John 16:33). Paul exhorted the brethren at Lystra, Iconium and Antioch to " . . . continue in the faith, and that we must through much tribulation enter into the kingdom of God" (Acts 14:21, 22). To the Roman Christians he wrote, " . . . we glory in tribulations also: knowing that tribulation worketh patience" (Romans 5:3). Now these heartaches, problems and perplexities experienced by all of God's people at various times are not to be confused with the GREAT TRIBULA-TION (Revelation 7:14). This designated seven year period is one of immense suffering for the *entire* world. It is an era of unthinkable tribulation. "Alas! for that day is great, so that none is like it . . . " (Jeremiah 30:7). There is nothing in past history to describe this period of time nor will there ever be anything to equal it in future years. Revelation chapters 6, 8, 9, 15 and 16 graphically describe the holocaust. The seven seals, seven trumpets and seven vials unfold the tragic and soon-coming scene. The clouds of doom and despair are lowered with the opening of the seven seals in Revelation 6:

First Seal

John declares: "And I saw when the Lamb opened one of the seals . . . and behold a white horse: and he that sat on him had a bow; and a crown was given unto him: and he went forth conquering and to conquer" (Revelation 6:1, 2).

Second Seal

"And when he had opened the second seal . . . there went out another horse that was red: and power was given to him that sat thereon to take peace from the earth, and that they should kill one another . . . " (Revelation 6:3, 4).

Third Seal

"And when he had opened the third seal . . . lo a black horse; and he that sat on him had a pair of balances in his hand. And I heard a voice in the midst of the four beasts say, A measure of wheat for a penny, and three measures of barley for a penny . . . " (Revelation 6:5, 6). Imagine! It will take a day's wages to buy a loaf of bread. It is coming — SOON!

Fourth Seal

"And when he opened the fourth seal, I heard the voice of the fourth beast say, Come and see. And I looked and behold a pale horse: and his name that sat on him was Death, and Hell followed with him. And power was given unto them over the fourth part of the earth, to kill with sword, and with hunger, and with death, and with the beasts of the earth" (Revelation 6:7, 8).

Fifth Seal

"And when he had opened the fifth seal, I saw under the altar the souls of them that were slain for the word of God, and for the testimony which they held: And they cried with a loud voice, saying, How long, O Lord, holy and true, dost thou not judge and avenge our blood on them that dwell on the earth?" (Revelation 6:9, 10).

Sixth Seal

"And I beheld when he had opened the sixth seal, and, lo, there was a great earthquake; and the sun became black as sackcloth of hair, and the moon became as blood; And the stars of heaven fell unto the earth . . . And the heaven departed as a scroll when it is rolled together; and every mountain and island were moved out of their places. And the kings of the earth, and the great men, and the rich men, and the chief captains, and the mighty men, and every bond-man, and every free man, hid themselves in the dens and in the rocks of the mountains; And said to the mountains and rocks, Fall on us, and hide us from the face of him that sitteth on the throne, and from the wrath of the Lamb: For the great day of his wrath is come; and who shall be able to stand?'' (Revelation 6:12-17).

Seventh Seal

The seventh seal in Revelation 8:1 depicts the lull before the storm. The catastrophic trumpet judgments are so horrendous that all heaven sits in awesome silence before the blitzkrieg begins. That is why the text reports: '' . . . there was silence in heaven about the space of half an hour.'' Then each of the seven angels sounds a trumpet before each calamitous judgment begins.

First Trumpet

''The first angel sounded, and there followed hail and fire mingled with blood, and they were cast upon the earth: and the third part of trees was burnt up, and all green grass was burnt up'' (Revelation 8:7).

Second Trumpet

''And the second angel sounded, and as it were a great mountain burning with fire was cast into the sea: and the third part of the sea became blood; And the third part of the creatures which were in the sea, and had life, died; and the third part of the ships were destroyed'' (Revelation 8:8, 9).

Third Trumpet

"And the third angel sounded, and there fell a great star from heaven, burning as it were a lamp, and it fell upon the third part of the rivers, and upon the fountains of waters; And the name of the star is called Wormwood: and the third part of the waters became wormwood; and many men died of the waters, because they were made bitter'' (Revelation 8:10, 11).

Fourth Trumpet

"And the fourth angel sounded, and the third part of the sun was smitten, and the third part of the moon, and the third part of the stars; so as the third part of them was darkened, and the day shone not for a third part of it, and the night likewise'' (Revelation 8:12). Wait, there is more! Verse 13 states: "And I beheld, and heard an angel flying through the midst of heaven, saying with a loud voice, Woe, woe, woe, to the inhabiters of the earth by reason of the other voices of the trumpet of the three angels, which are yet to sound!'' What are the three cataclysmic "Woes'' the three angels sound upon their trumpets?

Fifth Trumpet

"And the fifth angel sounded, and I saw a star

fall from heaven unto the earth: and to him was given the key of the bottomless pit. And he opened the bottomless pit; and there arose a smoke out of the pit, as the smoke of a great furnace; and the sun and the air were darkened by reason of the smoke of the pit. And there came out of the smoke locusts upon the earth: and unto them was given power, as the scorpions of the earth have power. And it was commanded them that they should not hurt the grass of the earth, neither any green thing, neither any tree; but only those men which have not the seal of God in their foreheads. And to them it was given that they should not kill them, but that they should be tormented five months: and their torment was as the torment of a scorpion, when he striketh a man. And in those days shall men seek death, and shall not find it; and shall desire to die, and death shall flee from them" (Revelation 9:1-6). The pains and pangs of Hell being unleashed upon the earth at this hour are but a beginning for the angel cries in verse 12: "One woe is past; and, behold, there come two woes more hereafter." What are they?

Sixth Trumpet

"And the sixth angel sounded, and I heard a voice from the four horns of the golden altar which is before God, Saying to the sixth angel which had the trumpet, Loose the four angels which are bound in the great river Euphrates. And the four angels were loosed, which were prepared for an hour, and a day, and a month, and a year, for to slay the third part of men" (Revelation 9:13-15). These demonic beings or demon-controlled humans compose the world's greatest army for " . . . the number of the army of the horsemen were two hundred thousand thousand (or two hundred million)" (Revelation 9:16). Their method of destroying mankind is undoubtedly through atomic incineration. Verse 18 declares: "By these three was the third part of men killed, by the fire, and by the smoke, and by the brimstone, which issued out of their mouths." There is more, for the angel cries in verse 14 of chapter 11: "The second woe is past; and, behold, the third woe cometh quickly." This third woe constitutes the seventh trumpet judgment.

Seventh Trumpet

"And the seventh angel sounded . . . and there were lightnings, and voices, and thunderings, and an earthquake, and great hail" (Revelation 11:15, 19). The blast of the seventh trumpet also begins the seven vial judgments. Revelation 15:1 reports: "And I saw another sign in heaven, great and marvelous, seven angels having the seven last plagues; for in them is filled up the wrath of God." This is undoubtedly the same wrath mentioned in Psalm 2:1-5 just before the King returns to establish His glorious kingdom. The rejected King becomes the reigning King after the wrath of God has been administered to a Christ-rejecting world. The text states: "Why do the heathen rage, and the people imagine a vain thing? The kings of the earth set themselves, and the rulers take counsel together, against the Lord, and against his anointed, saying, Let us break their bands asunder, and cast away their cords from us. [God] that sitteth in the heavens shall laugh: the Lord shall have them in derision. Then shall he speak unto them in his wrath, and vex them in his sore displeasure." This assuredly is the wrath of the seven seals, trumpets and vials combined. In concluding this chapter, let's look at the seven vial judgments.

First Vial

"And the first [angel] went, and poured out his vial upon the earth; and there fell a noisome and grievous sore upon the men which had the mark of the beast, and upon them which worshipped his image" (Revelation 16:2).

Second Vial

"And the second angel poured out his vial upon the sea; and it became as the blood of a dead man: and every living soul died in the sea" (Revelation 16:3).

Third Vial

"And the third angel poured his vial upon the rivers and fountains of waters; and they became blood" (Revelation 16:4).

Fourth Vial

"And the fourth angel poured out his vial upon the sun; and power was given unto him to scorch men with fire. And men were scorched with great heat, and blasphemed the name of God, which hath power over these plagues: and they repented not to give him glory" (Revelation 16:8, 9).

Fifth Vial

"And the fifth angel poured out his vial upon the seat of the beast; and his kingdom was full of darkness; and they gnawed their tongues for pain. And blasphemed the God of heaven because of their pains and their sores, and repented not of their deeds" (Revelation 16:10, 11).

Sixth Vial

"And the sixth angel poured out his vial upon the great river Euphrates; and the water thereof was dried up, that the way of kings of the east might be prepared" (Revelation 16:12).

Seventh Vial

"And the seventh angel poured out his vial into the air; and there came a great voice out of the temple of heaven, from the throne, saying, It is done. And there were voices, and thunders, and lightnings; and there was a great earthquake such as was not since men were upon the earth, so mighty an earthquake, and so great. And the great city was divided into three parts, and the cities of the nations fell: and great Babylon came in remembrance before God, to give unto her the cup of the wine of the fierceness of his wrath.

And every island fled away, and the mountains were not found. And there fell upon men a great hail out of heaven, every stone about the weight of a talent: and men blasphemed God because of the plague of the hail; for the plague thereof was exceeding great" (Revelation 16:17-21).

The final catastrophe following the twenty-one judgments just described, is the Battle of Armageddon (Revelation 16:16). It is closely associated, timewise, with the final or seventh vial, and becomes the battle of the ages. During the Tribulation Period, Russia marches to the Middle East. Gog, Magog, Meshech, Rosh and her allies are obliterated. God says: " . . . Behold, I am against thee, O Gog, the chief prince of Meshech and Tubal: And I will turn thee back, and leave but the sixth part of thee . . . " (Ezekiel 39:1, 2). Millions will die in this Mid-East war and "seven months shall the house of Israel be burying of them, that they may cleanse the land" (Ezekiel 39:12).

This invasion of the Middle East is not Armageddon, but leads to Armageddon — the climatic moment in world history when Christ returns with the armies of heaven to end war forever as pictured in Revelation 19:11-21. John states: "And I saw heaven opened, and behold a white horse; and he that sat upon him was called Faithful and True, and in righteousness he doth judge and make war . . . And the armies which were in heaven followed him upon white horses, clothed in fine linen, white and clean. And out of his mouth goeth a sharp sword, that with it he should smite the nations: and he shall rule them with a rod of iron: and he treadeth the winepress of the fierceness and wrath of Almighty God. And he hath on his vesture and on his thigh a name written, KING OF KINGS, AND LORD OF LORDS . . . And I saw the beast, and the kings of the earth, and their armies, gathered together to make war against him [the King of Kings] that sat on the horse, and against his army.'' The result is found in Verse 21: ''And the remnant were slain with the sword of him [Christ] that sat upon the horse, which sword proceeded out of his mouth: and all the fowls were filled with their flesh.'' This concludes earth's most terrifying hour. This is the end of the Tribulation Period. Christ immediately sets up His millennial Kingdom and then humanity beats their swords into plowshares and their spears into pruninghooks (Isaiah 2:4). Then universal peace begins — Utopia commences.

The Great Tribulation is near. Soon the Church of Jesus Christ will be evacuated before this judgmental hour begins. I am a pre-Tribulationist, proclaiming dogmatically that the Body of Christ misses this blood-soaked scene. I believe this for many reasons as we will see in the following chapters. If you have not prepared for the GREAT ESCAPE via the rapture, there is only one way to do it. I Thessalonians 4:16 declares: '' . . . and the dead in Christ shall rise first: Then we which are alive and remain shall be caught up together with them in the clouds to meet the Lord in the air: and so shall we ever be with the Lord." Notice this resurrection of the dead and living is *only* for those who are IN CHRIST. The only way to be IN CHRIST is to *receive* Him. John 1:12 states: "But as many as received him to them gave he power to become the sons of God . . . " Christ shed His blood for our sins and we can have redemption *only* " . . . through his blood . . . " (Ephesians 1:7). When one believes that Christ died for him and calls upon Christ for salvation, he instantly is IN CHRIST. Romans 10:13 states: "For whosoever shall call upon the name of the Lord shall be saved." Do it now!

A rash of booklets have appeared in recent days espousing the post-Tribulation viewpoint. One would think that the writers had just discovered undisclosed secrets, hidden from the foundation of the world. However, none of their arguments are new. Neither should one be impressed with their listing of scholars who propagate the theory. For every prophetical genius proposing the post-Tribulation view, there are fifty scholars who proclaim the GREAT ESCAPE, or the pre-Tribulation Rapture. However, names are meaningless on either side because *scripture* is the *final authority* on any given subject, including the meeting in the air. What saith the Holy Spirit? Let's work our way through the Bible, correlating texts.

Jacob's Time of Trouble

We begin with Jeremiah 30:7: "Alas! for that day is great, so that none is like it: it is even the time of Jacob's trouble . . . " This prophet, in chapters 30 and 31, summarizes Israel's endurance in the hour of Tribulation and depicts it as Jacob's or Israel's trouble. All the Old Testament prophets harmoniously affirm the truth. In Ezekiel 38 and 39 the northern army or Russian bear comes out of North against Israel. Seventeen different passages mark Israel as the victim. Ezekiel says: "And thou shalt come up against MY PEOPLE Israel . . . " (Ezekiel 38:16). Daniel described this horrible period of Tribulation in chapter 12, verse 1: " . . . and there shall be a time of trouble, such as never was since there was a nation even to that same time: and at that time THY PEOPLE shall be delivered . . . " Daniel's seventy weeks, of which the Tribulation Period is the closing segment, has to do with Israel: "Seventy weeks are determined upon thy people and upon thy holy city, to finish the transgression, and to make an end of sins, and to make reconciliation for iniquity, and to bring in everlasting righteousness, and to seal up the vision and prophecy, and to anoint the most Holy" (Daniel 9:24). The sixty-nine weeks totaling 483 years — already past — had to do with Israel. Why would God change His modus operandi or mode of operation for the seventieth week — the Tribulation Hour? The simple conclusion is that there is no change. God returns to His original program for the final week. This is again the reason that Satan, upon being cast to earth during the Tribulation Hour, goes after the woman (Israel) who brought forth the man child (Christ) in Revelation 12:12-17. The voice out of heaven cries: " . . . Woe to the inhabiters of the earth and of the sea! for the devil is come down unto you, having great wrath, because he knoweth that he hath but a short time. And when the dragon saw that he was cast unto the earth, he persecuted the woman which brought forth the man child [Christ]. And to the woman were given two wings of a great eagle, that she might fly into the wilderness, into her place, where she is nourished for a time, and times, and half a time, from the face of the serpent." Here we see God's loving protection for His covenant people for a time — one year, and times — two years, and for half a time or one-half-year. This totals 3½ years or 42 months — exactly one-half of the Tribulation Period. Verse 17 further corroborates the fact that Israel is the persecuted one, not the church, for " . . . the dragon was wroth with the woman, and went to make war with the remnant of her seed [Israelites] . . . " Only anti-literalists and anti-dispensationalists confuse the issue. They allegorize, spiritualize and pulverize the truth into mass confusion. They make Jews of all the redeemed or relegate the title of "Israelites" to Americans, Canadians and other Anglo Saxons. Little do they realize that there can be no harmony of the scriptures when one does not rightly divide the word of truth (II Timothy 2:15).

What is the truth? It is that God has *two* elect groups of individuals on this earth — Israel and the Church. Israel is the wife of Jehovah forever and the Church is the Bride of Christ. Romans 9 through 11 depict Israel's past (chapter 9); Israel's present (chapter 10), and Israel's future (chapter 11). During the Tribulation Hour, all Israel shall be saved (Romans 11:26). The 144,000 Jewish evangelists (Revelation 7:4-8) will proclaim the gospel of the Kingdom to all the world (Matthew 24:14), and all Israel will accept Messiah (Christ) as Saviour and King. Now these Israelites are the "elect" " . . . as touching the election, they are beloved for the fathers' sakes'' (Romans 11:28). This solves the problem of Matthew 24:22 which states: "And except those days should be shortened, there should no flesh be saved: but for the elect's sake those days shall be shortened." Post-Tribulationists vehemently cry: "You see, the elect are present for the judgments of the Father's elect wife!" The fact is that Jehovah chose or elected Israel to be His wife and Christ chose or elected His people to be His bride.

Concerning Israel, Deuteronomy 7:6 declares: "For thou art an holy people unto the Lord thy God: the Lord thy God hath chosen thee to be a special people unto himself, above all people that are upon the face of the earth." This promise is perpetual. "For the gifts and calling of God are without repentance [or change of mind]" (Romans 11:29). This is the reason that all Israel is going to be saved (verse 26). God keeps His covenants (verse 27), and Israelites are still the Father's "election" (verse 28). To the Christian, Christ says in John 15:16: "Ye have not chosen me, but I have chosen you . . . " We were chosen from before the foundation of the world (Ephesians 1:4), and our choosing is eternal. Now there is no difficulty whatsoever when men see both elections, but confusion reigns when the two are intermingled, spiritualized, allegorized and symbolized. Take God for what He states — literally — and the problems vanish.

Israel's Travail Points to the Returning King

The problem began when Christ came to earth the first time nearly 2,000 years ago. The Old Testament prophets predicted that a powerful potentate, a majestic king, would come to rule over Israel. This is why the wise men, in searching for the child, asked in Matthew 2:2, " . . . Where is he that is born King of the Jews?" What the people failed to see as they studied the prohets was that this Christ would suffer humiliation and pain before becoming a powerful ruler (Isaiah 53). Because of it, they rejected Christ. John 1:11 states: "He came unto his own [Israel], and his own received him not." This is why Christ commanded His disciples saying, " . . . Go not into the way of the Gentiles, and into any city of the Samaritans enter ye not: But go rather to the lost sheep of the house of Israel" (Matthew 10:5, 6). He would offer Himself as King to Israel first. In fact, John the Baptist cried: " . . . Repent ye: for the kingdom of heaven is at hand" (Matthew 3:2). However, the King was rejected just as Daniel predicted. He said in Daniel 9:26, "And after threescore and two weeks shall Messiah be cut off, but not for himself . . . " Now these are weeks or sevens of years. God's timetable amounts to seventy weeks or 490 years in His dealings with Israel.

The first seven weeks, or 49 years, had to do with the rebuilding of Jerusalem in troublesome times (Daniel 9:25). The second division of 62 weeks or 434 years signaled the time of Christ's death after the rebuilding of Jerusalem. The prophecy happened exactly on schedule. Christ came and offered Himself to Israel, but was rejected and "cut off" — but " . . . NOT FOR HIMSELF . . . " (Daniel 9:26). This was the crucifixion after the completion of His offer as King. Now Israel must pay the price for rejecting her King. So, a final week is coming when the Antichrist shall confirm the covenant with many for one week or seven years (verse 27). When this Antichrist usurps the throne that belongs to Christ, he " . . . shall destroy the city and the sanctuary; and the end thereof shall be with a flood, and unto the end of the war desolations are determined" (Daniel 9:26). Now, in the name of common sense, why would this final week or seven years be revamped to chastise the church which never rejected Christ — when the other 69 weeks dealt with Israel? Simple logic plus a super abundance of scripture make it clear that this is the time of Jacob's or Israel's trouble for rejecting their King. The chastisement creates an attitude of acceptance for the coming King at the close of the seventieth week. There is no doubt about it — Israel travails greatly before the King returns.

Jeremiah's prophecy proves it: "For, lo, the days come, saith the Lord, that I will bring again the captivity of my people Israel and Judah, saith the Lord: and I will cause them to return to the land that I gave to their fathers, and they shall possess it. And these are the words that the Lord spake concerning Israel and concerning Judah.

For thus saith the Lord; We have heard a voice of trembling, of fear, and not of peace . . . wherefore do I see every man with his hands on his loins, as a woman in travail, and all faces are turned into paleness? Alas! for that day is great, so that none is like it: it is even the time of Jacob's trouble . . . '' (Jeremiah 30:3-7). Daniel also describes the day of sorrow when a monstrous anti-Semitic dictator, satanically energized, speaks '' . . . great words against the most High . . . '' (Daniel 7:25). Jesus also said in Matthew 24:9, 21, 22: "Then shall they deliver you up to be afflicted, and shall kill you: and ye shall be hated of all nations for my name's sake . . . For then shall be great tribulation, such as was not since the beginning of the world to this time, no, nor ever shall be. And except those days should be shortened, there should no flesh be saved: but for the elect's sake [Israel] those days shall be shortened.''

Israel Preserved

The same prophets envision the physical and spiritual salvation of the nation of Israel. Jeremiah 30:7 states: '' . . . but [Israel] shall be saved out of it.'' Daniel cries in chapter 12, verse 1: '' . . . and at that time thy people [Jews] shall be delivered . . . '' Jesus also declared the shortening of the days for the preservation of the elect (Israelites): "But as the days of Noe were, so shall also the coming of the Son of man be'' (Matthew 24:37). Noah was preserved through judgment on the Ark. This pictures Israel's preservation through the time of judgment.

Israel's King

Notice also that Israel's physical and spiritual salvation has to do with the return of their King. This KING OF KINGS AND LORD OF LORDS shall ride to earth when "the daughter of Zion," a weeping wanderer "in Babylon," shall " . . . Be in pain and labour . . . like a woman in travail . . . " (Micah 4:10). When is our Lord coming back to earth? It will be "in that day" when "Jerusalem shall be taken, and the houses rifled" by international anti-Semitic bandits. "Then shall the Lord go forth, and fight against those nations . . . And his feet shall stand in that day upon the mount of Olives . . . And the Lord shall be king over all the earth . . . " (Zechariah 14:3, 4, 9).

When is our Lord coming back to earth? When shall sunset come for "the times of the Gentiles" and " . . . the Sun of righteousness arise" over a sorely bruised Israel "with healing in his wings . . . " (Malachi 4:2)? It will be "in that day" when "The kings of the earth set themselves, and the rulers take counsel together, against the Lord, and against his anointed [Israel], saying, Let us break their bands asunder, and cast away their cords from us. He that sitteth in the heavens shall laugh: the Lord shall have them in derision. Then shall he speak unto them in his wrath, and vex them in his sore displeasure. Yet have I set my king upon my holy hill of Zion" (Psalm 2:2-6). Then King Jesus " . . . shall have dominion also from sea to sea . . . and his enemies shall lick the dust . . . Yea, all kings shall fall down before him: all nations shall serve him" (Psalm 72:8-11).

Surely no reasonable, rational thinker will disagree with the facts presented to this point. Surely no one will try to place the bride of Christ into the texts or contexts used in this message. It is abundantly clear that God is dealing with Israel during the hour of Tribulation — not the Church. Christ's "elect" bride has been evacuated — the GREAT ESCAPE has occurred. The believers within the dispensation of grace, forming the Church, are gone. They vanished at the trumpet blast of I Thessalonians 4:16, 17 which declare: "For the Lord himself shall descend from heaven with a shout, with the voice of the archangel, and with the trump of God: and the dead in Christ shall rise first: Then we which are alive and remain shall be caught up together with them in the clouds, to meet the Lord in the air: and so shall we ever be with the Lord." From that point onward the Church is where Christ is — the bride with the bridegroom.

This is explicitly clear from the statement, "so shall we ever be with the Lord." When the seventieth week is finished for Israel, Christ returns to earth. Since the Church is forever where the Lord is, they return with the King to earth. Revelation 19:14 states: "And the armies which were in heaven followed him upon white horses, clothed in fine linen, white and clean." Jude 14 reports: ". . . Behold, the Lord cometh with ten thousands of his saints." Post-Tribulationists tell us that the Church, at the end of the Tribulation, goes up to meet Christ and immediately returns with the King. I cannot accept this "Yo-Yo" theory — up and down — presto whipto! This leaves no time for the Judgment Seat of Christ or the Marriage Supper of the Lamb. Contrary to this theory, Christ *does* rapture His Church into glory. The Judgment Seat occurs in the heavenlies as the Tribulation bombards the earth. Both "elect" groups are being prepared for the Millennium. Then, at the conclusion of the seventieth week, Christ returns with the army of believers who were part of the GREAT ESCAPE and immediately judges the nations on the basis of their treatment of His brethren or Israelites (Matthew 25:31-46). Notice that the nations are *not* judged on the basis of mistreating the Church — the body of Christ. This would be impossible since the Son of Man comes in His glory, with His angels to sit upon His throne as king — and *the believers* (in Revelation 19:11-16) *also return with Him at this moment!* How could they have been abused by the nations when they were absent from the earth? Take the Church out of the scene as the Bible does and see that the abused constitute the King's brethren — the Jews (Matthew 25:40).

Every anti-Semitic voice presently heard is indicative that the King is about to return.

However, before He comes to establish His kingdom, the GREAT ESCAPE, via the Rapture, takes place for Christ's bride. At this point, the most solemn question I can ask is: "Are you ready?" Have you trusted in Christ's shed blood for the remission of *your* sins? Don't delay! The Church may slip away in "the twinkling of an eye" at any moment (I Corinthians 15:52)!

3
The Great Escape

An indescribable holocaust, unparalleled in history is about to bombard planet earth. It is described as "the great tribulation" (Revelation 7:14), "the hour of temptation" (Revelation 3:10), "a day of great wrath" (Revelation 6:17) and an hour when the "wrath of God Almighty" is unleashed on all the world (Revelation 19:15).

Seven Years

This calamitous time of judgment lasts approximately seven years. Since the 69 weeks of Daniel total 483 years — each week representing seven years — it is only logical to make the final, seventieth week a period of seven years also. This harmonizes with the calculations of the second half of the Tribulation Hour described as a period of "forty-two months" (Revelation 11:2) or 1,260 days (Revelation 11:3).

The Tribulation's Purpose

When one considers God's purpose for the Tribulation, it is difficult to place the bride of Christ into such a horrendous scene. Why should Christ's virgin bride suffer the judgments of the seven seals, seven trumpets and seven vials? Why place her in the midst of the judgments recorded in Revelation chapters 6, 8, 9, 11, 15 and 16, when the church cannot be found beyond the third chapter of the book? The purpose of Christ during that worst hour in history is not to abuse

His bride, but to execute wrath upon an ungodly world. God does this in a two-fold manner:

1) He purges out any Jewish rebels before establishing His millennial kingdom. God states: "And I will cause you to pass under the rod [the Great Tribulation] . . . And I will purge out from among you the rebels, and them that transgress against me . . . and they shall not enter into the land . . . " (Ezekiel 20:37, 38).

2) He punishes Gentile rejectors. God continues: "And I will execute vengeance in anger and fury upon the [Gentiles], such as they have not heard" (Micah 5:15).

So, the Tribulation Hour is primarily a time of judgment upon a Christ-rejecting, God-rejecting world — both Jewish and Gentile. This judgment is so horrifying that Titus 2:13 becomes an absurdity if one must first look for seven years of heartache. The text states: "Looking for that blessed hope, and the glorious appearing of the great God and our Saviour Jesus Christ."

Deliverance From Wrath

The reason this hope is a blessed or happy one is that the Church escapes the turmoil of earth's most devastating hour. This fact is confirmed by the teaching of Jesus. He said that the days of the Son of man would be like the days of Noah and Lot (Luke 17:26-32). In Noah's day, Enoch, a type of the Church, was evacuated before the judgment of the flood while Noah, a type of Israel, was preserved through it. Lot, in his removal to Zoar before the fires fell, is also a type of the escaping Church before atomic incineration begins. Upon examining the story of Lot in Genesis 18:23-32, we discover that God informed Abraham that He would destroy the cities of Sodom and Gomorrah. Abraham immediately began bargaining with the Lord. " . . . Wilt thou also destroy the righteous with the wicked? Peradventure there be fifty righteous within the city: wilt thou also destroy and not spare the place for the fifty righteous that are within? That be far from thee to do after this manner, to slay the righteous with the wicked: and that the righteous should be as the wicked, that be far from thee: Shall not the Judge of all the earth do right?'' (Genesis 18:23-25). Abraham finally got the figure down to ten righteous people, but there were not even ten who were undefiled. Therefore, God had to destroy the cities. Lot and his family, however, survived. There was another way — the GREAT ESCAPE. The angels came and removed Lot and his family out of the city and took them to Zoar. Now listen to this shocking statement from the mouth of God in Genesis 19:22. He said: " . . . I cannot do any thing till [Lot] be come thither . . . '' God had to remove His people before He rained judgment upon the world of the ungodly. Then, and only then, did the Lord rain " . . . upon Sodom and upon Gomorrah brimstone and fire from the Lord out of heaven; And he overthrew those cities, and all the plain, and all the inhabitants of the cities, and that which grew upon the ground" (Genesis 19:24, 25). As it was in the days of Lot, so shall it be in the day of the Son of man or when the Son of man returns. Whether it is the GREAT ESCAPE for the Church or the preservation of the Israelites through the Tribulation, God's promises cannot fail.

The "day of great wrath" (Revelation 6:17), is meted out to sinners who "store up," "treasure up," yea accumulate "wrath against the day of wrath" (Romans 2:5). But this wrath is only for the wicked. Paul wrote: " . . . [God] which delivered us [Christians] from the wrath to come" (I Thessalonians 1:10), and again: "For God hath not appointed us to wrath, but to obtain salvation by our Lord Jesus Christ" (I Thessalonians 5:9). This salvation from wrath cannot be the eternal deliverance from Hell because the Christian already has that without Christ's return. The moment one believes, he is delivered from condemnation and " . . . is passed from death unto life" (John 5:24). Because of it, "there is therefore now no condemnation to them which are in Christ Jesus . . . " (Romans 8:1). The deliverance from wrath in I Thessalonians 1:10 has to do with Christ's return because the text states: " . . . [We] wait for his Son from heaven . . . which delivered us from the wrath to come." It does not take the return of Christ to deliver us from the wrath of Hell — salvation instantaneously accomplished this. But, the coming of Christ delivers us from the "wrath" of the coming Tribulation Hour. This is how God will

" . . . keep thee from [Greek, "ek," meaning "out of"] the hour of temptation which shall come upon all the world . . . " (Revelation 3:10).

Chronological Outline
Of The Book of Revelation

The book of Revelation is also written chronologically and beautifully sei ; forth the believer's deliverance from wrath. Revelation 1:19 states: "Write the things which thou hast seen . . . " (Chapter 1); "Write the things which are . . . " (Chapters 2 and 3) and "Write the things which shall be . . . " (Chapters 4 through 22). Presently the twentieth century finds us in Revelation, chapter 3. The churches of Philadelphia and Laodicia are both present in modern Christendom. To the lukewarm Laodicians God says: "So then because thou art lukewarm, and neither cold not hot, I will spue thee out of my mouth" (Revelation 3:16). Some portray this as professing Christians whom God spues out of His mouth while others think of them as lukewarm lackadaisical believers who meet Christ "ashamed" (I John 2:28). However, the important point is that the church of Philadelphia is snatched away before the "seal" judgments begin in Revelation 6. God tells this group, " . . . I also will keep thee from the hour of temptation, which shall come upon all the world, to try them that dwell upon the earth" (Revelation 3:10).

John sees the GREAT ESCAPE or evacuation of believers in chapter 4, verse 1. He says, "After this [after what? After the seven-church program in chapters 2 and 3 has run its course — chronologically] I looked, and, behold, a door was opened in heaven: and the first voice which I heard was as it were of a trumpet talking with me; which said, 'Come up hither, and I will shew thee things which must be hereafter.' " I believe this to be the Rapture because the twenty-four elders, picturing the saints of all ages — Old and New Testament believers — are already crowned and casting their rewards at Christ's feet in verses 10 and 11. The Judgment Seat has already taken place, the rewards distributed and all is well as the chapter ends. Then the Tribulation Hour, depicted in Revelation 6, continues until the Battle of Armageddon when Christ returns as King of kings and Lord of lords (Revelation 19:11-16). The crowning of the saints in chapter 4, plus the fact that the Church is conspicuously absent and not even mentioned after chapter 4, is certainly meaningful. Even post-Tribulation brethren are gone though they long to participate in the hour of wrath.

The Twenty-Four Elders

Now let's consider another great pre-Tribulational truth — the twenty-four elders. After the "come up hither" of Revelation 4:1, twenty-four elders are casting crowns at Christ's feet in verses 10 and 11. Then a throne is set up.

Around God's throne are twenty-four thrones on which sit twenty-four elders, " . . . clothed in white raiment; and they had on their heads crowns of gold" (Revelation 4:4). Who are the twenty-four elders? *This is of extreme importance for pre-Tribulation proponents:* the twenty-four elders are the representatives of God's people in both testaments — the saints of all ages. The book of Revelation unites the representative groups often. For instance, in describing the Holy City in Revelation 21:12-14, the names of the twelve tribes of Israel are posted on the gates while the names of the twelve Apostles are inscribed upon the city's foundations. Now twelve plus twelve equals twenty-four. Simple, isn't it? In chapter 5, verses 8 and 9, these twenty-four elders do something that is spine tingling. "[They] fell down before the Lamb [Jesus] having every one of them harps, and golden vials full or odours, which are the prayers of saints. And they sung a new song, saying, Thou art worthy to take the book, and to open the seals [dear Christ] thereof: for thou wast slain, and hast redeemed us to God by thy blood out of every kindred, and tongue, and people, and nation; And hast made us unto our God kings and priests: and we shall reign on the earth."

Here we witness the praise session of the ages — Old and New Testament believers, represented by twenty-four elders, praising the Lamb of God for shedding His blood. Someone says, "Old Testament believers were not saved by the blood." No one — BUT NO ONE — gets to heaven without the shed blood of Jesus! This is why Acts 10:43 declares: "To [Jesus] give all the [Old Testament] prophets witness, that through his name whosoever believeth in him shall receive remission of sins." Therefore, Old and New Testament believers, pictured by the twenty-four elders, are singing about the blood in Revelation 5:9 before the "seal" judgments begin in chapter 6 (the beginning of the Tribulation Hour). The Jews of old looked ahead to Calvary's shed blood as they offered their animal sacrifices while the Church looks back to the cross as the communion or memorial supper is conducted. Either way, " . . . it is the blood that maketh an atonement for the soul" (Leviticus 17:11).

Since the elders are already crowned — and since no one can be crowned until he is either resurrected if dead, or translated if living — it is obvious that the resurrection has occurred by Revelation 4:10. I Thessalonians 4:16 has transpired. We conclude, then, that the scene in Revelation 4 and 5 is the direct result of the Rapture, the GREAT ESCAPE, before the judgments begin in chapter 6.

In concluding this lesson, let's look at Christ's Church, His body and His bride. Will the Church go through the administration of God's wrath upon the earth? I believe not. Why? Millions upon millions of believers are already in heaven. All who have died "in Christ" for approximately 2,000 years are already with Christ. Paul said, " . . . to be absent from the body, and to be present with the Lord" (II Corinthians 5:8). Why should a handful of believers experience God's wrath while millions who lived and died the last two thousand years enjoy the blessings of heaven during the Tribulation Hour. For God to have 99 percent of His church with Him while one percent suffer untold agonies would be inconsistent.

Since the Greek word "ecclesia" translated "church" in English — means "a called out assembly," could not this definition extend to the very hour when the final "called out assembly" meets the other 99 percent of the Church already in glory? Why should a minority suffer God's vengeance while the others watch from heavenly places? We are also members of Christ's body. We are " . . . members of his body, of his flesh, and of his bones" (Ephesians 5:30). Should 99 percent of His body in heaven rejoice while the remaining one percent upon earth suffer? Perish the thought! In fact, since Christ is the head of the Body, He would actually be administering wrath to His own body if He left part of that body on earth for the Tribulation Period. Believers are also Christ's bride. Should one percent of the believers (constituting the Bride) languish in anguish while 99 percent abide at His side? Let's be consistent in our thinking! Love demands that all the remaining one percent join the 99 percent already in His presence, completing the Church, the Body and the Bride.

The Return of "The Body"

This same church, body and bride must go through a time of examination called the Judgment Seat of Christ. The Bride also experiences the Marriage Supper of the Lamb before returning with Christ to the earth. The post-Tribulation adherents, teaching a "Yo-Yo" theory — up and down, presto whipto, going to meet Christ and returning instantly — have no time interval for this Judgment Seat examination or Marriage Supper. It takes time to investigate God's people. II Corinthians 5:10 states: "For we must all appear before the judgment seat of Christ; that everyone may receive the things done in his body . . . " This is an impossibility in the post-Tributional arrangement of events because millions cannot be investigated in less than one second or the "twinkling of an eye" (I Corinthians 15:52). The "bob up to meet Him and bob down to reign" theory, if true, destroys the intervals of time demanded for the Judgment Seat of Christ and the Marriage Supper of the Lamb.

The Great Escape

I believe it is logically and abundantly clear that there *is* going to be a Rapture and that it *must* come *before* the Tribulation Hour. Common sense demands it and confusion reigns without it. Soon the Lord will break through the clouds. His church, body and bride will unite with members already in His presence, for " . . . them also which sleep in Jesus will God bring with him" (I Thessalonians 4:14). Then all the Church is investigated and prepared " . . . as a chaste virgin to Christ" (II Corinthians 11:2) to enjoy the Marriage Supper and honeymoon. Are you ready? Have you been washed in the blood?

4
Theological Proofs
of a Pre-Tribulation Rapture

Who is right — the pre-Tribulationists, the mid-Tribulationists, or the post-Tribulationists? Soon seven years of untold suffering and unprecedented heartache will enshroud the globe. This horrendous hour is called "the Great Tribulation" (Revelation 7:14). "Pre" means "before," "mid" stands for "middle" and "post" means "after." In other words, there are those who teach that the Church is to be evacuated via the Rapture *before* the Tribulation begins. They look with eager anticipation to the GREAT ESCAPE. Mid-Tribulationists believe that the Church experiences the first 42 months of earth's goriest hour and then is "snatched away" at the *halfway* mark. Post-Tribulationists believe that the Church goes through the *entire* seven years of turmoil. At the conclusion of this catastrophic era, the believers suddenly bob up to meet the Lord in the clouds and immediately return with Christ to establish His glorious Millennial Kingdom.

An Interval Demanded

The correct *conclusion* belongs to the *pre-Tribulational* school of thought. A comparison of scripture passages *demands* that there be an interval of time between the two appearings of Christ. The post-Tribulational "Yo-Yo" theory — where believers bob up and down, rising and returning in the "twinkling of an eye" — leaves no room for the Judgment Seat of Christ or the Marriage Supper of the Lamb. Both of these events are time-consuming and cannot fit into a scheme of interpretation where believers go up to meet the Lord and instantly return with Him for the establishment of His Millennial Kingdom. Time is demanded for the investigation of the believers' works. II Corinthians 5:10 declares: "For we must all appear before the judgment seat of Christ; that every one may receive the things done in his body . . . " Romans 14:12 adds: "So then every one of us shall give account of himself to God." This examination of every believer takes time. The post-Tribulational error leaves no vacancies for the greatest events in the history of the Church.

Should one argue that this judgment is the one described in Matthew 25 or Revelation 20 is the "great white throne judgment" at the end of time for sinners, He has immediately lost the debate. Rev. 20 is the "great white throne judgment." Matthew 25 is the judgment of Gentile nations. This is *not* the investigation of the Bride by the Bridegroom, but the judgment of the King as He prepares the nations of earth for His kingdom upon earth. Verse 34 states: "Then shall the King say unto them on his right hand, Come, ye blessed of my Father, inherit the kingdom prepared for you from the foundation of the world." This coincides with the return of the King of kings and Lord of lords in Revelation 19:16. This is the hour He establishes His 1,000-year reign upon the earth (Revelation

20:6). The Judgment Seat of Christ, con-
trariwise, is the investigation of Christ's virgin
(II Corinthians 11:2), preparing her for the marriage feast and honeymoon. There is no doubt as
to the time this examination occurs. I John 2:28
states: "And now, little children, abide in him;
that, when he shall appear, we may have confidence, and not be ashamed before him at his
coming." The verse begins with Christ's appearing and ends with His coming. It is at this time
that His people are either confident or ashamed
in His presence. This investigation of the Bride's
works takes approximately seven years. While
Israel is being judged on earth, the Bride is being
examined in heaven.

This testing of the Bride is necessary because
Christ wants His sweetheart presented to Him
" . . . not having spot, or wrinkle, or any such
thing; but that [she] should be holy and without
blemish" (Ephesians 5:27). This presentation of
the spotless Bride takes place at the Marriage
Supper of the Lamb. Christ, the Lamb of God
who takes away the sin of the world (John 1:29),
has His purified bride by His side as the myriad
of voices at the greatest marriage feast in history
unanimously cry: "Let us be glad and rejoice,
and give honour to him: for the marriage of the
Lamb is come, and his wife hath made herself
ready. And to her was granted that she should be
arrayed in fine linen, clean and white: for the
fine linen is the righteousness of saints. And he
saith unto me, Write, Blessed are they which are
called unto the marriage supper of the

Lamb . . . '' (Revelation 19:7-9).

Only a modern-day post-Tribulational Houdini could place the Church or Bride on earth in this chapter. Notice verse one, " . . . I heard a great voice of much people IN HEAVEN . . . '' In this same heaven, the judgment of all believers took place for " . . . his wife hath made herself ready" (verse 7). Her "fine linen, clean and white" picturing the "righteousness of saints" (verse 8), proves that the Judgment Seat already took place in heaven and she is now ready to sit next to her bridegroom for the Marriage Supper (verse 9). Watch the next movement. The Supper being ended, the Bride returns to earth with her bridegroom for earth's 1,000-year honeymoon. Verse 11 pictures Christ returning on a white horse, and " . . . the armies which were in heaven [His people] followed him . . . '' (verse 14). The purpose of the triumphant return is to purge the earth of its sinful rebels through the Battle of Armageddon (verses 17:21), making the millennial honeymoon one of peace and joy. This is true because Satan is bound for a thousand years. Then the saints take their thrones, and the Bride rules and reigns with her lover (Revelation 20:1-6). Now in the name of common sense, how can all this happen in the post-Tribulationist's scheme of interpretation? The Marriage Feast would still be sticking in the craw and severe indigestion would ensue if it all occurred in a moment of time. Certainly the Word of

God is on the side of the pre-Tribulationists!

The Restrainer

Another area of truth concerning the GREAT ESCAPE, or pre-Tribulation Rapture, that needs to be considered has to do with the ministry of the Holy Spirit. Jesus, before departing from earth to heaven, said: "Nevertheless I tell you the truth; It is expedient for you that I go away: for if I go not away, the Comforter will not come unto you; but if I depart, I will send him unto you. And when he is come, he will reprove the world of sin, and of righteousness, and of judgment" (John 16:7, 8). It is evident that the work of the Holy Spirit is that of conviction and restraint concerning sin. The Spirit of God does this through those whose bodies He indwells. I Corinthians 6:19 states: "What? know ye not that your body is the temple of the Holy Ghost which is in you, which ye have of God, and ye are not your own?" Every child of God is indwelled by His Spirit: " . . . Now if any man have not the Spirit of Christ, he is none of his" (Romans 8:9). Spirit-indwelled believers have a purifying effect upon the world. They are the "salt of the earth" and "light of the world" (Matthew 5:13, 14). Salt prevents spoilage and light dispels darkness. Think of the corruption and darkness that will prevail when the "salt of the earth" and "light of the world" are removed at the Rapture. No wonder Jesus said, "for then shall be great tribulation, such as was not since
280

the beginning of the world to this time . . . "
(Matthew 24:21).

Does the Bible teach such an evacuation of
believers? Is there really a GREAT ESCAPE
before the Tribulation begins? Definitely! The
second Epistle to the Thessalonians proves this
fact. In the first century, some post-
Tribulationists were already sowing seeds of dissent. They said that the Church was already
undergoing the trials of the Tribulation. They
even produced a falsified letter, forging Paul's
name, that stated the Church was in the hour of
trial. Recent post-Tribulational writers have
almost gone as far in falsifying facts. They even
print names of men who adopted their viewpoint
and the men named wonder how they arrived at
such a conclusion. Well, Paul, the misquoted
one, settled the mess by stating in II Thessalonians 2:1-8: "Now we beseech you, brethren, by
the coming of our Lord Jesus Christ, and by our
gathering together unto him, That ye be not soon
shaken in mind, or be troubled, neither by spirit,
nor by word, nor by letter as from us, as that the
day of Christ is at hand. Let no man deceive you
by any means: for that day shall not come, except there come a falling away first, and that
man of sin be revealed, the son of perdition;
Who opposeth and exalteth himself above all
that is called God, or that is worshipped; so that
he as God sitteth in the temple of God, shewing
himself that he is God. Remember ye not, that,
when I was yet with you, I told you these things?
And now ye know what withholdeth that he

might be revealed in his time. For the mystery of
iniquity doth already work: only he who now letteth will let, until he be taken out of the way.
And then shall that Wicked be revealed, whom
the Lord shall consume with the spirit of his
mouth, and shall destroy with the brightness of
his coming."

Beware of Deceivers

Paul, deeply perturbed by the forged letter,
states: "I understand that someone produced a
letter, supposedly written by me, stating that the
Church is presently experiencing the pangs of the
Tribulation Hour. Well, don't believe that lying
prattle. Don't be bothered, bewildered or shaken
over such a distortion of facts. I could not and
would not write such a letter simply because the
Tribulation cannot begin until two things occur.
First, there must be a falling away, and second,
the man of sin must be revealed" (paraphrased).
Scholars of the past rendered the terminology
"falling away" as "a catching away." They
talked about a time when the law of gravitation
would be broken and men would "fall away" via
the Rapture to meet the Lord in the clouds.
Other scholars believed that the Greek
"apostasias" meant that an apostasized departure from the faith would occur. The important
point to consider is that either must happen
before the man of sin — the lawless one, the
beast of the seventieth week — is revealed. This
introduction of the Antichrist to the world in-

augurates the Tribulation Hour. This means that the "day of the Lord" or Tribulation Period cannot begin until this monstrous maniac is identified to earth's citizens. Yet he cannot be revealed until the restraining influence of the Holy Spirit is removed: . . . " he who now letteth [Old English for "hinders"] will let, until he be taken out of the way. And then shall that Wicked be revealed . . . " (II Thessalonians 2:7, 8). This does not mean that the Holy Spirit must be removed from the earth. This is impossible because He, as God, is omnipresent, everywhere at all times (Psalm 139:7-11). So it means that His hindering or restraining power over sin — that keeps the Antichrist from mounting the throne — is removed. This happens as the Holy Spirit's temples — believers' bodies (I Corinthians 6:19) — are taken from the earth to heaven. Then the "salt of the earth" and "the light of the world" are removed. This immediately produces corruption and darkness on an unprecedented scale, allowing the world dictator to come to power. This begins the Tribulation Hour. Then the "beast" of the ages rules during earth's bloodiest hour, proclaiming himself as God, the Christ (II Thessalonians 2:4). He rules until Christ returns to earth at the conclusion of the seven years. Then " . . . the Lord shall consume [him] with the spirit of his mouth, and shall destroy [him] with the brightness of his coming" (II Thessalonians 2:8).

Watchfulness

The Church of Jesus Christ is also repeatedly told to watch for His coming. In order to avoid any confusion, let's stick with church truth — the Epistles of Paul. He says: "Therefore let us not sleep, as do others; but let us watch and be sober" (I Thessalonians 5:6). Again: "Looking for that blessed hope, and the glorious appearing of the great God and our Saviour Jesus Christ" (Titus 2:13). In fact, a special crown is presented to those who watch. II Timothy 4:8 states: "Henceforth there is laid up for me a crown of righteousness, which the Lord, the righteous judge, shall give me at that day: and not to me only, but unto all them also that love his appearing." So believers are to "watch" for the Lord — not for Tribulation, not for the Antichrist, not for persecution, and not for martyrdom, but for Christ! This is the blessed or happy hope.

Post-Tribulationists do not have an "imminent" hope for which to watch. Why? "Imminency," as applied to the Lord's return, does not mean "all at once," or a "rapidity in returning." Instead it is a constant expectation of Him on the basis that there is no revealed event that must precede His return. This is not so for post-Tribulationists who know from Daniel that when the Antichrist mounts his throne, the seventieth week or seven-year period of Tribulation begins. Revelation 11:2 informs them that since half of the Tribulation Hour is 42 months, then 84 months (from the rise of Antichrist), marks the day that Christ returns and consumes the world dictator with the brightness of His coming. In fact, Revelation 12:5 gives post-Tribulationists all the evidence necessary to count off the days to the very end because 1,260 days is presented as one-half of the horrendous period and 2,520 days as the completed schedule. So, if Antichrist came to power December 1, 2,520 days later he would be toppled at Christ's return. This is not "imminency" but exact mathematical calculation. One would not have to "watch" for the imminent return of Christ, but "count" toward the "expected day."

This viewpoint *contradicts the words of Jesus* who said in Matthew 24:36: "But of that day and hour knoweth no man, no, not the angels of heaven, but my Father only." Post-Tribulationists could count off the seven seal judgments, the seven trumpet judgments, and the seven vial judgments. They could then bob up to greet the Lord, and bob down for Armageddon. They even get in on that! In the meantime, they have missed the crowning of the saints and the Marriage Supper of the Lamb because both took place in heaven while they were still on earth. They had no time intervals for such pleasures. They shot up and splashed down like a defective space vehicle, missing it all. Well, praise God this will *not* happen for any part of Christ's Church — even the post-Tribulationists. Like it or not, they will be there. Christ cannot have one percent of His Church on earth while 99 percent is in glory. His body must be there in its entirety. His bride cannot be defective — missing fingers or toes — at the Marriage Supper of the Lamb. So, until the GREAT ESCAPE, look up, watch for and *expect* His "imminent" return.

Friends, are you ready? Christ shed His blood to save *you*. The acceptance of the Lord Jesus Christ as personal Saviour is the *only way* to be ready for Christ's return. Bow your head now and receive Christ today!

PART

VII

The Judgment
Seat of Christ

1
Judgment and God's Word

Five different, diversified and distinct judgments are presented in the Bible. Men who do not rightly divide the Word of truth (II Timothy 2:15) often confuse this fact by conglomerately linking the various texts concerning judgment into one mass hodgepodge. I will not be guilty of this practice. Instead, I will differentiate and briefly describe each of the five judgments, also noting where they may be found in Scripture.

Judgment number one is of the believer's sin: Nineteen hundred years ago, Christ came down from heaven's glory to shed His precious blood for a world of ungodly sinners. He did not die for His own sin, for He knew no sin, but became sin for us (II Corinthians 5:21). Through this substitutionary death — dying for you and me — all who *receive* this Christ can have the past, present and future stains of sin immediately forgiven, forgotten, obliterated and liquidated, because " . . . the blood of Jesus Christ [God's] Son cleanseth us from **ALL** sin" (I John 1:7).

As soon as the "washing of regeneration" takes place (Titus 3:5), God cries, " . . . their sins and their iniquities will I remember no more" (Hebrews 8:12). The result of being so completely washed in the blood is that "There is therefore now no condemnation to them which are in Christ Jesus . . . " (Romans 8:1). This is true because Christ was already judged in the sinner's place. Oh, what love, what compassion. Is it any wonder that Paul declares in Hebrews 2:3: "How shall we escape, if we neglect so great salvation . . . "

The second judgment is of the believer's service.

This investigative probe into a believer's lifetime of works will form the basis of our present study. We will discuss this "Bema Seat" judgment in chapter 2.

The third judgment is of Israel:

During the tribulation hour, an enemy comes against Israel from the North (Ezekiel 38 and 39). Then the armies of the world also converge on the Middle East (Zechariah 14:2), and this period of bloody devastation becomes ". . . the time of Jacob's trouble . . . " (Jeremiah 30:7).

The fourth judgment is of the nations:

Matthew 25 pictures the return of Christ to this earth. The text correlates to and is synonymous with Revelation 19:11-16 when

288

Christ returns to earth as "King of kings and Lord of lords." Before He establishes His Millennial Kingdom upon earth for 1,000 years (Revelation 20:4), He purges the earth of its rebels (Matthew 25:31-46). The righteous are then allowed to enter God's earthly Kingdom utopia for 1,000 years, and eventually heaven, eternally. This transition is observed in I Corinthians 15:24-25 which state: "Then cometh the end (Millennium), when he shall have put down all rule and all authority and power. For he must reign, till he hath put all enemies under his feet."

The fifth and final judgment is of the wicked:

Commonly called, "The Great Judgment Day," this solemn universal trial is described in Revelation 20:11-15. John says, "And I saw a great white throne, and him that sat on it, from whose face the earth and the heaven fled away; and there was found no place for them. And I saw the dead, small and great, stand before God; and the books were opened: and another book was opened, which is the book of life: and the dead were judged out of those things which were written in the books, according to their works. And the sea gave up the dead which were in it; and death and hell delivered up the dead which were in them: and they were judged every man according to their works. And death and hell were cast into the lake of fire. This is the second death. And whosoever was not found written in the book of life was cast into the lake of fire."

Friends, the hour is coming when every unsaved, unregenerate sinner must meet a holy God for a detailed review of his life upon planet earth. When God's books are opened, every offender's tongue shall be silenced. There will be no hope then, but there is now! Why? Because Christ died for our sins (I Corinthians 15:3). This means that the guiltiest of mortals can immediately be absolved by trusting in the merits of the shed blood of Jesus. Don't procrastinate — do it today! Then you, too, will know the blessedness of John 3:18 which declares: "He that believeth on [Christ] is not condemned . . . " because the believing are " . . . passed from death unto life" (John 5:24).

2
The Judgment Seat of Christ

Romans 14:10 states: " . . . we shall all stand before the judgment seat of Christ." II Corinthians 5:10 adds: "For we must all appear before the judgment seat of Christ; that every one may receive the things done in his body, according to that he hath done, whether it be good or bad." Millions of God's children, internationally, think that they can live nominal Christian lives and still be fully rewarded. They think that they can play "fast and loose" with the world without suffering loss. This is but wishful thinking! The day is coming when every blood-bought believer must stand before a holy God for a scrutinizing investigation. This becomes abundantly clear when one traces the English term "judgment seat" to its Greek origin. There the term is "bema seat." When Paul used the terminology in the first century, every educated mind immediately knew the severity of the warning, because their thinking took them to the runner's track in Athens, Greece. It, like modern-day sports stadiums, contained thousands of seats. However, there was one seat differing from the rest in that it was uplifted and elevated. The judge of the contest, who sat there, had no obstruction to mar his view of the racing participants. He could see every movement clearly. Does this not picture "the God of Holiness" elevated upon His throne watching the Christian's race of life? He sees where we go, hears what we say and watches our every move. Yes, "For the eyes of the Lord run to and fro throughout the whole earth . . . " (II

Chronicles 16:9). God cries " . . . mine eyes are upon all their ways . . . " (Jeremiah 16:17) and because of it, " . . . all things are naked and opened unto the eyes of him with whom we have to do" (Hebrews 4:13).

God is watching His people and keeping records for the day when " . . . we must all appear before the judgment seat of Christ; that every one may receive the things done in his body, according to that he hath done, whether it be good or bad" (II Corinthians 5:10). Therefore, it behooves each one of us to place Christ first in our daily walk and talk. We cannot live for the flesh and self and hear Christ say in that day, "Well done, thou good and faithful servant." There must be a battle fought and won. There must be scars traded for crowns. Rewards must be earned. Paul who " . . . [bore] in [his] body the marks [scars] of the Lord Jesus" (Galatians 6:17), was " . . . [pressing] toward the mark for the prize of the high calling of God in Christ Jesus" (Philippians 3:14). Salvation was his as a gift, but only works of hardship, suffering and perhaps death could bring him the prize or crown to lay at Jesus' feet (Revelation 4:10-11). It is also true for *you,* dear Christian. You, too, must *know* the " . . . fellowship of his sufferings . . . " to receive the prize of the high calling of God in Christ Jesus (Philippians 3:10-14).

Wait! There is more. We are just beginning to explore the depths of this judgment. As we delve further into this subject, we discover that God also will investigate the **motives** behind one's works. In other words, the question will be: "**Why** did you do what you did when you did it? Why were you a pastor, an evangelist, a missionary? Why did you hold the office of deacon, elder or Sunday School teacher? Why did you sing or perform solos? What was your motive in being a counselor, an usher, a bus driver? What purpose was there in desiring to be a full-time Christian worker? Was it for power, prestige or pride? Was it to be noticed, to be lauded and applauded?" Christian, will you answer this question in your own heart *this very moment?* **Why** are you doing what you are doing when you are doing it? **What is your motive**?

If there is an iota of self-glorification behind **any** act of service, the rewards will be sparse — if any! Listen to the Saviour in Matthew 6:1-6: "Take heed that ye do not your alms before men, to be seen of them: otherwise ye have no reward of your Father which is in heaven. Therefore when thou doest thine alms, do not sound a trumpet before thee, as the hypocrites do in the synagogues and in the streets, that they may have glory of men. Verily I say unto you, They have their reward. But when thou doest alms, let not thy left hand know what thy right hand doeth: That thine alms may be in secret: and thy Father which seeth in secret himself shall reward thee openly. And when thou prayest, thou shalt not be as the hypocrites are: for they love to pray standing in the synagogues and in the corners of the streets, that they may be seen of men. Verily I say unto you, They have their reward. But thou, when thou prayest, enter into thy closet, and when thou hast shut thy door, pray to thy Father which is in secret; and thy Father which seeth in secret shall reward thee openly." Christ continues in verses 16-19: "Moreover when ye fast, be not, as the hypocrites, of a sad countenance: for they disfigure their faces, that they may appear unto men to fast. Verily I say unto you, They have their reward. But thou, when thou fastest, anoint thine head, and wash thy face; That thou appear not unto men to fast, but unto thy Father which is in secret: and thy Father which seeth in secret, shall reward thee openly."

There is no doubt as to the meaning of Christ's startling words. He declares that there are two places to be rewarded — here upon earth as one seeks the praise of men, or later in heaven when the Father Who saw the works performed in secret, without notoriety, rewards those who did the job simply out of love for Him. When Jesus returns to call His people unto Himself in the twinkling of an eye and the judgment begins, what will your motives have been in the Christian race? The motives issue will then be made manifest. I Corinthians 4:5 states: "Therefore judge nothing before the time, until the Lord come, who both will bring to light the hidden things of darkness, and will make manifest the counsels [or motives] of the heart . . . " This teaching is also propounded in I Corinthians 3:11-15: "For other foundation can no man lay than that is laid, which is Jesus Christ. Now if any man build upon this foundation gold, silver, precious stones, wood, hay, stubble; Every man's work shall be made manifest: for the day shall declare it, because it shall be revealed by fire; and the fire shall try every man's work of what sort it is. If any man's work abide which he hath built thereupon, he shall receive a reward. If any man's work shall be burned, he shall suffer loss: but he himself shall be saved; yet so as by fire." Again, there is no doubt about the explicit teaching within this portion of scripture. It states: "The fire shall try every man's work of what **SORT** it is." Now notice some interesting observations concerning this judgment.

1. **The judgment is only for the people of God** — those who have built upon the foundation of the Lord Jesus Christ.

2. **All of God's people present some form of "works" to Christ at the Bema Seat.** The fire then tests every man's work. Every man? Every man!

3. **Though all worked to some degree, a difference in quantity and quality is observed.** Some works are precious and good — the gold, the silver and the precious stones. Others — the wood, the hay and the stubble — are bad.

4. **The difference is tested by purging fires.** The good works survive while the wood, hay and stubble are reduced to a mass of incinerated rubble. Christian, will what you are presently doing in the service of God abide the fires of Christ's Bema Seat? Will your works endure the test? Will your final result be rewards or rubble? Stop

and think! Why do you do what you do when you do it? What is your *motive* as you serve?

5. **The disintegrated ashes bring sorrow and loss.** Yes, " . . . [they] shall suffer loss: but [they themselves] shall be saved; yet so as by fire" (I Corinthians 3:15). Notice that the lukewarm, the indifferent and the careless shall be present. They do not miss heaven because of their faults! Instead, they shall be saved as by fire — **by the skin of their teeth!** They made heaven only to sorrow over their waywardness for a millennium of time as we shall presently see. Their loss was not of salvation, but of rewards. They suffered loss (rewards), but they themselves were saved, though as by fire. It is obvious, then, that the wayward lose out with God. Yet the loss is not of eternal life but of rewards. Eternal life is freely bestowed upon all who believe as a gift apart from works (Romans 6:23), and cannot be forfeited, but crowns can be earned and lost, accumulated and liquidated.

6. **Quality works, consisting of gold, silver and precious stones, performed for the glory of God to win the souls of men, when tested and found genuine, will earn crowns for the faithful for all eternity.** These crowns will then be placed at the feet of Christ as an eternal memorial of one's love for a lifetime of service. The scene is portrayed in Revelation 4:10-11. The twenty-four elders pictured in the text are the representatives of all of God's people in both testaments — the twelve patriarchs of Israel and the twelve Apostles of Christendom. These same twenty-

four stalwarts of both eras have their names combined upon the gates and foundations of the future Holy City in Revelation 21:12-14. So there is no doubt as to who they are. They represent all the faithful blood-bought people of God down through the ages. The thrilling scene is described as follows: "The four and twenty elders fall down before him that sat on the throne, and worship him that liveth for ever and ever, and cast their crowns before the throne saying, Thou art worthy, O Lord, to receive glory and honour and power; for thou hast created all things, and for thy pleasure they are and were created" (Revelation 4:10-11). Christian, do you long to lay a crown at the feet of the Saviour on the coronation day? Or will you be off in the background ashamed (I John 2:28), having experienced a humiliating entrance into the presence of God (II Peter 1:11)? It need not be so. A change can be made today. Confession of failure is longingly desired by your heavenly Father (I John 1:9). Rededication and redirection can be your experience this very moment. Utter that prayer of confession today and make a new start immediately so that you, too, may hear from the precious lips of Jesus, "Well done, thou good and faithful servant."

3
Triumph or Tears

One day soon, every Christian must meet God for an investigative judgment of his entire life. This moment shall be a time of jubilant victory for some. Jesus said, "He that receiveth a prophet in the name of a prophet shall receive a prophet's reward; and he that receiveth a righteous man in the name of a righteous man shall receive a righteous man's reward" (Matthew 10:41). Paul adds: "If any man's work abide which he hath built thereupon, he shall receive a reward" (I Corinthians 3:14).

On the other hand, it shall be a time of weeping for others. Paul, dealing with this hour of judgment, states in II Corinthians 5:11: "Knowing therefore the terror of the Lord, we persuade men . . . " Terror? Yes, terror! How often Christians hilariously shout: "Praise the Lord, Jesus is coming soon!" Though this will undoubtedly be the most joyous event of the ages for some, it will be a time of intense and immense sorrow for others. I John 2:28 declares: "And now, little children, abide in him; that, when he shall appear, we may have confidence, and not be **ASHAMED** before him at his coming."

Notice carefully that when Christ returns, **all** believers are summoned into His presence — the confident and the ashamed. The confident appear before the tribunal with "good works" whereas the ashamed have naught but "bad works" (I Corinthians 5:10). This is exceedingly important to understand because multitudes today think that one sin can keep a child of God out of heaven. The text plainly states that the "ashamed" meet Christ at His appearing. At the sound of the trumpet, when the dead in Christ rise first and living believers join the dead to meet Christ in the clouds (I Thessalonians 4:16), the "ashamed" also enter heaven, but the abundant entrance is reserved for those who earned it upon earth (II Peter 1:11).

Please do not argue with me. If English means anything — and it does — this text **proves** that the wayward go home to meet Christ though *ashamed*. Since one can only bear shame for error and wrongdoing, then it is dogmatically clear that the wrongdoers meet Christ at His appearing or return. I grant you that they are embarrassed and lose all of their rewards, but they are nevertheless present at the roll call of the ages, though "saved as by fire" (I Corinthians 3:15), or "by the skin of their teeth" to use a modern-day expression. What produces their embarrassment and humiliation as believers?

Neglected Opportunities

Multitudes of God's people **could** do so much more for Christ **if they would,** *but* the flesh stands in the way. When they do serve, it is often with selfish motives. Their hue and cry is, "What will I get out of this? What is in it for **me**?" The result? Modern Christianity has become big business. Religious performers today charge exorbitant rates. Some receive $1,000 or $2,500 for a performance. What a judgment of terror awaits these mercenary "gospel entertainers." Though saved by fire, their works will dissolve into incinerated ashes. The wood, hay and stubble will disintegrate because they had their reward. **About face, Christian!**

Then again, there are those who have little or no time for spiritual exercises. They seldom read God's Holy Word, seldom attend God's house, seldom give their tithes and never win souls. **This is sin!** James 4:17 states: "Therefore to him that knoweth to do good, and doeth it not, to him it is sin." These sins of omission — failing to do God's will — also produce remorse in that day.

Friend, if I am describing you, it is not too late to change. As long as one has the breath of life, he can decide to do the will of God. Confess your sins, seek again your first love for Christ, rekindle the flame of devotion to the Lord Jesus immediately. Then use your opportunities to serve Him wisely. One who obeys God will not be sorry.

The faithful will be rewarded a hundred fold at the Bema Seat. **Scholars calculate this to be a 10,000 percent yield.** No wonder Paul said in II Corinthians 9:6: " . . . He which soweth sparingly [meagerly] shall reap also sparingly; and he which soweth bountifully [abundantly] shall reap also bountifully." One cannot outgive God at 10,000 percent interest. Galatians 6:7, often quoted to the unsaved but directed to Christians concerning giving, states: "Be not deceived; God is not mocked [or fooled]: for whatsoever a man soweth, that shall he also reap." Christian, your heavenly mansion will only be as beautiful as you build it now. Jesus said in John 14:2: "In my Father's house are many mansions . . . " The literal rendering should state: "In my Father's house are numerous and differing kinds of dwelling places." Not all mansions will be identical. Building blocks for one's eternal home are being sent ahead from earth. Jesus said, "Lay not up for yourselves treasures on earth, where moth and rust doth corrupt, and where thieves break through and steal: But lay up for yourselves treasures in heaven . . . " (Matthew 6:19-20). If one's earthly treasure is piled up in stocks and bonds and banks, he has had his reward. On the other hand, if the treasure is sent ahead, it awaits the believers with added and fantastic dividends. Take you choice, Christian. You can have it here for seventy years, die and leave it for the ungodly to spend; or you may send it ahead for eternal blessing. Hang on and lose it, or let go and retain it forever. **It is up to you!**

May I share a most heart-moving experience with you? When Rexella and I were in Hershey, Pennsylvania, a man sitting in a wheelchair asked that he might speak to us. As we reached the area where he sat, he began to weep saying, "I am an invalid, as you can see. I have multiple sclerosis and osteo-arthritis. The pain is more than I can humanly bear. In fact, my pain-destroying medication costs me one hundred dollars per month. Nevertheless, I have made a decision after much prayer. I want to give you the hundred dollars and omit this month's medicine. I know my pain will be unbearable, but it is the least I can do for Christ who suffered so much for me. Take it and use it for His glory." Rexella and I, both in tears, replied, "We cannot accept this money for your medicine." He again wept audibly saying, "Would you deprive me of a blessing? Take it for the glory of God and the salvation of souls."

How many thousands who have a superabundance of material things — stocks, bonds, bank accounts and possessions — do nothing but tip God occasionally. Do you think that it won't make a difference at the time of rewards? Do you honestly feel that it will be the same for all? "Be not deceived; God is not mocked: for whatsoever a man soweth, that shall he also reap" (Galatians 6:7). We are all going home soon — either confident or ashamed. Will it be a time of victory or anguish, triumph or tears, for you? It is not too late to make a new start.

Neglected Holiness

Then, too, there will be tears over neglected holiness. No doubt about it. God demands that His people live holy lives. "For God hath not called us unto uncleanness, but unto holiness" (I Thessalonians 4:7). "Who hath saved us, and called us with an holy calling . . . " (II Timothy 1:9). "Follow peace with all men, and HOLINESS . . . " (Hebrews 12:14). " . . . Be ye holy; for I am holy" (I Peter 1:16). This means that we are not to fashion ourselves

" . . . according to the former lusts . . . " (I Peter 2:11) and that we are to put on Christ and not make any provision for the flesh, " . . . to fulfill the lusts thereof" (Romans 13:14).

How different from the lowly standards held by many carnal church members who constantly play "musical chairs" with the pagans and God-haters of this world. These indifferent backsliders run with the world, visit its clubs, casinos and theaters, all under the guise of being curious. They, like Lot who desired Sodom, want to spend time in Las Vegas and get away from it all. The getting away is really from God. The cursing, drinking, gambling and vulgarity matters not as the flesh is on a spree. Are they saved? God alone really knows! One thing is certain — if they are Christ's, their double standards will be investigated, "For we must all appear before the judgment seat of Christ; that every one may receive the things done in his body, according to that he hath done, whether it be GOOD or BAD" (II Corinthians 5:10). Oh, what weeping, what wailing, what travail, what heartache and heartbreak as they meet Jesus face to face. Their entrance into God's presence will not be "abundant" (II Peter 1:11). They shall be tremendously "ashamed" (I John 2:28). The "terror of the Lord" will be meted out in judgment (II Corinthians 5:11) and they then suffer the loss of all rewards (I Corinthians 3:15). No wonder the lukewarm are weeping. They blew it all. They suffered the loss of all things except salvation.

This loss extends beyond the loss of rewards for a meaningless life. It includes losing, through foolish living, rewards previously earned during years of spiritual service. God has a system of addition and subtraction, pluses and minuses, on His books. Therefore, one's accumulation of "good works" can be wiped out swiftly through disobedient living. You do not believe it? **Here is proof:** "Look to yourselves, that we lose not those things which we have wrought [or earned], but that we receive a full reward." (II John 8). God says, "Be careful how you live, where you go, how you serve, if you want a **full** reward." Again, " . . . hold that fast which thou hast, that no man take thy crown" (Revelation 3:11). In simpler terminology, God says, "Hang on to your earned crown and do not let anyone entice you, mislead you, drag you down or destroy the good works already accumulated or you will suffer loss."

Paul, led by the Holy Spirit, also declares in I Corinthians 9:27: "But I keep under my body, and bring it into subjection: lest that by any means, when I have preached to others, I myself should be a castaway [a reject for rewards]." He could not mean the loss of salvation by the term "castaway" because we have already seen that the "ashamed" are present at heaven's roll call though saved by fire. Instead, Paul is saying, "Look, I am a red-blooded man with desires similar to others. However, I will not allow my flesh to control me. Instead, I constantly battle and batter my fleshly appetites into subjection.

Yes, I keep my bodily appetites under control lest I lose everything I have ever earned." Now if this be true for Paul, it is equally true for all. In fact, Paul's service record is unparalleled in the history of Christendom. No one suffered as he did except the Lord Himself. Listen to the list of "good works" Paul accumulated in II Corinthians 11:23-27. He states: " . . . in labours more abundant, in stripes above measure, in prisons more frequent, in deaths oft. Of the Jews five times received I forty stripes save one. Thrice was I beaten with rods, once was I stoned, thrice I suffered shipwreck, a night and a day I have been in the deep; In journeyings often, in perils of waters, in perils of robbers, in perils by mine own countrymen, in perils by the heathen, in perils in the city, in perils in the wilderness, in perils in the sea, in perils among false brethren; In weariness and painfulness, in watchings often, in hunger and thirst, in fastings often, in cold and nakedness." Wow! What a servant of God — beaten, battered, stoned, crushed, robbed, persecuted, hated and starved. Surely this portfolio of earned works would bring Paul heaven's greatest "Oscar." It would if he remained faithful. Remember, he said as quoted earlier, "If I did not keep my body under and bring it into subjection, I myself would be a castaway, disapproved and rejected for heaven's 'Emmy Awards.' Therefore, I fight the good fight of faith — fight the world, the flesh and the devil — so that my Saviour will say to me at that day, 'Well done, thou good and faithful servant.' "

How about you Christian? If the judgment took place within the next 24 hours, would you lose some or all of your rewards? Millions are going home ashamed, embarrassed and red-faced.

Tears in Heaven

The result will be intermittent weeping for 1,007 years. This is proven by studying the chronological outline of the book of Revelation. Let's look at it.

Revelation 1:19 states: "Write these things which thou hast seen, and the things which are, and the things which shall be hereafter." One immediately notices the three tenses of the English language — past, present and future. Write the things which thou hast seen — past, chapter 1. Write the things which are — present, chapters 2 and 3, and write the things which shall be — future, chapters 4 through 22. We are presently awaiting the homegoing of the believers. This occurs in Revelation 4:1 with the words, "Come up hither." The seven years of Tribulation follow in chapters six through 18. Christ returns to earth as King of kings and Lord of lords (chapter 19:11-16). He rules the earth for 1,000 years (chapter 20:4-6), and judges the world after the thousand years (chapter 20:11-15). Then, finally and forever, God wipes all tears away from their eyes (Revelation 21:4). Chronologically, this is after the Tribulation, after the Millennium. In other words, from the Rapture call in Revelation 4:1 onward, there is intermittent and spasmodic crying for the next 1,007 years.

Is your foolish episode with the world that important to you? Will it be worth it all when you see Jesus? *Do not lose out on rewards eternally for a short fling presently!*

Two Judgments Simultaneously

In dwelling further on the teaching of "tears" in God's presence, we discover that the weeping takes place simultaneously with the Tribulation Hour. Two judgments are occurring at the same period of time. One is in heaven; the other upon earth. One is a judgment of believers regarding service; the other a judgment of Israel. One is called the "Bema Seat" judgment; the other, the Tribulation Hour. Both prove to be heartbreaking for the participants.

Let's look at the Tribulation Period for a few moments. This is the time of Jacob's trouble (Jeremiah 30:7), and Jacob represents Israel. Satan, the old devil, hates Israel. She was used of God as a channel for producing His only begotten Son on earth. Revelation 12:5 states: "And she [Israel] brought forth a man child . . . " Because of Israel's connection with Christ's birth, the nation has always been Satan's prime target of hatred. He has relentlessly persecuted her throughout the annals of history and increases his persecution during the Tribulation Hour. His attack is most vicious when he realizes that the end of his power struggle for world supremacy over Jehovah God is about to cease.

307

Therefore, Revelation 12:13 states: "And when the dragon saw that he was cast unto the earth, he persecuted the woman which brought forth the man child." This is the world's bloodiest hour. Seven seal, seven trumpet and seven vial judgments are unleashed upon planet earth. These produce murder, starvation, war, militarism, earthquakes, hail, fire, oceanic disruptions, cosmic catastrophes, pestilence, inflation, sores, infections, pain, pollution, darkness and finally **ARMAGEDDON!** The hour is so bleak, dreary and hopeless that earth's inhabitants are crying to the mountains and rocks to fall on them (Revelation 6:16). **Earth's most agonizing hour will make men desire death over life.** Simultaneously, the people of God are being examined at Christ's Judgment Seat. This, too, will be an unpleasant situation because the Holy Spirit speaks about the "terror of the Lord" in connection with the investigation of believers' works (II Corinthians 5:11). I have no doubt that some believers will be so ashamed, so embarrassed, so humiliated and so frightened to face the fireworks (I John 2:28), that they will want to exchange heaven for earth, the Judgment Seat exposure for the Tribulation woes. They would rather cry for the mountains to fall on them than to meet Christ with a wasted life. Small wonder the song writer said, "Must I go in empty-handed, my Redeemer thus to meet?"

What sadness, yea, what vehement crying shall then ensue as rewards are lost forever. Christian, disobedience to the commands of Christ is not worth a millennium of spasmodic weeping.

4

The Rewards of Righteousness

Chapters two and three of this study concerned the victor's triumph and the backslider's blues. We have learned that, when the Lord Jesus appears, some Christians will rejoice while others will weep remorsefully. In this concluding chapter, I want to discuss the five crowns which will be distributed at the Judgment Seat of Christ. They will be presented by the Lord Himself as rewards of righteousness to those who recognized and followed His holy calling (II Timothy 1:9), allowing Him to fulfill His purpose in their lives. They were conformed to His image (Romans 8:29) in every area.

The Watcher's Crown

This meritorious award is given to all who longingly and desiringly watch for Christ's return. Paul declares in II Timothy 4:8: "Henceforth there is laid up for me a crown of righteousness, which the Lord, the righteous judge, shall give me at that day: and not to me only, but unto *all them also that love his appearing.*" Imagine, God gives a special crown to believers who fix their eyes and hearts heavenward in watchfulness of Christ's return. This is reasonable when one realizes that "expectancy" and "purity" are closely related. One cannot longingly look for Christ's return and practice abominable sins. The two never coexist in a rational mind. That is why I John 3:2-3 state: "Beloved, now are we the sons of God, and it doth not yet appear what we shall be: but we know that, when he shall appear, we shall be like him; for we shall see him as he is. And every man that hath this hope [of His appearing] in him *purifieth himself, even as he is pure.*"

Adulterers, fornicators, homosexuals, drunkards, drug addicts, extortioners, swindlers, liars and worldlings are not anxiously awaiting Christ's return. Neither are carnal believers who neglect the Bible, prayer, God's house, soulwinning and personal holiness. No, those who look daily and expectantly are not among the worldlings who sit in bars, theaters, rock concerts, gambling casinos and other pagan dens. They do not want to be found there when Jesus comes. Their desire — " . . . that blessed hope, and the glorious appearing of the great God and our Saviour Jesus Christ" (Titus 2:13) — makes them consistently live for His return. They want to be commended, congratulated and crowned in their fight to the finish. They do not want a confrontation producing consternation and castigation at that day. They long to hear Jesus say, "Well done, thou good and faithful servant." Because the Saviour's appearing is closely aligned with holiness of life, it is to be expected that the carnal rebel and refuse the teaching of prophecy. They cry, "Do not preach prophecy! It is but sensational and speculative nonsense anyway. Instead, tell us about ' . . . Parbar westward, four at the causeway, and two at Parbar' (I Chronicles 26:18)." This does not hit us where we live!

One should expect this from the indifferent, the lethargic, the worldly and the backslidden. They definitely do not want to hear about a time when they must meet Christ with wasted lives because His appearing means the disintegration and dissolution of their selfish, substandard works. They know that they are going to be among the "ashamed" (I John 2:28), and that they shall be "saved as by fire" (I Corinthians 3:15). They hate to think of meeting Jesus empty handed and being "rejects" at the Judgment Seat. Small wonder they dislike this Bible doctrine. But, like it or not, it will happen! May I, therefore, plead with preachers, "Preach the message of Christ's return. Present the signs. Tell the people the moment is near. Beg them to keep their eyes fixed on heaven so that you and they will receive the watcher's crown." Only those who "look," receive!

The Runner's Crown

The background for this award is found in I Corinthians 9:24-27. Paul says, "Know ye not that they which run in a race run all, but one receiveth the prize? So run, that ye may obtain. And every man that striveth for the mastery is temperate in all things. Now they do it to obtain a corruptible crown; but we an incorruptible. I therefore so run, not as uncertainly; so fight I not as one that beateth the air: But I keep under my body, and bring it into subjection: lest that by any means, when I have preached to others, I myself should be a castaway." Consider this tremendous portion of scripture with me expositorily. The writer says in verse 24 that though there are numerous runners — and he undoubtedly has the athletic field of Athens, Greece in mind — yet only one becomes the winner. The analogy is that though tens of thousands of believers have run and are in the race of Christian service, competing for "good works," it will be but a minority who receive the runner's crown. Hence, the admonition, "Run that you may obtain."

Next, we observe the rules of the race. The Greek athletes were *temperate* in all things, subjecting their bodies to the most stringent health rules. They trained, they exercised and they abstained from anything that would render them unfit for the big day. Verse 25: "And every man that striveth for the mastery [victory] is temperate [under self-control] in **ALL** things . . . " Is every habit under control in your life? There are those who say, "I don't think a little cigarette can keep me out of heaven." I agree. *In fact,* I think it may get you there *sooner*! However, it, along with other uncontrolled bodily habits, will get you there "ashamed." It will help reduce your runner's crown into incinerated rubble (I Corinthians 3:15). The crown is only for victors, for winners who have battered the cravings of the body into submission. This explains Paul's words in verses 26-27: "I therefore so run, not as uncertainly; so **FIGHT** I, not as one that beateth the air . . . " I am not just shadow boxing. I cannot afford it in the fight against the world, the flesh and the devil. Instead, " . . . I keep under my body, and bring it into subjection; lest that by any means, when I have preached to others, I myself should be a castaway" (a reject for heaven's rewards, God's "Oscars"). It is abundantly obvious, as cited frequently in this chapter, that the term "castaway" has nothing to do with salvation. This is evident because the "ashamed," saved-by-fire crowd, goes home at the Rapture to weep. No, the Greek word from which we get the English term "castaway," means "to be disapproved" for crowns. Therefore, I again plead with the lukewarm to enthrone Christ in the heart. Get your first love rekindled. Serve Him with all your might. Throw off every encumbrance of the flesh, including tobacco. Yes, " . . . let us lay aside every weight, and the sin which doth so easily beset us [trip us], and let us run with patience the race that is set before us" (Hebrews 12:1). The result? An incorruptible crown (I Corinthians 9:25).

Paul concludes with a final scene of the race by saying, "The Greek runners subjected their appetites to the strictest regimentation imaginable simply to win the race and receive 'a corruptible crown,' a wreath of laurel leaves that would decay and die in a few days time." Then, by way of analogy, he again says, "If God's people batter their fleshly wants into submission, they, shall receive an **incorruptible** crown that endures for eternity." Child of God, it will be worth it all when we see Jesus.

Adoniram Judson and his sweet wife, Ann, were missionaries in India and Burma. During their tour of service, Adoniram was arrested as an enemy agent when his homeland, England, and the nation in which he served became disenchanted with one another. Immediately, Judson was imprisoned. The tiny cell in which he was incarcerated was so crowded and small that the prisoners had to take turns sleeping. There was not enough room for all of them to lie down. The hot sun beating upon the dingy cell caused unbearable suffering through heat prostration. The stench also became obnoxious as the men were never allowed to bathe.

One day the government officials decided to punish the prisoners and Judson was hoisted into the air by his thumbs. Pain filled his body as he remained suspended in midair for hours at a time. His precious helpmeet, Ann, would come by the cell daily, look inside and weep. However, this soldier of the cross always encouraged her man by saying, "Don't despair, Adoniram. God will give us the victory."

As the days and weeks passed, faithful Ann no longer made the visits and Adoniram's loneliness increased. No one had informed him that she was dying. All he had now was a memory of his sweetheart saying, "God will give us the victory." Months later, upon his release, he immediately began the search for Ann. As he approached the area where he formerly lived, he saw a child so begrimed with dirt that he failed to recognize the little one as his own. He then dashed into the tent and saw the form of one so small and weak from malnutrition, that she appeared to be a skeleton. Her beautiful flowing hair had also fallen and she was bald. As Adoniram called, she failed to respond. It seemed as though she were already dead. He took her in his arms and wept. The hot tears dropping on her angelic face revived Ann and she said, "Don't despair, Adoniram. God will give us the victory."

Adoniram lost his sweetheart, but not his faith and courage. He continued under dire circumstances to preach and build churches, and when this man of God was buried, scores of churches had come into existence through his labors. Adoniram and Ann ran the race faithfully unto the end and experienced the "abundant entrance" I have been proclaiming. What will **your** homegoing be like, Christian?

The Shepherd's Crown

This award is mentioned in I Peter 5:1-4 and is undoubtedly reserved for faithful ministers. In the text, the Apostle Peter says, "The elders which are among you I exhort, who am also an elder, and a witness of the sufferings of Christ, and also a partaker of the glory that shall be revealed: Feed the flock of God which is among you, taking the oversight thereof, not by constraint, but willingly; not for filthy lucre, but of a ready mind; Neither as being lords over God's heritage, but being ensamples to the flock. And when the chief Shepherd shall appear, ye shall receive a crown of glory that fadeth not away.'' Peter, in writing to the elders or spiritual shepherds, exhorts his fellow minister's to ''feed the flock.'' God so loves His precious people that He wants the pastors to meet the nutritious needs of His children, spiritually. Hence, the shepherds are to feast on the Word of God daily in order to meet the needs of the hungry. This takes discipline and perseverance. It means that the golf game, the tennis court and other recreational amusements must be in second place. It means that the obedient preacher cannot wait until the last minute to prepare the ''Saturday Night Special'' for the Lord's Day.

Again, ministers are to lead exemplary lives. They are not to be power-crazy dictators. Their leadership must be in love. They are to rule the church as God's appointed directors, *but with compassion.* As rulers they are not to be board-dominated ''puppets'' — an *insult* to God and His Word. That's right! I Timothy 3:4-5 state: A minister should rule '' . . . well his own house, having his children in subjection with all gravity; For if a man know not how to rule his own house, how shall he take care of [or rule] the church of God?''

This God-appointed leader, the pastor, must be obeyed. Are you shocked? Hebrews 13:17: ''Obey them that have the rule over you, and submit yourselves: for they watch for your souls, as they that must give account, that they may do it with joy, and not with grief: for that is unprofitable for you." Imagine! God's shepherds are to be **obeyed.** This is specifically true as they teach doctrine and ethics. Those who ignore these commandments will suffer great embarrassment at the Bema Seat. They will weep as their spiritual guardians, their pastors, report their disobedience, stubbornness and carnality. Is this truth hard to accept? Hebrews 13:17 again states: " . . . they watch for your souls, as they **MUST** give an account, that they may do it with joy and not with grief," victory and heartache, triumph and tears, as the reports are presented.

This does not mean that the shepherd is free from investigation. **He, too,** must obey the Word he preaches, must live according to the God-demanded requirements mentioned in I Timothy 3:2-7 which say, "A bishop [or preacher] then must be blameless, the husband of one wife, vigilant, sober, of good behavior, given to hospitality, apt to teach; Not given to wine, no striker, not greedy of filthy lucre; but patient, not a brawler, not covetous; One that ruleth well his own house, having his children in subjection with all gravity; For if a man know not how to rule his own house, how shall he take care of the church of God? Not a novice, lest being lifted up with pride [becoming arrogant] he fall into the condemnation of the devil [who also fell through pride, Isaiah 14:12-14]. Moreover he must have a good report of them which are without [the unsaved world]; lest he fall into reproach and the snare of the devil." Shepherds who make these God-ordained standards their goal receive an **ex-**

clusive crown at that day, for I Peter 5:4 declares: " . . . when the chief Shepherd shall appear, ye shall receive a crown of glory that fadeth not away."

The Soulwinner's Crown

Heaven's fourth crown is awarded to soulwinners. Daniel 12:3 declares: "And they that be wise shall shine as the brightness of the firmament; and they that turn many to righteousness as the stars for ever and ever." Stand outside on a clear night, fix your eyes upon heaven and study God's breathtaking creation. Stars, billions of miles away, twinkle as plainly as the flickering candle on the dining room table. No wonder Christians joyfully sing, "O God, how great Thou art."

An even more majestic scene is portrayed for the future as children of God who won souls are coronated with star-studded crowns. Hallelujah! Yes, " . . . they that turn many to righteousness as the stars for ever and ever." Is it any wonder that Proverbs 11:30 states: " . . . he that winneth souls is wise?" The inference here is: "he who does not win souls is foolish." Why? He casts aside eternal rewards as though they were bubble gum wrappers. Wise men have more sense than this. They do not trample on God's commands. Instead, they longingly obey Matthew 28:19: "Go ye therefore, and teach all nations . . . " Mark 16:15: " . . . Go ye into all the world, and preach the gospel to every creature.'' Luke 14:21: '' . . . Go out into the highways and hedges, and compel them to come in . . . '' Acts 1:8: '' . . . ye shall be witnesses unto me both in Jerusalem, and in all Judaea, and in Samaria, and unto the uttermost part of the earth.'' They love God and will not allow business or pleasure to stand in the way of the *highest calling* in the world — the winning of souls for eternity. They heed the warning of Jesus about the bushel of business and the bed of relaxation and pleasure of hindrances to the candle's flame (Mark 4:21). Their love for Christ and the souls of men make them press forward for the '' . . . prize of the high calling of God in Christ Jesus'' (Philippians 3:14). They want to present their troubles of grace to Jesus, not the husks of a barren life. They want a soulwinner's crown and a crown they receive as they, with Paul, triumphantly present their converts in that day saying, ''For what is our hope, or joy, or crown of rejoicing? Are not even ye [converts] in the presence of our Lord Jesus Christ at his coming?'' (I Thessalonians 2:19). At this great roll call, will **you** be able to make a presentation to the Saviour? Will **you** have any spiritual children? Will **you** receive a crown that shines like the brightness of the firmament? Don't procrastinate, become a soulwinner today! Then and **only then** will you be coronated with heaven's glittering ''Oscar.''

The Sufferer's Crown

The fifth and final crown is presented to those who have suffered for the sake of Christ and the Gospel. James 1:12 states: "Blessed is the man that endureth temptation [testing and trials]: for when he is tried, he shall receive the **CROWN OF LIFE,** which the Lord hath promised to them that love him." Some will receive this glorious reward for having experienced the taunts and jeers of sinners. Jesus said, "Blessed are they which are persecuted for righteousness' sake: for theirs is the kingdom of heaven. Blessed are ye, when men shall revile you, and persecute you, and shall say all manner of evil against you falsely, for my sake. Rejoice, and be exceeding glad: for great is your reward in heaven . . . " (Matthew 5:10-12).

The reward will also be presented to those who bore illness and infirmity with a smile believing that " . . . all things work together for good to them that love God . . . " (Romans 8:28). Some believers constantly praise the Lord in the midst of adversity while others continuously grumble in the midst of prosperity. Some Christians gripe so much that they will even complain about heaven's streets of gold, saying, "The glitter affects my eyes!" **God help us!** *How different from the saint who lost five sons in the service.* Her minister, in a state of frustration, went to the godly little lady's home to share the sad news. When he arrived, she greeted him with the words, "I already know. The Lord spoke to me

during my prayer time. Which one is it?" The
pastor replied, "All five." She said, "Praise the
Lord! Praise the Lord! The last time my boys
were home I led all five of them to the Saviour.
Had they died prior to that furlough I would
never have seen them again. Now they are
already on heaven's shore awaiting mom's
homecoming. Isn't God good?" *Oh, what a
reward this suffering saint shall receive at the
great coronation day!*

The Sufferer's Crown is also given to those
who are faithful unto the end. Revelation 2:10
declares: " . . . be thou faithful unto death, and
I will give thee a crown of life." Again I want to
emphasize that this is not a reward for salvation,
but for service, and is presented to those who remain faithful throughout life. It is the same
crown mentioned previously in James 1:12
presented to all who bore trial and testing out of
love for the Lord Jesus.

Child of God, the time is at hand for the
distribution of heaven's awards. Where do **you**
stand at this moment? What rewards would **you**
receive were Jesus to come today? He is coming
soon, and immediately upon His arrival the judgment of the believer's service record begins.
That's right. The investigation begins at the **appearing** of Christ. Luke 14:14 states: " . . . thou
shalt be recompensed [rewarded] . . . " When?
" . . . at the resurrection of the just." I Peter 5:4
adds: "And when the chief Shepherd shall appear, ye shall receive a crown of glory that fadeth
not away." I John 2:28 also verifies the time by

stating: "And now, little children, abide in him; that, when he SHALL APPEAR, we may have confidence, and not be ashamed before him AT HIS COMING."

Our Eternal Testimony

When we are rewarded, we shall present our crowns at the feet of Jesus along with millions of other saints from all ages (Revelation 4:10, 11). This will be an awesome event. Let me illustrate.

Eight men wrote the New Testament. Seven were murdered. Matthew was slain with an halberd. Mark was dragged through the streets of Alexandria by a team of wild horses until dead. Luke was hanged in an olive tree. John, thrown into a caldron of boiling oil, survived the painful ordeal but was disfigured for life and banned to the isle of Patmos. One day he undoubtedly saw his seared face reflected in a stream of water and wept. God said unto him, "Son, cheer up. I will allow you to write I John 3:2 which promises new bodies to all of my children." It says, " . . . when he shall appear, we shall be like him; for we shall see him as he is." What joy must have filled the suffering servant's soul as he realized a better day was coming in which he would be changed to be like Jesus.

Paul was beheaded. Jude and Peter were crucified and James was battered to death with a fuller's club. **Now get the future picture**: The great hour has arrived and all God's children are present. The investigation begins. What will each of us say as we stand with such an array of heroes — believers who gave all, who proved their first love for Christ during an entire lifetime, even unto death!

Christ's return may be tomorrow, next week, next month or next year. We know not the day or the hour when Jesus shall break through the blue to call us home. However, we do know that it is near, even at the door. Therefore, my closing question is: **Are you ready?** Could you bear the investigative judgment were it to take place tomorrow? Would you be "ashamed," "embarrassed," "red-faced" and "broken-hearted?" Would tears of sorrow intermittently flow from your eyes for the millennial age? Is your present disobedience worth such heartache? Would you not rather serve God with all your heart and hear Him say, "Well done, thou good and faithful servant?" **It is not too late to make a change,** to reverse your lifestyle and put Christ first. I ask you to obey I John 1:9 now. It says, "If we confess our sins, he is faithful and just to forgive us our sins, and to cleanse us from all unrighteousness." Do it. Then live for Him. **It will be worth it all when we see Jesus,** for then we will hear Him say, "Well done, thou good and faithful servant" (Matthew 25:13-30).

Other Books by Jack Van Impe

AIDS Is for ~~Life~~ Death

Documented factual information about this deadly modern-day plague. Hundreds of authoritative medical and news reports listed alphabetically by subject for instant reference.

The Walking Bible

The "inside" story of Dr. Jack Van Impe. Forty years of the triumphs and tragedies of a remarkable man of God. New updated version includes new chapters and photographs.

Sin's Explosion

Though sin permeates and inundates the land, God specializes in bringing sinners to himself when sin is rampant. Includes scores of stirring quotes from great revival leaders. This book a must for every library.

Heart Disease in Christ's Body

Shocking! Explosive! Documented! A ringing defense of historic, biblical fundamentalism, proving that today's brand of fundamentalism differs from that of the founders, and a call for love and cooperation among all members of the body of Christ.

11:59 . . . and Counting!

What does the future hold for you and your loved ones? The questions that plague humanity are answered in this detailed account of mankind's march toward the Tribulation, Armageddon, and the hour of Christ's return.

Israel's Final Holocaust

Over 240,000 in print! One of the most helpful explanations of Israel's role in end-time Bible prophecies ever published. What will the final holocaust be . . . and how will it affect you?

ALCOHOL: The Beloved Enemy

Liquor and the Bible. Filled with wisdom and reasoning, this important book thoroughly covers the alcohol question. Includes historic background, current research, and statistics that may shock you. Bible help for a major problem. Every verse on the subject of wine from Genesis to Revelation is explained.

Revelation Revealed

Re-released! yes, you *can* understand what many consider to be the most complex book in the Bible. Dr. Van Impe's verse-by-verse teaching reveals the meaning of this prophetic treasure.

Great Salvation Themes

Do you have unsaved loved ones . . . and don't know quite how to reach them? This book includes inspired messages by Dr. Van Impe that have been used to win thousands of souls through radio, TV, and city-wide crusades.

The Baptism of the Holy Spirit

Dr. Van Impe's easy-to-understand study of who the Holy Spirit is, what He does, and why His baptism is for every believer. Includes what the Bible says about the personality, attributes, gifts, fruit, and power of the Holy Spirit.

God! I'm Suffering, Are You Listening?

Why do good people go through seemingly senseless suffering? Dr. Van Impe explains from a biblical perspective why even Christians suffer and the best way to make the most of misfortune.

The Happy Home: Child Rearing

Many parents are confused about how to raise their children to love and serve God. Dr. Van Impe provides sound Bible principles, as well as practical advice for raising children to be happy Christian adults.

America, Israel, Russia, and World War III

What will the end of the world be? Is a nuclear holocaust inevitable? Dr. Van Impe explains how Bible prophecy is being fulfilled, and the roles America, Israel, and Russia wil play in the Battle of Armageddon.

Escape the Second Death

Five powerful salvation messages especially directed to the unsaved. A great witnessing tool. Explains the Bible way to be born again. (Excerpted from *Great Salvation Themes.*)

Exorcism and the Spirit World

What every Christian should know about Satan, demons, and demonic activity. Reveals the dangers of association with the occult, describes Satan worship, and tells how to defeat demon forces through the delivering power of the Holy Spirit.

The True Gospel

The only "good news" is that Christ died for our sins, was buried, and rose again. There is no other good news. Dr. Van Impe also covers Christ's last seven sayings upon the cross, and the importance of His resurrection.

**Everything you always wanted
to know about Prophecy**

But didn't know who to ask! Dr. Van Impe answers questions on the Rapture, the Judgement seat of Christ, the Tribulation, and more. Headlines and international events interpreted in the light of Christ's soon return. This booklet will challenge you to live a life of holiness and service.

Can America Survive?

NEW EDITION! This dynamic book deals with where we've come from as a nation, where we are now, and what the future holds. Thoughtful, biblical answers for more than 30 compelling questions facing every concerned Christian today!

The Judgment Seat of Christ

Sheds light on the misunderstood subject of God's judgment. Covers the five judgements of the Bible, including the judgment of works, and a special section on the believer's crowns to be awarded on Judgment Day.

This Is Christianity

Millions who claim to be Christians including church members are not because they have never been born again. The message of this book will help you understand this vital subject and know what it means to be a follower of Christ.

The Cost of Discipleship and Revival

To be a true follower of Jesus Christ, the Bible says you must take up your cross and die to self. But just what kind of price do you have to pay? Find the answer, plus keys to revival, in the pages of this enlightening book.

What Must I Do to Be Lost?

Are you trusting in the traditions of men, your church, your good works? All the doctrines of the church will not get you into heaven. There is only one way to be saved — find out how in the pages of this book.

Religious Reprobates and Saved Sinners

A time message by Dr. Van Impe that distinguishes "religion" from genuine salvation. If you've ever wondered how to separate the wolves from the sheep, you must read this frank, tell-it-like-it-is booklet!

AIDS: 150 Million 1991

Now in print! Contains the unedited transcript of the TV special, documenting the dangers of this deadly disease. A shocking exposé!

1. 714 = 731 - 1000.

Gaurdian Angel pe

1 - 503 - 714 - 731 - 1000